Undoing the Revolution

In the series *Politics, History, and Social Change*, edited by John C. Torpey

ALSO IN THIS SERIES:

Rick Fantasia, *French Gastronomy and the Magic of Americanism*
Donald S. Pitkin, *Four Germanys: A Chronicle of the Schorcht Family*
John Torpey and David Jacobson, eds., *Transformations of Warfare in the Contemporary World*
Heribert Adam and Kogila Moodley, *Imagined Liberation: Xenophobia, Citizenship, and Identity in South Africa, Germany, and Canada*
Aidan McGarry and James Jasper, *The Identity Dilemma: Social Movements and Collective Identity*
Philipp H. Lepenies, *Art, Politics, and Development: How Linear Perspective Shaped Policies in the Western World*
Andrei S. Markovits and Emily Albertson, *Sportista: Female Fandom in the United States*
Nicholas Toloudis, *Teaching Marianne and Uncle Sam: Public Education, State Centralization, and Teacher Unionism in France and the United States*
Philip S. Gorski, *The Protestant Ethic Revisited*
Étienne Balibar, Sandro Mezzadra, and Ranabir Samaddar, eds., *The Borders of Justice*
Kenneth H. Tucker Jr., *Workers of the World, Enjoy! Aesthetic Politics from Revolutionary Syndicalism to the Global Justice Movement*
Hans-Lukas Kieser, *Nearest East: American Millennialism and Mission to the Middle East*
Ernesto Verdeja, *Unchopping a Tree: Reconciliation in the Aftermath of Political Violence*
Rebecca Jean Emigh, *The Undevelopment of Capitalism: Sectors and Markets in Fifteenth-Century Tuscany*
Aristide R. Zolberg, *How Many Exceptionalisms? Explorations in Comparative Macroanalysis*
Thomas Brudholm, *Resentment's Virtue: Jean Améry and the Refusal to Forgive*
Patricia Hill Collins, *From Black Power to Hip Hop: Racism, Nationalism, and Feminism*
Daniel Levy and Natan Sznaider, translated by Assenka Oksiloff, *The Holocaust and Memory in the Global Age*
Brian A. Weiner, *Sins of the Parents: The Politics of National Apologies in the United States*
Heribert Adam and Kogila Moodley, *Seeking Mandela: Peacemaking between Israelis and Palestinians*
Marc Garcelon, *Revolutionary Passage: From Soviet to Post-Soviet Russia, 1985–2000*
Götz Aly and Karl Heinz Roth, translated by Assenka Oksiloff, *The Nazi Census: Identification and Control in the Third Reich*
Immanuel Wallerstein, *The Uncertainties of Knowledge*
Michael R. Marrus, *The Unwanted: European Refugees from the First World War through the Cold War*

Vasabjit Banerjee

Undoing the Revolution

Comparing Elite Subversion of Peasant Rebellions

TEMPLE UNIVERSITY PRESS
Philadelphia • Rome • Tokyo

TEMPLE UNIVERSITY PRESS
Philadelphia, Pennsylvania 19122
tupress.temple.edu

Published 2019

Portions of Chapter 2 originally appeared in Vasabjit Banerjee, "The Religious Origins of Class Coalitions: Elite Participation in Religiously Motivated Peasant Rebellions in Mexico, Zimbabwe, and India," *International Political Science Review* 36.5 (2015): 545–561.

Library of Congress Cataloging-in-Publication Data

Names: Banerjee, Vasabjit, author.
Title: Undoing the revolution : comparing elite subversion of peasant rebellions / Vasabjit Banerjee.
Description: Philadelphia : Temple University Press, [2019] | Series: Politics, history, and social change | Includes bibliographical references and index. |
Identifiers: LCCN 2018044539 (print) | LCCN 2018056672 (ebook) | ISBN 9781439916933 (E-book) | ISBN 9781439916919 (cloth : alk. paper) | ISBN 9781439916926 (pbk. : alk. paper)
Subjects: LCSH: Peasant uprisings—India—History—20th century. | Peasant uprisings—Mexico—History—20th century. | Peasant uprisings—Zimbabwe—History—20th century. | Land reform—India—History—20th century. | Land reform—Mexico—History—20th century. | Land reform—Zimbabwe—History—20th century. | Elite (Social sciences)—India—History—20th century. | Elite (Social sciences)—Mexico—History—20th century. | Elite (Social sciences)—Zimbabwe—History—20th century.
Classification: LCC HD1537.I4 (ebook) | LCC HD1537.I4 B37 2019 (print) | DDC 303.6/2—dc23
LC record available at https://lccn.loc.gov/2018044539

♾ The paper used in this publication meets the requirements of the American National Standard for Information Sciences—Permanence of Paper for Printed Library Materials, ANSI Z39.48-1992

Printed in the United States of America

9 8 7 6 5 4 3 2 1

To my father, who mused about how human nature made revolutions impossible

Contents

Acknowledgments

Writing a scholarly book is possible only with the financial, intellectual, and personal support of many organizations and individuals. This book, which germinated in my dissertation at Indiana University, was fostered and meaningfully structured by my dissertation committee members, Jack Bielasiak, Michael Dodson, Armando Razo, and Regina Smyth. Without their encouragement and painstaking reviews, I could not have written a broad comparative historical analysis of agrarian societies in three continents across the span of the twentieth century.

The project began when the Center for Latin American and Caribbean Studies (CLACS) at Indiana University, along with the Tinker Foundation, helped underwrite a preliminary research trip to Mexico in 2007. Subsequently CLACS supported my fieldwork there in 2009 via the student exchange program with the Centro de Investigaciones y Estudios Superiores en Antropología Social (CIESAS) in Mexico City.

Also, I thank Peter Guardino and Bradley Levinson at Indiana University for their help with and support of my research on Latin America. Romana Falcón from El Colegio de Mexico, Jeffrey Weldon from the Instituto Tecnológico Autónomo de México (ITAM), and Joy Langston from Centro de Investigación y Docencia Económicas (CIDE) also provided invaluable insights on the Mexican Revolution and the formation of the postrevolutionary regime.

My research on India was enhanced by support from Security and Political Risk Analysis, India (SAPRA), in New Delhi. In particular, Indranil

Banerjie, who headed the organization, has supported my development as a scholar on South Asia since 2004. I am thankful to the Dhar India Studies Program and its former director Sumit Ganguly for their support, including an India Studies Fellowship in 2005, which allowed me to come to Indiana University. My dissertation benefited tremendously from the help of Paranjoy Guha Thakurta, who provided both financial support and insights into Indian politics during my fieldwork in India in 2010.

I conducted my research on Zimbabwe via a generous postdoctoral fellowship from the Department of Sociology at the University of Pretoria. The late Tony Emmett, a gentleman, a scholar, and an activist, had made the initial connections and proposed my candidacy. At Pretoria, my postdoctoral adviser, Jonathan Hyslop, and the head of the department, Janis Grobbelaar, provided invaluable advice and encouragement and studiously overlooked my neophyte assumptions about southern African politics and society. Andries Bezuidenhout and Irma du Plessis adopted me intellectually and helped mold my approach to understanding political development in the region as a multilayered and interconnected process spanning different countries and the public and private spheres. They also indulged my tastes for expensive tea and coffee. Sepetla Molapo provided me with the most helpful insights into regional labor histories. Sakhela Buhlungu's observations on the quotidian aspects of southern African anticolonial struggles were immensely helpful in cultivating a feel for the uncertainty, hope, and machinations of the period.

With regard to Zimbabwe, a subject I had to master within a short period of time, I received critical help from two junior colleagues. Splagchna N. Chikarara at the University of Pretoria acted as a guide on my brief trip to Zimbabwe, which was under the Mugabe regime at the time, and continued to help me thereafter with insights into Zimbabwean culture and politics. Bryan Mathison provided crucial help by exploring new and old research on Rhodesia's economy and foreign relations.

In addition to those mentioned earlier, an entire village of academics fostered the writing of this book and my development as a scholar. They include Ishita Banerjee and Saurabh Dube from El Colegio de México, for their insights on the Indian anticolonial movement and for several excellent dinners; Bill Bianco from Indiana University, whose tips on writing I employed extensively; and Jeffrey Isaac from Indiana University, who provided support and feedback during the dissertation-writing process.

Brian Shoup from Mississippi State University, who heard my ever-evolving theory, deserves a special thank-you. Underneath the theory and empirical evidence lies the methodological rigor that Karen Rasler at Indiana University introduced to me. This book's effort to understand the role of international economic actors, in contrast to purely domestic-level explanations of rebellions and state formation, was first inspired by the observations of Rafael Khachaturian, my graduate school friend at Indiana University.

I owe James C. Scott a thank-you for patiently listening to my theory of rebellion and state formation, on the sidelines of a visit to Bloomington, Indiana, and responding with clarificatory questions that helped streamline the theory. During his visit to Bloomington, Indiana, the late Christopher Bayly provided critical insights into the shifting role of Indian merchants in the anticolonial movement. Catherine Boone's reassurance—during a visit to Bloomington, Indiana—that I was on the right track in terms of the role of localized elite-peasant coalitions and national-level intraelite competition was also crucial in shaping the core theory of this book. When I visited him at his home in Harare, the late Samuel Moyo helped me understand the evolution of the Black African middle class in Zimbabwe in terms of broader modernization theory. Alois Mlambo at the University of Pretoria connected me to local scholars in Harare for my trip to Zimbabwe.

The insights of James Mahoney at the Institute for Qualitative and Multi-Method Research (IQMR) in 2008 were tremendously helpful in structuring my dissertation. The training that I received at the IQMR workshop, which also introduced me to a broad social and professional network, would not have been possible without the amazing understanding and support of Colin Elman during a particularly difficult time in my life.

Special thanks are due to Fern Bennett, Amanda Campbell, Sharon Laroche, Jan Peterson, James Russell, and Jessica Williams in the Department of Political Science at Indiana University for facilitating everything from paychecks and presentations to the intricacies of submitting a dissertation. Quintara Miller and Kamicca Brown at Mississippi State University and Rosa Da Costa–Bezuidenhout at the University of Pretoria administered my various research trips during the transformation of my dissertation into a book.

Indiana University's Student Academic Center and Chip Frederick provided me with a steady job to support myself through the dissertation-writing period. William Rasch gave me a most generous postdoctoral position in Indiana University's Department of International Studies to complete the research.

I owe a special thank-you to Timothy Rich, my co-author on numerous scholarly and media articles, who has been a friend since the start of my graduate career, a trusted counselor, and a source of support. I am also grateful to my dear friend and co-author Anand Jha for his insights on India's political economy and novel takes on North Indian politics and society.

I especially thank the late Elaine Salo, as well as Srobana Bhattacharya, Nicolas Blarel, Dallas Breen, James Chamberlain, Aurelian Craiutu, Michelle

Deardorff, Forrest Fleischman, Robert Holahan, Prashant Hosur, Ekrem Karakoc, Prakash Kashwan, Kenneth C. Morrison, and Manjeet Pardesi..

Ryan Mulligan, acquisitions editor at Temple University Press, who has been a strong advocate for the book, patiently guided me through the publication process. The anonymous reviewers coordinated by Temple University Press offered excellent suggestions. Reviewer number four, who provided the most comprehensive and detailed comments on the segments concerning Zimbabwe, helped improve this work via several rounds of revisions. Reviewer number two, whose recommendations helped clarify the broader theory and organization of the empirical chapters, not only helped make this book more readable but also afforded lessons for my future book-length projects. I thank Susan Deeks for her careful work, which involved three languages, in the copyediting phase. A special note of appreciation goes to Joan Vidal, senior production editor, and Gary Kramer, publicity manager, at Temple University Press, who have been so gracious with a first-time book author.

Every historically oriented study uses the time and resources of various archives and libraries, and my book is no exception. I owe a special debt of gratitude to, among others, the librarians and archivists at the Centro de Estudios de Historia de México and the Instituto Nacional de Estudios Históricos de las Revoluciones de México in Mexico City and the Indian Institute of Public Administration Library and Parliament Library in New Delhi. It also behooves me to acknowledge the invaluable help my work on Zimbabwe received from the Margaret Thatcher Foundation's digital archives.

My family and friends provided emotional and financial support, as well as understanding and encouragement, during the often isolating and demanding process of dissertation and book writing, which spanned a decade. They include my father-in-law, D. Peter Holmes, and my sisters and brothers-in-law Emily and Andy Nordstrom and Elizabeth Holmes and Matthew Stuart. My elder brother, Vikramjit Banerjee, provided invaluable insights into the Indian legal system during the colonial and postcolonial period, and my elder sister, Tamanna Varma, provided boarding and lodging (and Scotch) during my fieldwork in Delhi. My cousin, philosopher, and guide, Ananda Roop Ganguly, and sister-in-law, Diane Ganguly, were always there for personal and professional advice and sometimes critical financial support. My cousins Ranajit, Debajit, Sudeshna, and Susmita Banerjee also provided immense support.

My best friend, counselor, and wife, Carolyn Holmes, warrants a very special mention for tolerating my extended mental and physical absences, editing numerous versions of my dissertation, and providing unflagging support during the lonely writing process. In addition, her comprehension of southern African social structure and politics and her vast knowledge of extant research on the region were invaluable in transforming the dissertation into a book.

Finally, this book relies on personal values that I learned from two people: stubborn persistence and a love for history from my late father, Sourya K. Banerjee, and dogged ambition and a love for geography from my mother, Sucheta Banerjee.

A book is both a journey and a destination. I traveled and lived in three countries to complete the book, met and sought help from more people than it would be humanly possible to recall, and had experiences and insights that cannot be represented by pages drafted using a social science theory. This book also symbolizes the end of all of that, only with the hope that the shards of gathered knowledge wound together by strings of theory can reflect some deeper truths about the painful transitions of agrarian societies into modernity.

Portions of Chapter 2 originally appeared in Vasabjit Banerjee, "The Religious Origins of Class Coalitions: Elite Participation in Religiously Motivated Peasant Rebellions in Mexico, Zimbabwe, and India," *International Political Science Review* 36.5 (2015): 545–561.

Undoing the Revolution

Introduction

A Theory of Peasant Rebellions and Elite Victories

I woke up to the bone-jarring sensation of the potholed Beitbridge-Harare highway, somewhere near the town of Masvingo in southeastern Zimbabwe, and witnessed the dazzlingly bright morning sunlight reflect over the Lowveld. This was a landscape I had seen many times in neighboring South Africa, but in Zimbabwe it appeared inexplicably unnatural. Chicken-wire fences and wooden posts were visibly separating nothing from nothing. There intermittently appeared hamlets of decrepit brick-and-mortar homes with battered tin or tiled roofs, usually accompanying an emaciated general store.

Cleared areas for cultivation sporadically appeared, with maize growing in small, irregularly shaped plots. These cornfields did not resemble their blandly lush counterparts in midwestern America; instead, they looked like gaunt products of hand-strewn seeds and little irrigation. I turned to my research assistant, Mr. Chikarara, and asked, "There's something strange about this place, isn't there?" He replied nonchalantly, "Those were the White farms." At that moment, I was struck by the scale of what happened after the "fast-track land-reform programme" of 2000: the countryside looked like a postapocalyptic reversion of human progress. Abandoned by the government after hasty land redistribution from White farmers, poor Black peasants, without training and equipment, were attempting to grow crops in these miserable plots. The revolutionary promise of land reform had been ignored for two decades, only to be perversely fulfilled, and all of it to keep a coterie of leaders in power.

The fate of Zimbabwean peasants brings to the fore an often ignored question: why do rebellions in agrarian societies create state institutions dominated by elites, even as the peasants—the largest segment of the population—struggle and risk the most to rebel? The key to understanding the causes of peasants' remarginalization, I argue, lies in the roles that elites play during the rebellions and in the subsequent bargains that form new state institutions. Dissenting elites' participation in rebellions is critical, because, given their poverty and large population size, peasants face nearly insurmountable barriers to fostering and maintaining collective action. For individual peasants barely eking out a living, participating in rebellions is too costly and risky. Who will till their fields and herd the cattle? Where can they get weapons and food to sustain a rebellion? What about the inevitable retaliatory attacks on their lives, liberty, and property? And if non-rebels can also enjoy the freedom and wealth that may result from rebellion, then why bear the costs and risk it all?

I argue that the peasants' inability to bear the costs and risks of rebellion creates a window for participation by dissenting elites, who provide the resources peasants need, from food and finances to leadership and weapons, to overcome barriers to collective action. At times, such elites even use their resources to goad peasants into rebellion. Nevertheless, in both scenarios, elite participation is critical to rebellion's success. After rebelling, however, allied elites retain their advantage in resources, which, combined with their small numbers, facilitates intraelite cooperation. As a result, elites bargain among themselves, co-opt sections of the peasantry, and select or capture state institutions to best reflect their own interests. Peasants' interests are disregarded.

The comparative studies presented in *Undoing the Revolution* evaluate the processes of rebellion and state formation in three different agrarian societies during distinct time periods spanning the twentieth century: revolutionary Mexico from 1910 to 1930, late-colonial India from 1920 to 1947, and White-dominated Zimbabwe (Rhodesia) from the mid-1960s to 1980. To collect and present the evidence, I use a qualitative approach centered on historiographical sources, which are strongly supplemented with archival data from India, Mexico, the United Kingdom, and the United States, as well as insights from local scholars acquired during visits to Mexico, India, and Zimbabwe.

I present regional rebellions thematically across different countries—for example, Chapter 2 compares rebellion centered on religion in northwestern Zimbabwe, southern India, and western-central Mexico. This comparative approach reveals both the need for elite participation and the variety of causes that incentivize elites to participate, extending from sharing ascriptive identities such as religion with peasants to elites' own political and economic grievances.

These subnational-level studies of rebellions and subsequent national-level studies on conflict resolution and state formation reveal two major findings. First, the critical class for explaining the success of peasant rebellions is, paradoxically, not peasants but local elites, who join such rebellions for three primary reasons: shared religion, political exclusion, and economic grievances. Second, these allied elites capture rebel organizations, bargain among themselves, and entrench their interests within new and existing institutions. Furthermore, during the bargaining over state institutions, the preferences of the elites are contingent on whether they are domestic or foreign and whether they control mobile assets such as capital and high skills or fixed assets such as land and natural resources.

The subnational and national-level studies presented here contribute to research on both peasant rebellions and state formation in agrarian societies. The necessity of elite participation in overcoming collective-action barriers to peasant rebellion is counterintuitive. This approach challenges the established consensus on the causes and processes of rebellions, which focuses on how peasants attempt to overcome such barriers on their own (Scott 2009; E. Wood 2003). Instead, *Undoing the Revolution* underscores the need for coalitions among classes using a model of strategically rational action based on economic interests to reaffirm, at the subnational level, Barrington Moore's (1966) national-level theory of revolutions in agrarian societies, as well as its more contemporary rational-choice (Acemoglu and Robinson 2006) and historiographical extensions (Tudor 2013).

More important, perhaps, *Undoing the Revolution* deepens our understanding of a topic overlooked by scholarship on the outcome of peasant rebellions: conflict resolution and state formation that reempower elites and remarginalize peasants, a reality that characterizes revolutions from China and Russia to those studied here. Prominent scholars using both bottom-up, peasant rebellion–based (Scott 1977, 2009) and top-down, state institution–centric explanations (Skocpol 1979) ignore the outcome of revolutions. Even those who emphasize the critical role of "marginal elites" (Wickham-Crowley 1992, 41) and "middle peasants" (Wolf 1969) in fomenting and leading revolutions in agrarian societies ignore how these groups shape postrevolutionary institutions. The findings from the national-level studies presented here, however, demonstrate that postrevolutionary regimes in such societies disregard and exclude peasants because rebellions, paradoxically, empower elites.

Finally, *Undoing the Revolution* challenges the assumption of comparative studies of revolutions that classes arise from, and revolutions are motivated by, factors at the domestic level (Acemoglu and Robinson 2006; Boix 2003; Moore 1966; Rueschemeyer, Stephens, and Stephens 1992); the effects of export-oriented, cash-crop enclaves on class coalitions (Paige 1975); or the weakening of the state itself due to foreign wars (Skocpol 1979). Rather, the studies of rebellion and state formation presented here demonstrate that both international and domestic investors in cash crops, natural resources, and finance can ally with peasant rebels and, after threatened or actual state collapse, bargain with one another to select new state institutions. Consequently, my theory accounts for intraelite differences centered on the types of assets they control, as well as their domestic and foreign origins.

In this vein, the next section defines the central concepts of the study before presenting the theory around which my analyses of subnational rebellions and national-level state formation revolve. Specifically, it addresses the question of why elite participation is critical to the success of peasant rebellions and how allied elites subsequently bargain to select institutions. The third section explains why revolutionary Mexico, late-colonial India, and White-dominated Zimbabwe (Rhodesia) were especially suitable for verifying the theory, along with the evidence and methods used to verify the theory. I conclude with an outline of the book, which shows how individual chapters verify the theory.

Peasant Rebels and Elite Victors: A Theory

Despite extensive research, scholars who focus on peasant rebellions either ignore the subsequent stage of state formation (Popkin 1979; Scott 1977, 2009; Weinstein 2006; E. Wood 2003) or assume that institutions simply reflect the interests of victorious social classes (Acemoglu and Robinson 2006; Moore 1966; Rueschemeyer, Stephens, and Stephens 1992; Skocpol 1979). The resultant gap in our understanding of the connections between rebellion and state formation in agrarian societies leaves an important question unanswered: why are peasants who risk everything to rebel unable to create postrevolutionary states that best reflect their class interests? This continued marginality is demonstrated repeatedly by elite-dominated state formation in diverse societies across time, from eighteenth-century France to late twentieth-century Mozambique.

To address the gap, this section presents a theory of rebellion and state formation that highlights the critical role of elite classes in helping peasants overcome barriers to collective action. After defining the main groups of actors and concepts, I present the theory in three broad segments: the causes of rebellions, especially the role of elites who deliver resources to peasants;

the effects of elite participation on peasant rebellions; and how subsequent intraelite bargains establish new state institutions.

The theory revolves around two social classes: peasants and elites. Peasants control their own labor; elites fall into two categories based on whether they control fixed assets such as land and natural resources, which cannot be moved out of their country of origin, or mobile assets such as high skills and capital, which can be moved abroad (Boix 2003). In addition to possessing different resources, these classes also differ in size: in agrarian societies, peasants are the most numerous, while elite classes are small. Also, while peasants belong to a particular society, elite classes can either originate in the society or be foreign actors with assets in the society.

A caveat: although an individual's class identity is primarily contingent on the type of assets he or she controls, empirical studies nuance the categorization of individuals or groups within a class through historiographical research and self-identification. Thus, in some areas groups that own small parcels of land can self-identify as peasants, while in other areas scholars classify only landless agricultural laborers as peasants. Similarly, owners of mobile assets referred to as the "bourgeoisie" or "middle classes" can extend from village moneylenders and storekeepers who also own land to merchants who export cash crops or own urban businesses and even banks. Owners of fixed assets can be landlords with seigniorial rights that span centuries; those who grow cash crops on vast tracts of land; or simply landed homesteaders. Because their wealth depends on particular locations—which, moreover, require buildings and equipment for extraction—owners of natural resources such as mines and oil wells are also classified as fixed asset owners.

In this book, I follow Doug McAdam and his colleagues' (2001) archetypal conceptualization of mobilizations, which centers on the characterization of participating actors and processes, to define rebellions. In terms of actors, rebellions involve governments as a "claimant," as an "object of claims," or "a party to the claims" (McAdam, Tarrow, and Tilly 2001, 5). With regard to process, rebellions are "episodic, public, collective interactions among makers of claims and their objects" (McAdam, Tarrow, and Tilly 2001, 7). The observable outcomes of rebellions, therefore, extend from peaceful protests, marches, tax withholding, and hunger strikes to social banditry and armed insurrections, all of which can be classified as spontaneous and organized rebellion (Lichbach 1994, 394–399). However, this classification excludes everyday forms of individual peasant resistance such as theft, gossip, and the shirking of work (Scott 1985) because they are discrete, uncoordinated, and secretive actions by individuals or small groups that frequently center on grievances against specific people.

States, which rebellions attack and rebels later seek to reestablish, comprise a combination of formal and informal institutions "that structure political, economic, and social interaction" (North 1991, 97). Formal institutions are created by written laws and regulations and enforced by individual bureaucrats and official organizations, which instantiate the state's monopoly of legitimate coercion over a population in a given territory (Weber [1922] 1978, 54). Informal institutions consist of unwritten traditions; affective loyalties centered on ethnicity, language, and religion; patronage networks; and corruption (Bratton 2007). Formal and informal institutions can complement and interact with one another (Helmke and Levitsky 2004), with such "practices and alliances" acting "to promote a variety of sets of rules, often quite distinct from those set out in the state's own official laws and regulations" (Migdal 2001, 20).

Extant research posits three different causes of rebellions against established state institutions and the incumbent elites therein: grievances against existing political and economic institutions; political opportunities; and resources to overcome barriers to collective action. Rebels' grievances can center on a lack of political representation or economic advancement. Such grievances are frequently interrelated because state institutions and policies, such as taxation, affect the distribution of wealth across groups, and the distribution of wealth, in turn, affects groups' capacity to influence politics. Therefore, rebels in agrarian societies can become aggrieved by a lack of political opportunities to make economic gains (Popkin 1979) or fight against the introduction of institutions that threaten their subsistence (Scott 1977, 2009).

In tandem with political and economic grievances, cultural identities motivate rebellions. Grievances related to ethnicity, language, and religion can act alone or in conjunction with grievances that arise from political and economic marginalization (Hasenclever and Rittberger 2003). By themselves, religious and ethnic grievances extend from demands against the state to practice a religion freely, speak a language, or demonstrate an ethnic identity to demands that a particular religious or ethnolinguistic group dominate state institutions. Religion can also be used to frame notions of injustice and tyranny; to assign responsibility to individuals and groups for these problems; and, subsequently, to provide resolutions such as rebelling to defend religious beliefs or capturing the state (Benford and Snow 2000, 615).

Theories of opportunity structures posit that people rebel when they perceive changes in political and economic institutions that affect "the degree to which groups are likely to be able to gain access to power and to manipulate the political system" (Eisinger 1973, 25). Specifically, apertures in formal institutions, and consequent rebellions, occur when existing institutions are threatened by instability in alignments among incumbent elites, the development of multiple independent centers of power within a regime, and a decline in the state's capacity for repression (McAdam, Tarrow, and Tilly 2009, 263).

In contrast to these theories, *Undoing the Revolution* demonstrates that elite grievances and apertures in the incumbent institutions, and the fracturing of ruling elite coalitions therein, cannot in and of themselves explain successful rebellions. Local rebellions are difficult to carry out because they require resources to start and sustain themselves. Individual peasants should refuse to participate in rebellions. They not only might face significant opportunity costs, such as hours lost in terms of tending their land and cattle; they also risk property damage, injury, and even death from violent repression. Furthermore, the probability that an individual peasant's participation could affect the outcome of a rebellion is extremely low, while nonparticipation could still allow the individual to enjoy the public goods achieved by successful rebellion, such as social welfare policies and better infrastructure—a problem that is often called the "rebel's dilemma" (Lichbach 1994, 387).

Poor peasants, who make up the majority of agents carrying out rebellions (Acemoglu and Robinson 2006), consequently need elite entrepreneurs to provide collective and selective resources, such as information, leadership, and financial incentives, to make the benefits of rebelling outweigh the considerable costs (Lichbach 1994; McCarthy and Zald 2001; Popkin 1988; Wickham-Crowley 1992). Indeed, the need for resources—and therefore for elite allies—is apparent even in rebellions motivated by religion: religious organizations provide intangible and tangible resources that facilitate the initiation and sustaining of conflicts (De Juan 2008). Furthermore, religious and ethnic identities' cross-class appeal reduces prospective elite participants' fears that they will be attacked and their property expropriated by rebelling peasants. Also, religious organizations' provision of resources as well as monitoring and enforcement of participation reduce the cost burden for participating elites.

Elite-peasant alliances can form after a rebellion has broken out (Figure I.1), in which case resources help to sustain and expand the rebellion. Or elites can encourage peasant rebellions (Figure I.2) by providing resources that reduce the costs of peasant participation. Because the increased intensity of elite-peasant interactions centers on shared cultural identities (Walter 2002, 83–84) and lowers barriers to information and enforcement of participation (Olson [1965] 1971), the need for elite support necessitates cross-

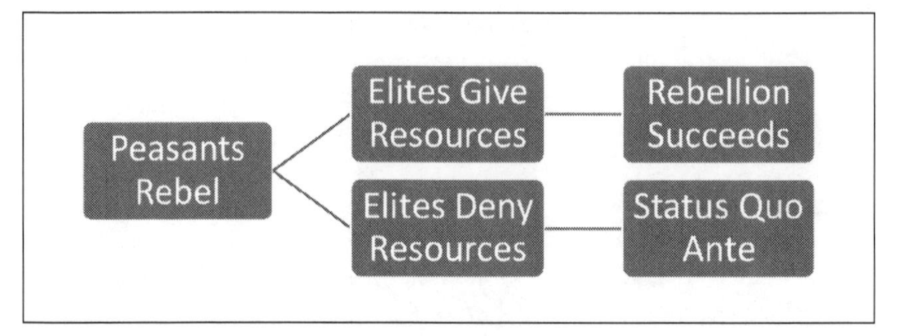

Figure I.1. Peasant uprisings followed by elite resources. (Created by the author.)

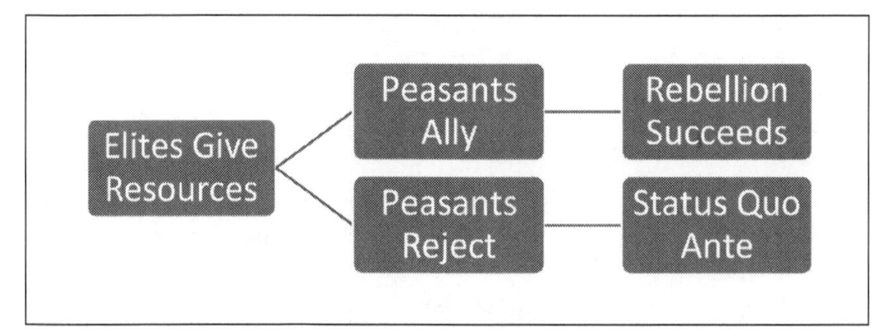

Figure I.2. Elite resources followed by peasant alliances. (Created by the author.)

class alliances at the subnational level, as opposed to the national level. The Janus-faced nature of revolutions portrayed in studies of regional rebellions—instantiated simultaneously in subnational rebellions and seeking nationwide social and institutional transformation—therefore, arises from this phenomenon of localization, compelled by peasants' need for resources.

After allying with peasants, political leaders from or backed by the elite classes decide the rebels' strategies and reshape peasants' grievances to align with elite interests. To do this, the elites selectively offer goods and services to peasant members of political parties or client networks while monitoring and punishing recalcitrant peasants (Lichbach 1994). Even when the political leaders emanate from the peasant class, the resources needed to maintain political organizations and the strategies to acquire and sustain support make them dependent on economic elites. As a result, economic elites' interests shape political leaders' decisions, which, in turn, determines the fate of peasant rebels.

Therefore, unlike peasants, economic elites may not be visibly represented on the political stage. They may influence politics by contributing money to political leaders to sustain their popular organizations, or their share of the economy may implicitly pressure politicians who seek to retain popular support. This phenomenon is present in all three countries I studied. The political-economic effects of the elites' ambitions and actions become evident only via the influence they exert in bargains struck among political leaders to select new state institutions.

When congeries of rebellions cause the prerevolutionary state to approach collapse, or to actually do so, the rebelling elites leverage their smaller numbers and greater resources to bargain among themselves and co-opt segments of the peasantry in order to select new state institutions that support their interests. As a result, postrevolutionary states are formed not by peasants but by elites, institutionalizing the "systematic tendency for 'exploitation' of the great by the small" (Olson [1965] 1971, 29).

Specifically, whereas repressive state institutions become the targets of rebellion, the central obstacle to reestablishing peace after successful rebellions is rebel leaders' fear that post-conflict institutions and incumbent elites will co-opt other groups and sections of their own groups to empower themselves and renew repression (Hartzell, Hoddie, and Rothchild 2001, 199). Underlying this fear is the view that new political institutions will be determinants of de jure political power, as well as de facto political power "possessed by groups as a result of their wealth, weapons, or ability to resolve collective action problems" (Acemoglu and Robinson 2008, 266–267). Agreements between belligerent groups to end conflict therefore evolve into informal and formal institutions to share or divide power "to limit the capacity of any one party to the conflict to dominate the postwar state and use its advantaged position to harm the interests or survival of its rivals" (Hoddie and Hartzell 2003, 306).

The local rebels are led by political leaders or political-military warlords, both backed by economic elites. Political leaders control political parties with recognized organizational structures and hierarchy of leaders. Political-military warlords extend from leaders of political parties with armed wings or charismatic leaders whose military prowess allows them to build personalist popular organizations. Unlike their political counterparts, economic elites control natural resources, are financiers and bankers, or are landlords producing cash crops for export.

The phase of competition and bargaining among different rebel factions to form new state institutions is influenced by the prerogatives of the political and economic elites who are empowered through rebellions. Thus, the willingness of rebel leaders to compromise is contingent on two necessary and jointly sufficient factors: (1) the increasing costs and risks of continued conflict and (2) whether agreements are preferred by the economic elites underwriting the popular organizations that support the rebel leaders.

TABLE I.1. ELITE ORIGINS, ASSETS, AND PREFERENCES		
Location of elites	**Type of assets**	**Preference on peace**
Foreign	Fixed	Oppositional
Domestic	Fixed	Conditional
Foreign	Mobile	Supportive
Domestic	Mobile	Supportive

Furthermore, peace agreements and the selection of state institutions by implication are shaped by three possible preferences of economic elites regarding the cessation of conflict between the rebel leaders that they support: opposition, conditional acceptance, and support for peace. These preferences are determined by the economic elites' origins (Reno 1998) and the specific assets that they control (Boix 2003). If the economic elites are foreign and control fixed assets, such as land or natural resources, they might continue to support rebel leaders and sustain or exacerbate conflicts because new state institutions could heavily tax, or even nationalize, their assets. Paying off local rebel leaders, however, would protect these holdings. In contrast, domestic elites who control similar fixed assets would prefer nationwide peace agreements that are contingent on those agreements' predicted effects—that is, agreements leading to institutions that secure their assets. Finally, domestic and foreign elites who control mobile assets, such as financiers and bankers, favor peace agreements that encourage macroeconomic stability, which benefits them. The alignment of elite location and asset type with their preferences regarding peace agreements is shown in Table I.1.

The elite preferences presented in the table highlight the internal contradiction of peasant rebellions: they are quickly co-opted by elites, and peasants' interests rarely shape new institutions. Rather, political leaders responding to economic elites create institutions that marginalize peasants and serve elite interests. Though peasants may share solidary bonds (Moore 1966) or inhabit moral economies (Scott 1977, 2009), their poverty and large population size render them "incapable of asserting their class interest in their own name" and "finds its final expression in the executive power which subordinates society to itself" (Marx [1852] 1954, 106).

Comparing Mexico, India, and Zimbabwe: Their Relevance and Methods of Comparison

Comparing the selected cases confirms the critical role of elites in peasant rebellions—specifically, the factors that lead to their participation, their capture of such rebellions, and the elite competition and bargains that determine state formation. This section therefore allays concerns that the selected cases, comparative methods, and evaluation of evidence were undertaken arbitrarily or handpicked to confirm the posited theory. Specifically, it explains why revolutionary Mexico, colonial India, and White-dominated Zimbabwe are used to verify the theory. The comparative research design is subsequently presented to explain how it reveals the shared and distinct dynamics of rebellions and state formation of each society. The section concludes with a discussion of the types of evidence used and how such evidence is analyzed.

The proposed theory of rebellions and state formation is tested on Mexico from 1910 until the mid-1930s, India between 1920 and 1947, and Zimbabwe from 1965 until 1980. These cases were selected because they were very different in terms of their institutional systems and cultures; they are similar only in the factors of interest to the broader study. Such a combination is especially suitable to highlight the common factors that caused subnational rebellions and state formation that paradoxically benefited elites and marginalized peasants.

The three countries' institutions and cultures varied significantly. Mexico inherited Spanish state institutions as a colonial legacy. Its population was primarily of mixed-race European and indigenous ancestry and Catholic. India inherited British colonial institutions. Its population was divided by more than twenty languages; two major religions (Hinduism and Islam); and, within Hinduism, by caste. Zimbabwe also inherited British colonial institutions but of a variety that favored British settlers with special property rights and political representation. Its population was divided along racial lines between the minority Whites and Black Africans, a group that, in turn, was ethnically divided between the majority Shona and minority Ndebele.

With regard to shared preconditions, during the period under study all three societies were agrarian in that the majority of the people lived in rural areas and depended on agricultural and related activities, such as ranching, for their livelihood. Moreover, the subnational social and economic differences in these societies facilitated the tracking of "spatially uneven effects of processes of economic and political transformation" that characterize developing societies (Snyder 2001, 93). There were five distinct regions in Mexico: the relatively industrialized north; the southeast, centered on plantations; the variegated southwest, which had ranchers and landlords; the west, where homesteaders and ranchers predominated; and the center, where plantations competed with smallholders. The regions of colonial India directly administered by the British centered on the largest provinces: the United Provinces in the north and Bengal Presidency in the east, dominated by large landowners called *taluqdars* and *zamindars*; the Punjab in the northwest, characterized by prosperous homesteaders; and the peninsular south, dominated by the Bombay Presidency in the southwest and the Madras Presidency in the southeast, both characterized by smallholding farmers called *ryots*. There were also distinct subregions, such as the Malabar Coast in the southwest. Zimbabwe—or Rhodesia, as it was called during the period under study—was also divided into two major regions centered on indigenous ethnic groups. The north and east were primarily inhabited by the Shona, who composed approximately 80 percent of Zimbabwe's indigenous populace. The region was characterized by a humid subtropical climate suitable for intensive and extensive agriculture, especially tobacco, but also maize and wheat. Thus, it became the center of the land grants for White colonial settlers. The warm semiarid south and southwest, mainly suitable for cattle raising, were dominated by the Ndebele, who composed the other 20 percent of the country's indigenous population. The region's economic activity centered on the city of Bulawayo, Zimbabwe's economic and commercial capital.

In terms of the proximate causes and ultimate outcomes of rebellions, comparisons of subnational rebellions across the three countries demonstrate that resources garnered from elite participation were critical to their success. The first comparative study of rebellions in Mexico and India shows that elite participation itself is necessary and sufficient to cause successful rebellions. The second study, of religiously motivated rebellions, explains why shared religion propels elite participation in peasant rebellions. The third comparative study demonstrates that elite participation in peasant rebellions is also driven by combinations of political and economic grievances, as opposed to only economic or political ones. Furthermore, a common theme in the studies of regional rebellions is the co-optation of rebelling peasants by elite organizations, which provided the necessary resources to begin and sustain rebellions, whether these organizations were dominated by Mexican warlords, India's Congress Party, or the Zimbabwe African National Union (ZANU).

Finally, the three national-level studies reveal that new state institutions were shaped by elite bargains: between domestic and foreign (primarily American) business and landed interests in Mexico; between rural middle class and domestic business interests in India; and between international (specifically, British) investors in natural resources across Africa in Zimbabwe. As a result, peasants' interests became marginalized in all three societies: by the absence of political freedom in postrevolutionary Mexico, the denial of wealth redistribution in postcolonial India, and the lack of both in postindependence Zimbabwe.

The source materials for the study of nine regional rebellions and three cases of state formation combine primary and secondary sources. The secondary sources extend from economic, anthropological, and sociological to historiographical studies of the periods under analysis. The primary sources include public records and declassified government reports from various archives in Mexico, India, Britain, and the United States. Contemporaneous reports from private companies, newspapers, and monographs by relevant actors are also used. Evidence from these sources was contextualized through conversations and correspondence with local scholars in Mexico, India, and Zimbabwe.

How Peasant Revolts Empower Elites: A Road Map from Rebellions to State Formation

The organization of *Undoing the Revolution*—from a comparative focus on subnational rebellions across countries to considering state formation in each country—aims to highlight that peasant rebellions cannot achieve substantive redistribution of power and wealth because the inequality of resources continues to favor elite classes. In this vein, the individual chapters answer specific research questions based on several broader inquiries. Why are coalitions between elites and peasants critical to successful rebellions? What are the effects of cultural values, such as religion, on elite participation? Do elites ally with peasants as a result of grievances caused by political and economic marginalization? What are the immediate effects of elite participation on these rebellions? Under what conditions do political, political-military, and economic elites agree to cease conflict? And finally, how do elite bargains shape new state institutions?

Chapter 1 compares an uprising in northern Mexico and two rebellions in colonial northern India to test four explanations for successful peasant rebellions: grievances caused by exclusionary political institutions; grievances caused by marginalizing economic institutions; new political opportunities; and collaboration between rebelling elites and peasants. The findings demonstrate that elite partnership with peasants in northern Mexico and the second rebellion in northern India was critical to the success of these rebellions because the elites delivered resources unavailable to the larger and poorer peasantry—including funds and organizing capabilities—that lowered barriers to collective action. In contrast, a lack of elite participation led to the failure of the first rebellion in northern India. The effects of economic and political grievances and of new opportunities in determining the success of rebellions are shown to be inconclusive.

Chapter 2 explains why elite classes participate in religiously motivated peasant rebellions. The chapter compares the Moplah Rebellion in colonial India, the Cristero Rebellion in revolutionary Mexico, and the Chimurenga

Rebellion in White settler–controlled Rhodesia (Zimbabwe) to test three common explanations for elite participation: low inequality between elites and peasants; moderate political repression or opportunity; and shared religious organizations with peasants. The findings reveal that elite cooperation is contingent on shared religion because it creates cross-class ideologies and lowers the costs of elite participation. The effects of inequality of wealth and political opportunities are, therefore, inconclusive.

Chapter 3 investigates the role of grievances in driving elites to participate in peasant rebellions. In the vein of the prior studies, the chapter compares northwestern, eastern, and peninsular southern India to southeastern, southwestern, and central Mexico to test three explanations for elite participation: low inequality between elites and peasants; political opportunities; and elite grievances against political and economic marginalization. The comparison demonstrates that elite cooperation was caused by grievances against political and economic marginalization, and such grievances could be distinct from those of rebelling peasants. The effects of lower inequality and political opportunities, however, remain inconclusive.

Chapter 4 evaluates the conditions under which political-military leaders create peace agreements to establish postrevolutionary state institutions. Using the case of Mexico from 1910 to 1930, the chapter presents an intuitive explanation centered on the co-optation of peasant rebels into elite-controlled organizations; the rising costs of continued conflict; and the dependence of political-military leaders on domestic and international economic interests. The findings demonstrate that Mexican warlords, called "caudillos," joined peace agreements under two conditions: (1) when the costs and risks of competing to retain power became intolerable and (2) when their economic backers incentivized such agreements. The critical precondition was the absorption of peasants into caudillo-controlled organizations. Furthermore, the chapter highlights that the type of assets controlled by supporting economic elites determines whether they oppose, conditionally accept, or actively favor such peace agreements. Foreign investors whose investments in natural resources did not rely on domestic producers opposed such agreements. Landowners accepted peace agreements, but only if the agreements ensured their local dominance. Domestic financial and industrial elites favored peace agreements.

Chapter 5 resolves the important puzzle of why democratic leaders in developing countries choose economic strategies that profit elites and marginalize peasants whose support is needed to retain power. Using the case of India from the 1930s until decolonization in 1947, the chapter reveals that the outcome of the competition between dominant economic interests in late-colonial India led to the inauguration of policies benefiting domestic industrialists, at the cost of foreign investors and landowners. In particular, the findings demonstrate how domestic capitalists, primarily centered in the western Indian city of Bombay, came to influence the anticolonial Congress Party, which subsequently dominated the postcolonial state institutions. Moreover, the account of the competition among economic elites provides a novel explanation for the partition of India: threatened by postcolonial land reforms, Muslim landowners from northern and northwestern India collaborated with a Muslim peasant rebellion against Hindu landlords in eastern India to exit the polity and form Pakistan.

Chapter 6 assesses how postrevolutionary institutions can deny peasants both political freedom and economic development. The chapter centers on the explanation that Britain's actions in Rhodesia/Zimbabwe through the period of conflict were contingent on its investments in Africa. Initially, Britain's dependence on South Africa pushed it to a policy of inaction toward Rhodesia's White minority regime. Subsequently, the rise of Nigeria, and South Africa's relative decline, led to Britain's renewed efforts to resolve the conflict in 1978–1980. Through the Lancaster Agreement of 1979 and the elections in 1980, Britain's primary interests were to avoid the costs of Whites' fleeing from Rhodesia to Britain and retain the sympathy of Black African countries and the support of South Africa. These aims led to parallel policies of inaction against voter intimidation by ZANU and covert machinations to forge a coalition government that included the Whites. The broader theory that domestic owners of fixed assets accept regimes that protect their local assets is also reaffirmed by a study of White Rhodesians, whose economic and political power was based on the racialized control of agricultural land and natural resources. Specifically, as the costs of continued conflict became intolerable, White Rhodesians unsuccessfully attempted a negotiated transition to Black majority rule with guarantees for the White minority.

The Conclusion begins with a summary of the findings, then discusses the book's core contributions to research on peasant rebellions and the formation of state institutions. The second segment addresses *Undoing the Revolution*'s relevance to policy making. Most important, the findings imply that inequality of wealth in agrarian societies makes elites indispensable and renders peasants unable to avoid alliances, co-optation, and, ultimately, marginalization, even after successful rebellions. Consequently, international efforts to build responsive state institutions in such societies may be futile because states are inevitably captured by economic elites and their political interlocutors.

1

The Critical Elites

Class Coalitions in Peasant Rebellions of Colonial India and Revolutionary Mexico

This chapter evaluates four causes of peasant rebellions: (1) preexisting political institutions that moderately exclude elites and peasants (McAdam, Tarrow, and Tilly 2009, 263); (2) preexisting institutions that deny opportunities for economic advancement to elites and peasants (Bates 1981, 2001; Popkin 1979); (3) new political opportunities (McAdam, Tarrow, and Tilly 2009; Skocpol 1979); and (4) rebelling peasants' collaboration with elite leaders and organizations.

Comparing rebellions in northern Mexico from 1910 to 1920 with those in colonial northern India from 1930 to 1934—two societies with very different cultures and institutions—reveals four common causes of successful rebellions: (1) elite-peasant coalitions; (2) economic repression of peasants; (3) political repression of peasants; and (4) political repression of elites. These shared causes are subsequently evaluated via a comparison with two rebellions in northern India, from 1917 to 1920 and 1930 to 1934, with culture and institutions held constant to uncover the factors whose variance caused the former rebellion to fail and the latter to succeed. This within-case comparison shows that, because economic and political repression of peasants and the political repression of elites remained constant during both periods, the primary explanation for successful rebellions is collaboration between elites and peasants. The overall findings thereby demonstrate that the character of elite-peasant relationships—including autonomous peasant initiatives in shaping such relationships—substantially determines the outcomes of peasant rebellions.

In terms of the theoretical insights of the broader study on popular rebellions and institution formation presented by the book, this particular chapter demonstrates that elite-peasant alliances play a distinct role in explaining successful rebellions. Consequently, it challenges existing arguments that individual-level political and economic opportunities, or lack thereof, cause such rebellions (Bates 1981, 2001; Popkin 1979). In turn, the importance of elite-peasant alliances justifies the subsequent investigations into the factors that help or hinder them and, perhaps more importantly, show how elites come to control such rebellions. Thus, the bottom-up nature of the coalitions portrayed here—wherein elites and peasants support or reject each other's organizations and leaders—challenges the characterization of poor peasants as passive and malleable (Brass 1997; Woodward 1995) by demonstrating that their autonomous engagement influences elite decisions.

To reiterate the definitions of different social classes that underlie the book's central theory, elite classes can be divided into groups that own land (landowners and landlords) or capital (bourgeoisie or middle class), while peasant classes own only their labor or land sufficient for subsistence. However, the categorization of individuals and groups as belonging to a class is also contingent on historical research and self-identification.

On the basis of these criteria, laborers in northern Mexico's newly constructed industries (apart from those who worked on the region's vast haciendas) either continued to own small plots of land or were pushed into urban areas as a result of landlessness while their families remained in the agricultural sector. Consequently, these segments of the population are classified as peasants. Northern India, by contrast, had a more prototypical peasantry, who either controlled small plots of land, paying rent to local landlords, or were landless wage laborers who worked on land owned by others.

The discontented elites in northern India were landed farmers who owned more extensive acreage than poor peasants and urban professionals (primarily lawyers, physicians, teachers, and journalists). The incumbent elites were *zamindars* and *taluqdars*—landlords with large holdings who had seigneurial rights supported by the colonial government. The urban dissident elites of northern Mexico were a broader segment than their Indian counterparts: they were not only professionals, such as lawyers and schoolteachers, but also men who owned small businesses and even skilled technicians from regional industries. Rural dissident elites were small farmers and ranchers who owned and managed their land and property. The incumbent elites were large industrialists and hacienda owners backed by the prerevolutionary national government.

Based on these definitions, Tables 1.1 and 1.2, which represent the three individual studies (northern India over two distinct time periods and north-

TABLE 1.1. CAUSES OF PEASANT REBELLION: A VERY DIFFERENT COMPARISON					
Case	**Economic repression**	**Political repression**	**Political and economic opportunity**	**Elite-peasant participation**	**Outcome of rebellions**
Northern Mexico, 1910	Peasant: Yes Elite: Yes	Peasant: Yes Elite: Yes	Peasant: Yes Elite: Yes	Collaborative	Success
Northern India, 1930	Peasant: Yes Elite: No	Peasant: Yes Elite: Yes	Peasant: No Elite: No	Collaborative	Success

TABLE 1.2. CAUSES OF PEASANT REBELLION: A MOST SIMILAR COMPARISON					
Case	**Economic repression**	**Political repression**	**Political and economic opportunity**	**Elite-peasant participation**	**Outcome of rebellions**
Northern India, 1918	Peasant: Yes Elite: No	Peasant: Yes Elite: Yes	Peasant: No Elite: No	Separate	Failure
Northern India, 1930	Peasant: Yes Elite: No	Peasant: Yes Elite: Yes	Peasant: No Elite: No	Collaborative	Success

ern Mexico), evaluate the following explanations for the success or failure of rebellions: economic grievances against extant institutions; political representation within extant institutions; political opportunities; and elite participation.

Table 1.1, which illustrates the very different comparison of northern Mexico in 1910–1920 and northern India in 1930–1934, shows that all of the posited causal factors *except* economic grievances can explain the success of rebellions. However, Table 1.2, which illustrates the most similar comparison of northern India in 1917–1920 and 1930–1934, reveals that the critical causal factor is peasants' acceptance of elite leadership and organization.

Based on the factors represented in Tables 1.1 and 1.2, studies of the rebellions in northern Mexico and northern India, respectively, are presented. The conclusion summarizes the findings, explicates limitations, and suggests other societies where the theoretical insights could be used to comprehend the origins of rebellions.

Northern Mexico: Elite Leaders and Peasant Soldiers

The study of northern Mexico in 1910 shows the critical role of elite-peasant collaboration in the regional rebellions headed by Francisco Villa and the Sonoran generals. Beginning with an analysis of the region's prerevolutionary institutions, the study explains how institutions politically excluded non-incumbent elites yet gave them economic opportunities. The analysis subsequently demonstrates the critical role of peasant support for elite leaders and organizations in the regional rebellions.

Northern Mexico consisted of the provinces of Sonora, Chihuahua, Coahuila, Nuevo Leon, Tamaulipas, Durango, Zacatecas, Nayarit, and San Luis Potosí. Characterized by arid plains, the region was better suited to raising cattle than to agriculture. By the prerevolutionary period, Chihuahua, Coahuila, and Sonora had also developed mining industries producing copper, lead, and zinc. The region comprises two areas with different geographic characteristics: the Huasteca region in the northeast, traversing the states of San Luis Potosí, Hidalgo, Tamaulipas, and northern Veracruz, is characterized by mountains and valleys of the Sierra Madre Oriental range; and the area of La Laguna, located around the Nazas and Aguanaval rivers, became a center of intensive cotton cultivation in the states of Coahuila and Durango.

In terms of demography and occupation, prerevolutionary regional society remained agrarian. For example, the industrial sector employed only 4,000 laborers and mining employed fewer than 10,000 laborers, compared with the 35,000–45,000 agricultural laborers in Chihuahua (Sección de Estadística de la Secretaría de Gobierno 1910, 229). The agrarian nature of the Mexican economy meant that northern industrial laborers were usually small farmers or landless agricultural laborers with social and familial linkages to the agricultural sector (Besserer, Diaz, and Santana 1980, 1325).

The inequality and poverty of the agrarian sector, however, decreased with the continuing growth of the region's mining-related industries. During the immediate prerevolutionary years in Chihuahua, which later became the epicenter of the rebellion led by Pancho Villa, agricultural laborers were paid 35 centavos to 1.5 pesos per day (Sección de Estadística de la Secretaría de Gobierno 1910, 216) while their urban counterparts' pay ranged from 50 centavos to 5.5 pesos per day (Sección de Estadística de la Secretaría de Gobierno 1910, 229).

Nevertheless, the urban laborers' higher wages were offset by workdays of up to sixteen and a half hours, from 4:30 A.M. until 9:00 P.M. (Navarro 1957, 510–511). In Sonora, fear that higher wages in the industrial sector could decrease the availability of cheap agricultural labor led political authorities to lower the minimum wages in the industrial sector, according to Antonio I. Villareal, a rebel leader and future minister of agriculture and development (*Bisbee Daily Review* 1906). Landlords also took special and extralegal measures to retain cheap labor, such as hiring temporary workers during the harvest, using debt bondage, and installing private prisons, as in the haciendas of Rafael Izábal, a local representative of the prerevolutionary government of Porfirio Díaz (Camin 1977, 51).

The economic conditions of peasants and laborers worsened when the

U.S. economy suffered a major financial crisis in 1907. The subsequent recession was acutely felt in northern Mexico because of its dependence on investments from and exports to the United States; it resulted in widespread unemployment in the industrial sector and reduced demand for agricultural products. Export losses in 1908 were 92 percent, amounting to $14,667,195; mineral exports decreased by $12,000,000 from 1907; and the price of silver fell by 30 percent, zinc by 28 percent, and lead by 10 percent (Cahill 1998). By comparison, in central and southern Mexico only the export of sisal was affected, declining in value by $960,000 (Cahill 1998, 805).

In addition to landlords, peasants, and laborers, urban bourgeoisie had a significant presence in northwestern Mexico; the rural bourgeoisie were primarily located in the northeast. The urban bourgeoisie contained professionals, small-business owners, and craftsmen who relied on northern industries. In Sonora, urban industrialization starting in 1880 resulted in a 40 percent increase in the state's population. Centered in small mining and border towns, this population created an urban and rural bourgeoisie of merchants, professionals, and commercial farmers (Carr 1973, 326–334).

In more rural Chihuahua, the rural bourgeoisie of small farmers controlled a significant portion of the agricultural land, despite prevailing inequalities in landownership. Although there were nineteen large haciendas of more than 100,000 hectares and more than twenty-three moderate-size ones of 40,000 hectares, 230 small haciendas of approximately 1,000 hectares or more (Almada 1964–1965, 59) and 2,615 ranches of 15–20 hectares each operated by owners and their families also existed (McBride 1929, 98–99).

Despite creating a regional bourgeoisie, state institutions mostly favored large landlords who controlled politics. For example, irrigation works and a railway system in the La Laguna area, which facilitated the commercial cultivation of cotton, interacted with prerevolutionary laws for the colonization of unclaimed land to concentrate landownership in an exclusive group of hacienda owners (Velez 1970, 32–33).

Furthermore, although the bourgeoisie initially profited from the prerevolutionary economic policies, they increasingly found avenues for political representation closed (Carr 1973, 326–329). Given the close links between political and economic power in the Porfirian system (Haber, Razo, and Maurer 2003), such political exclusion affected their economic opportunities. In Chihuahua, the lack of political connections prevented extant landed farmers from obtaining uncultivated or non-demarcated lands, while speculation in land made acquisitions prohibitively expensive for them (Wasserman 1973, 314).

The situation worsened after the effects of the U.S. financial panic of 1907 began to be felt in 1908. Minister of Finance José Yves Limantour decreed that the banks could collect all of their loans within six months, saving the politically connected bank owners at the expense of small-business owners and landed farmers whose sources of income had already decreased (Beals 1932, 397). When the recession officially ended in 1910, the effects remained, with continued low prices for minerals and cost-cutting undertaken by the mining companies (Fay 1911, 269–271). Consequently, this eliminated the most important markets for landed farmers and small-business owners (Wasserman 1973, 316).

The Rebellions of 1910–1915

Even before the recession, laborers' grievances caused unrest during the strikes at the Cananea copper mines in January 1906 (E. Meyer 1980; Sonnichsen 1971), which spread to the textile mills of Orizaba, in Veracruz, and the railway companies of Chihuahua. Laborers expressed similar demands: shorter work hours, parity in pay and treatment for Mexican workers with their foreign counterparts, and better prospects for promotion (Sandoval 2009). Notable by their absence, however, were demands for a change in government; rather, striking laborers requested the benevolent intervention of the Porfirian government (Anderson 1974).

Although the factory owners, backed by government forces, crushed the strikes, they revealed a nascent alliance between dissenting elites and workers. The leadership, articulation of grievances, and organizing of laborers was provided by politicians from the urban bourgeoisie (Cockcroft 1967). Prior to the strikes, the rural bourgeoisie itself had exhibited opposition to the regime through the rebellion of 1893 in the state of Coahuila (Richmond 1980, 50).

Landed farmers' support for the rebellions of 1910 centered on the acquisition of land and local political power, which was acknowledged by local political leaders (Camin 1977, 371). The farmers sought to elect municipal authorities who could help them control the local economy by favorably demarcating uncultivated land and village commons and stopping forcible dispossessions (Archivo General Agrario n.d., Pasaje 23/75, Guadalupe Victoria 23/170, Peñon Blanco 25/176, Ignacio 23/692). In the Huasteca area, landed farmers and ranchers determined the direction and results of the 1910 rebellion (Falcón 2004, 376). Paradoxically, in some parts of Huasteca, the same factions of ranch owners who had competed to control politics in the prerevolutionary era rebelled after 1910 (Schryer 1986).

The operational relationship between peasants and urban laborers and the bourgeoisie was based on the type of resources the bourgeoisie provided, such as organizational and leadership skills and the ability to network with neighboring communities and rebellions in other regions (Falcón 2004, 376–377). Individual rebellions in the rural areas were led by small merchants and landed farmers who had been trained in tactics and weapons operation during stints in the prerevolutionary army. They included Francisco (Pancho) Villa in Chihuahua, Álvaro Obregón in Sonora, Adalberto Tejada in the Huasteca area, Saturnino Cedillo in San Luis Potosí, and Calixto Contreras in Durango. In the urban areas, the leadership was provided by professionals and small merchants, such as Adolfo de la Huerta and Plutarco Elías Calles. Given their education and high social status, many urban leaders were teachers, such as Esteban Baca Calderón from Nayarit.

During the early revolutionary period, reformist elites (dominated by large landowners) exemplified by President Francisco Madero did not recognize the rebelling elites' grievances. When he received a delegation from Durango headed by Calixto Contreras in 1911, Madero talked about the need for democracy and liberty while Contreras talked about land reform, leading Contreras to leave with coldness and clear hatred for Madero (Martínez and Ramírez 1988, 136). Another delegate informed Madero that peasants from his municipality of Peñón Blanco had mobilized for the agrarian promises, as they interpreted them, in Madero's revolutionary manifesto, the Plan de San Luis (Sanginés 2006, 130–131).

The reformist elites' inability to placate the rebels led to the proliferation of local rebellions under Saturnino Cedillo of San Luis Potosí (Falcón 2004, 376–377) and Adalberto Tejeda in northern Veracruz (Falcón 1986, 320). National leaders such as Pancho Villa presided over agglomerations of such local rebellions (Katz 1998). For example, in the state of Durango, ostensibly under Villa's control, four autonomous rebel groups operated, headed by the former rustler Tomás Urbina, the former muleteer Domingo Arrieta, the former blacksmith Orestes Pereyra, and the former landed farmer Calixto Contreras (Altamirano 2000, 128–131; Rouaix 1946, 277–282).

As a result, the subsequent revolutionary government under President Venustiano Carranza started supporting the interests of landed farmers, in terms of access to water (Estado de Coahuila, Comisión de Gobernación y Justicia 1912), and debarred owners of large haciendas from levying tolls on traveling vendors and merchants for passing through their lands (Richmond 1980, 54). Carranza also imposed higher taxes on uncultivated land (usually owned by large landowners) to incentivize their transfer to landed farmers (Estado de Coahuila, Comisión de Gobernación y Justicia 1912).

Although the Sonoran-dominated national government that followed the Carranza presidency permitted large landowners to officially control land, de facto control of land had already shifted to the rural bourgeoisie (Plana 2000, 89). Consequently, the Sonorans established the Comisión Algodonera de la

Laguna and the Comisión Interventora de la Laguna in October 1915. The Comisión Algodonera was created to centralize the allocation and distribution of cotton, adjust prices, and distribute resources to cotton cultivators, regardless of the size of their holdings (Cervantes 1916). The Comisión Interventora, however, which ostensibly was created to confiscate property owned by Villa's supporters, also prevented large landowners, whose property Villa had confiscated, from automatically retaking control of such land (Plana 2000, 73). This duality, wherein the postrevolutionary government officially favored large landowners while unofficially overseeing a transfer of land to landed farmers, could explain decreasing demands for land redistribution in northern Mexico.[1]

Northern India: Elite Organizations and Peasant Members

The studies of northern India in 1917–1920 and 1930 also demonstrate that peasant acceptance of elite leaders and organizations determine the success of rebellions. The salience of peasant-elite coalitions is highlighted by the fact that institutional conditions—political exclusion of the bourgeoisie and political-economic exclusion of peasants—as well as political opportunities remain constant throughout. The variance lies in elites and peasants rebelling separately in 1917–1920 and collaboratively in 1930, the latter rebellion leading to land reforms and broadening of political representation. The studies of the two rebellions are preceded by brief descriptions of the geographic and cultural contexts of northern India to contextualize the region's political economy.

The United Provinces—one of colonial India's most populous and densely populated provinces, with approximately 96 million people (United Kingdom, Government of India 1908, 35, 1909, 454)—constituted the largest area of northern India. The other province in the region was Bihar, which administratively was part of Bengal from 1757 until 1912 but had a society, economy, and institutions that were similar to those of the United Provinces. A riverine plain centered on the Ganges and its tributaries and distributaries traversed both provinces. The fertile alluvial soil and plentiful water made the area suitable for growing food crops, mainly wheat, as well as cash crops, such as tobacco, poppies, indigo, and sugarcane (Sinha-Kerkhoff 2014).

Before discussing the landownership systems that determined the region's socioeconomic structure, it is important to note the existing religious identities, which varied significantly from the predominantly Roman Cath-

1. For data from 1915 to 1920, see Departamento Agrario, Mexico, ""Memoria del Departamento Agrario, Apendice Estadistico 1936/1937," 64, reprinted in Tobler 1988, 500–501.

olic identity of northern Mexicans. In the United Provinces, Hindus made up approximately 85 percent, and Muslims made up 14 percent, of the population (United Kingdom, Government of India 1908, 45).

Northern India's economy was agrarian, which meant that colonial institutions pertaining to control, use, and taxation of land determined the region's politics. As demonstrated below, such institutions favored landlords. Although peasants received some rights via modifications in land tenure laws, landlords circumvented them, and peasants' control of land remained insecure.

The colonial land tenure and taxation system, introduced via the Permanent Settlement Act of 1793, was modified as the territory under British control expanded through the early and mid-nineteenth century. Consequently, two different systems evolved that were applied to distinct parts of the region, contingent on which system existed in an area before colonization (Raychaudhuri 1983, 13). However, despite the variations elucidated below, landlords generally collaborated with the British administration, which viewed landlords as the natural and traditional leaders of the peasantry (S. Butler 1906; Robinson 1974, 16–19).

In the province of Bihar and southern parts of the United Provinces, the *zamindari* system was based on the Permanent Settlement Act, which created a segment of hereditary revenue collectors who fixed rents for the peasantry and paid a prearranged tax to the government. In effect, the *zamindar* had alienable, rentable, and heritable lands (Kuhnen 1982, 61) that could be auctioned by the government if *zamindars* did not pay the requisite taxes (B. Chaudhuri [1983] 2005, 89).

In practice, such a system fostered rack-renting, wherein further subletting of land created layers of peasants underneath the *zamindar*, from cultivators with long-term rights to occupy land to those with temporary rights, as well as landless wage laborers (Jannuzi 1974, 11). The situation was worsened for peasants by high population pressure on cultivable lands (A. Das 1983, 25), landlords' exactions of illegal rents, and forced labor called *begar* (Hauser 1961, 24).

Despite its goal to institutionalize landlordism, the Permanent Settlement Act had uneven effects on the still larger feudal landowners from the precolonial era called *taluqdars* or *jagirdars* (Eric Stokes [1983] 2005, 41). Although *zamindars* flourished in Bihar, the feudal landowners of the precolonial era were wiped out as economic and political actors.[2]

---

2. Bihar was part of Bengal province when the Permanent Settlement Act was passed. Bihar was recognized as a separate province in 1912. Thus, the land laws applicable in Bengal applied there, which created the same effects. For further study, see Wadhwa 1981.

The exceptions to this decline were the *taluqdars* in the Oudh area of the United Provinces, who survived and influenced the provincial economy and politics until the 1930s (Reeves 1966). Their survival was due primarily to colonial land tenure and rent policies in Oudh that undercut peasants' grievances and strengthened landlords. For example, under the Oudh Rent Act of 1886 (which ostensibly gave tenants the right to use and inherit land that they occupied), tenants who occupied land and paid rent for seven years would develop inheritable usufruct rights (Baden-Powell 1892a, 250–251), while their rent could not be increased more than 6.25 percent each year ("United Kingdom, Government of India, 1886. Oudh Rent Act" 1990, chap. 4, sec. 38, art. 2). However, these rights were not inheritable; nor did fulfillment of the seven-year occupancy obligation incur any privileges to the peasants. The *taluqdars* could and did eject tenants just before their seven years of occupancy ended and would renew or accept tenants based on payments of large, up-front fees (Reeves 1991, 94–95). Moreover, the Encumbered Estates Act of 1870 permitted the government to temporarily take over the management of *taluqdars'* financially insolvent estates, thus protecting them from creditors or auctioning (Reeves 1991, 94–95).

Another distinct set of land laws applied to the northwestern areas of the United Provinces. There the British introduced laws favoring peasants over landlords (Edward Stokes 1959, 115). Peasants had more rights against landlords and paid less in rent (Baden-Powell 1892a, 194), and rent could not be increased for ten years (United Kingdom, Government of India 1892, chap. 3, sec. 77). Peasants also developed heritable occupancy rights after twelve years of cultivating and paying rent on a plot of land (United Kingdom, Government of India 1892, chap. 2, sec. 8). Given the absence of special protections for *taluqdars*, this area consequently became dominated by smaller landlords, who were also called *zamindars* (Metcalf 1969, 157–158).

Although they economically disadvantaged peasants, these institutional variations also divided landlords' interests, as manifested in their varied organizations: the *taluqdars'* interests were represented by the British Indian Association of Oudh, while the Agra Province Zamindars' Association, founded in 1914, and the United Provinces' Zamindars' Association–Muzaffarnagar, founded in 1896, represented small landlords from the northern areas of the province (Reeves 1991, 66–67).

In terms of their effects on other economic groups, the British institutions fostered the growth of landed farmers. Some had their origins in landlord families whose holdings had declined due to inability to pay rent and subdivisions among inheritors (V. Pandey 1992, 46). Others had their origins as merchants and minor officials who had bought land (Cohn 1969, 78–79). In Bihar, landed farmers had significantly more land than the average peasant, who controlled (in terms of rights to use) 5.19 acres. The landed farmers acted as moneylenders to the peasants, as well as low-level administrators for local landlords (B. Misra 1963, 73). In short, the landed farmers behaved as a rural bourgeoisie.

Furthermore, with 11 percent of the population living in towns (B. Misra 1963, 34), and with twelve towns of more than 100,000 people (four containing more than 250,000), the United Provinces was one of the most highly urbanized provinces in British India (Spate and Ahmad 1950, 260). The high levels of urbanization signaled the existence of an urban bourgeoisie composed of indigenous bureaucrats and professionals. According to the Provincial Census taken in 1921, the total number of professionals and members in the liberal arts—practitioners of medicine and law (lawyers and paralegals), who were locally referred to as *mukhtars* and *wakils*; teachers and professors; journalists and writers; engineers and architects, and so on—was 206,409, and there were 414,607 members of the public administration (classified as liberal arts), extending from judges to low-level bureaucrats (United Kingdom, Government of India, Edye, and Tennant 1923, 334).

The Failed Mobilization of 1917–1920: Elite Leadership sans Peasant Followers

In 1917, Mahatma Gandhi was invited by local leaders to intervene on behalf of peasants against European indigo planters in the Champaran district of Bihar. In turn, Gandhi's involvement transformed the Champaran movement into a coalition of urban professionals, headed by lawyers and the landed farmers (Pouchepadass 1974). One of these local leaders, Rajendra Prasad, eventually became the first president of independent India.

However, despite the successful Champaran movement, the peasants of the northern region refused to join the Indian National Congress (INC)–dominated Kisan Sabhas (Peasant Associations), in order to start mobilizing. Rather, the peasants independently mobilized under the leadership of landed farmers during the years following World War I. These initial mobilizations were caused by the scarcity and high prices of basic commodities due to the war, made worse by forcible war loans that *taluqdars* imposed to support the British government (Mittal and Kumar 1978, 36).

Confusingly, the peasant movement was also organized around Kisan Sabhas, although they were not operationally associated—that is, they did not take orders from the United Provinces Kisan Sabha established in 1917 or the Oudh Kisan Sabha established in 1920, both of which were controlled by urban leaders associated with the INC. Rather, the peasant organizations centered on local leaders and local causes.

In Pratapgarh district in the Oudh Area, two landed farmers, Jhinguri Singh and Sahdev Singh, established a local Kisan Sabha in 1917 (Sushil Srivastava 1995, 97). Around 1918 or 1919, they invited Baba Ram Chandra, a social activist who had lived in Fiji as an indentured laborer, to start a campaign against the *taluqdars*. By 1920, the Kisan Sabha had acquired support even from the low-caste peasants, who suffered the most under the *taluqdars* (Mittal and Kumar 1978, 39–40). Baba Ram Chandra led demonstrations to stop illegal ejections from land (Siddiqi 1978, 154) and, according to official reports, helped articulate demands enshrined in the "Kisan pledge" to stop illegal rents and forced labor (United Kingdom, Government of India, and Mehta 1920, 109–110).

Disparate movements to improve tenurial rights and lower land rents, headed by local Kisan Sabhas, began to break out in the northern region. The colonial government remarked that different leaders calling themselves Baba Ram Chandra were heading various movements (Mittal and Kumar 1978, 48). In Fyzabad and Sultanpur, two districts adjoining Pratapgarh, another autonomous Kisan Sabha movement arose in 1920, led by Suraj Prasad, who claimed that he was Baba Ram Chandra (Crawley 1971, 102–103). Suraj Prasad was not a peasant; rather, he had been a teacher and had spent time in Calcutta.

Furthermore, the local Kisan Sabha movement overlapped with the Eka (Unity) movement in the districts of Hardoi, Unnao, and Kheri. Beginning in 1920 and continuing until 1921, the movement consisted of poor Hindu and Muslim peasants fighting the *zamindar* landlords (K. Kumar 1994, 191). There is some debate regarding the support it received from landed farmers.[3] Nevertheless, even colonial authorities recognized that the causes of the Eka movement were similar to others in northern India, which were grievances against that combination of illegal and legal rents sought by landlords (United Kingdom, Government of India, and Faunthorpe 1922, 273).

The economic oppression of peasants, however, did not initially attract elite participation. The contemporary provincial leadership of the INC consisted mainly of urban professionals, such as lawyers, teachers, journalists, doctors, and even a few landlords (G. Pandey 1978, 50). The appeal by the local Kisan Sabhas to the provincial INC leaders failed, despite Baba Ram Chandra's personal request to the Allahabad-based Oudh Kisan Sabha (United Kingdom, Government of India, and Mehta 1920). The future first prime minister

---

3. Although Majid Siddiqi (1978, 202) posits that the movement's leader asked for cooperation from the landlords, others argue that such cooperation was sought by local INC representatives, not by the Eka movement's peasant leadership (K. Kumar 1994, 200; G. Pandey 1979, 373–374).

of independent India, Jawaharlal Nehru, then a young lawyer and urban organizer for the INC, was unable to comprehend the reasons behind the peasant mobilization. He wrote that Baba Ram Chandra had agitated the peasantry, lacked a political agenda, and had appealed to provincial INC leaders only when he became unable to control the excited peasants (Nehru 1936, 62).

Similarly, the local Kisan Sabha movement in the border districts of Bihar, led by Swami Bidyanand, failed to garner support from Gandhi himself (Crawley 1971, 98). Lacking elite support, such spontaneous peasant uprisings frequently became violent: peasant tenants in the district of Fyzabad looted landlords' properties (Crawley 1971, 105)—and were crushed by the local authorities (Mittal and Kumar 1978, 48). The Eka movement was also neglected by the INC, which ironically intervened to reconcile peasants with landlords (K. Kumar 1994, 201).

The landlords and their colonial sponsors, moreover, responded to these rebellions with a mixture of amelioration and repression. With the guidance of colonial officials, landlords set up Aman Sabhas (Peace Associations) to air peasant grievances and attempt public reconciliations (Reeves 1966). Along with the Aman Sabhas, the landlords' strongmen and the local police violently repressed new peasant uprisings (Nehru 1921).

In terms of institutional responses, the government and the landlords agreed to change parts of the Oudh Rent Act of 1886 (Reeves 1991, 96–97). However, the modifications introduced in the 1921 amendments to the Oudh Rent Act fell short of popular expectations because they did not permit full inheritance of usufruct rights over land tenure. Instead, the amendments permitted limited heritable tenancy wherein some peasants could occupy land for their lifetime, and their descendants could control that land for five years after the original tenant's death (Saxena 1935, 271). Although tenants who controlled land on contract got their tenures extended from seven to ten years, if they died before the tenure's completion, their descendants could use the land only for the remainder of the tenure period (Saxena 1935, 467). In essence, lack of elite allies and the consequent inability to continue the movement resulted in minor concessions, which left intact the landownership and rent systems.

Peasant Mobilizations of 1930: An Elite-Peasant Alliance

Between 1920 and 1931, the urban bourgeoisie in northern India benefited economically. Despite some reclassification of categories in the 1931 Census, there were 332,420 professionals and members in the liberal arts (United Kingdom, Government of India 1933, 214), a 62.09 percent increase over the 1921 Census (United Kingdom, Government of India 1923, 333). Moreover, the category of Public Administration and Liberal Arts, covering employees and dependents in judicial and administrative positions, was 533,612 (United Kingdom, Government of India 1933, 214), an increase of 77.7 percent over the 1921 Census (United Kingdom, Government of India 1923, 334).

The increasing numbers of urban professionals and officials during the prior decade implied their growing capacity as political actors. Indeed, unlike the earlier uprising, the INC started the 1930 peasant movement to extend its support base to the significantly more populous rural sector (Siddiqi 1978, 143). In terms of attracting peasants, Nehru had been co-opting the autonomous Kisan Sabhas, which spontaneously arose between 1917 and 1920, into the Oudh Kisan Sabha (K. Kumar 1994, 105–106). In addition to peasant support, the INC's rural focus attracted support from landed farmers and rural merchants, who joined the party through the 1920s and early 1930s (C. Bayly 1970, 325–332; Brennan 1972, 182–183).

Despite the amalgamation of peasants and elites, methods of political protest through institutional channels versus mass mobilizations—albeit in peaceful marches, demonstrations, and no-rent campaigns—were initially a point of contention between rebelling elites. For example, the activists in the United Provinces Kisan Sabha wanted to participate in the provincial legislative council elections, while the Oudh Kisan Sabha's leadership intended to boycott the election. Even colonial officials such as William Crawley feared that the United Provinces Kisan Sabha threatened the landlords' majority in the provincial Legislative Council (Simon 1930, 1:117–118).

Such internal differences and official wariness, however, overlooked the fact that electoral institutions were not designed to represent popular demands: the restrictive literacy, tax, and property qualifications for voting precluded the participation of all peasants and most landed farmers. In the United Provinces, for example, the landlords' control over the Legislative Council relied on electoral rules that overrepresented them to manufacture artificial majorities (Reeves 1991, 82).

Nevertheless, the lack of institutional channels of representation did not keep the INC from further strengthening its support and organization among peasants. It did so by selectively repressing and co-opting autonomous peasant uprisings via the establishment of control over ongoing peasant mobilizations and the removal of recalcitrant peasant leaders. Gandhi was complicit in imprisoning the popular Baba Ram Chandra to avoid escalating the autonomous Kisan Sabha mobilization the local leader headed (Mittal and Kumar 1978, 47–48). Moreover, the INC dissociated itself from violent autonomous movements, such as the Eka movement headed by Madari Pasi (K. Kumar 1994, 201).

The extent of the INC's command of regional peasants became evident during the Civil Disobedience Movement of 1930–1931, in the wake of the

Great Depression that reduced prices of agricultural produce while land rents remained high (Neale 1962, 176). The movement began with an official INC declaration on January 26, 1930 (Sitarammya 1969, 357–369), which demonstrated that the INC was a popular organization demanding land reforms (Reeves 1991, 220). Consequently, the British recognized the rising peasant-elite coalition in the electoral area. The Simon Commission Report of 1930 and the Government of India Act of 1935 removed landlords' special representatives in the United Provinces. Moreover, the report called for taxes on agricultural income, which targeted landlords (Simon 1930, 2:78, 97, 257).

The INC's victory was further ensured by the landlords' internal divisions and inability to co-opt rebel elites and peasants. Internal divisions among landlords resulted in the establishment of two separate parties in 1934. The smaller landlords from the northwestern area created the National Agriculturalists Party of Agra. The larger landlords from Oudh created the National Agriculturalists Party of Oudh. The former insisted that their party was a coalition of propertied interests—that is, the urban and rural bourgeoisie and the landlords—while the latter organization wanted only landed farmers and landlords as members (Reeves 1991, 212–213).

The landlords' continued disunity and the growing strength of the INC-led mobilization hastened the landlords' decline through the 1930s (Reeves 1991, 169–174). Some landlords sought to avert defeat by supporting religious parties that could unite communities across class lines. The Muslim landlords supported the All-India Muslim League (Brass 1970), while the Hindu landlords patronized the Hindu Mahasabha (Reeves 1964, 341–349). Although this strategy helped some landlords, communal divisions further fractured the landlords as a united group.

The United Provinces' Legislative Council elections of 1937 confirmed the defeat of the landlords as a political force. This time, the proportion of eligible voters had been extended to 11 percent of the population, with 140 general seats. Out of the total 228 seats, eighty-seven were reserved for candidates elected from various groups, including sixty-four reserved seats for Muslims; six for landlords; three for merchants; six for women; three for labor; two for Europeans; two for Indian Christians; and one for Anglo-Indians (Chiriyankandath 2001, 70, table 1.3).

To take advantage of the new electoral laws, the landlord parties fielded 111 candidates, second only to the 159 candidates fielded by the INC. The two religious parties—the Muslim League and the Hindu Mahasabha—fielded thirty-eight and ten candidates, respectively. But despite their efforts and funds, the landlords managed to acquire only twenty-five seats, including eleven from seats reserved for Muslims and six from those reserved for landlords (Reeves 1991, 224–229).

After its victory in the United Provinces, the INC government "stopped ejection proceedings against tenants for the recovery of outstanding rent" (Kudaisya 2006, 218). Similarly, in Bihar the INC government passed pro-peasant legislation during 1937 and 1938. The legislation of 1937 gave tenants "rights over uncultivated land" that was not being directly cultivated by landlords. The following year, agricultural incomes higher than 5,000 rupees per annum were made taxable, and it was even suggested that the *zamindari* system be abolished (B. Misra 1970, 430).

It is important to note, however, that despite the fact that such changes negatively affected landlords and seemingly favored peasants, the primary beneficiaries were landed farmers whose holdings remained intact and whose rents were lowered (Saraswati Srivastava 1976, 325). A decade later, 98.51 percent of the 2,016,783 *zamindars* qualified as landed farmers who controlled 42.23 percent of the land (India, Government of United Provinces 1948, 341–343).

Conclusion

This chapter tests political repression, economic marginalization, political-economic opportunities, and the nature of elite and peasant participation (i.e., separate or collaborative) as factors that lead to successful peasant rebellion. The comparative analyses reveal that elite-peasant collaboration—specifically, peasants' acceptance of elite leaders and organizations—is the key determinant of successful peasant rebellion.

The findings from the analysis of peasant rebellions in two very different cases—northern Mexico in 1910–1920 and northern India in 1930—appear to demonstrate the salience of political and economic institutions in determining elite rebellion. However, the findings regarding political opportunities do not explain such alliances: two economic crises in India did not result in the weakening of incumbent institutions and elites, and the economic crisis in Mexico increased repression but reduced support among bourgeois elites.

This chapter thus takes a first step toward explaining the critical role of class coalitions in determining the success of peasant rebellions. Two contemporary cases of peasant rebellions, in Colombia and Nepal, appear to support the insights presented here and suggest modifications. The peasant rebellion in Colombia has been under way for more than fifty years. Researchers agree that the peasants' mobilization was caused by economic inequality, particularly as it related to the control of land by traditional landlords and agro-capitalists, and by the political marginalization of peasants through the elite pact underlying the National Front, which originated during the civil war called La Violencia of 1948–1958 (Brittain 2010; Zamosc 1986).

However, elites played a central role in both peaceful and violent mobilizations. The urban bourgeoisie led by President Carlos Lleras Restrepo's Alianza Nacional de Uniones de los Campesinos (ANUC) fomented peaceful peasant mobilization (Zamosc 1986). With regard to violent rebellion, intellectuals and members of the Partido Comunista Colombiano (PCC) supported the peasant-centric Fuerzas Armadas Revolucionarias de Colombia (FARC) movement in the 1960s, providing representation in electoral politics (Brittain 2010; Leongómez 2005). Furthermore, the PCC attempted to co-opt and repress segments of the FARC (Aguilera Peña 2014).

Similarly, the decade-long Maoist insurgency in Nepal (1996–2006) was fought by repressed peasants. Murshed Mansoob and Scott Gates (2005) argue that peasant grievances regarding inequality of landholdings were the critical factors in the rebellion, while Alok K. Bohara and Neil J. Mitchell (2006) show that violent repression and rugged terrain also increased peasant violence. Nevertheless, the urban bourgeoisie, represented by the leaders of mainstream political parties on the center left and right, delivered direct and indirect support at critical junctures to the Maoists (Hacchethu 2008–2009).

2

The Religious Origins of Elite Participation

Class Coalitions and Religiously Motivated Peasant Rebellions in Mexico, Zimbabwe, and India

This chapter evaluates three explanations for why elites participate in peasant rebellions: (1) when mass grievances related to inequality are low (Acemoglu and Robinson 2006); (2) under conditions of moderate repression or political opportunities (McAdam, Tarrow, and Tilly 2009, 263); and (3) if they share a common religion with the masses (Marwell and Oliver 1993; Polletta and Jasper 2001).

The comparison of Zimbabwe's Chimurenga against White-minority rule from 1972 to 1979 with colonial India's Moplah Rebellion of 1921–1922 and revolutionary Mexico's Cristero Rebellion of 1926–1929, using an indirect comparative research design that leverages both the very different institutional and cultural characteristics of all three cases and variations in the outcomes of peasant rebellion, demonstrates that elite-peasant alliances are caused by shared religious beliefs. Variations in grievances based on inequality, by contrast, did not affect elite participation. Because moderate political opportunities remained a constant in all three cases, this factor also cannot be used to explain the variation in outcome. These societies' shared religions integrated elites and peasants by creating collective identities, while common religious organizations provided resources that reduced costs for participating elites. Where shared religious identity and institutions were not present, rebellions did not inspire cross-class participation.

The study of Zimbabwe reveals that, although the root cause of the Chimurenga was unequal control of land between White settlers and indigenous Africans, religion, centered on spirit mediums, cemented the alliance between indigenous elites and peasants. The rebellions in India and Mexico confirm this pattern, even though they were regional rather than national in scope. In Mexico and Zimbabwe specifically, shared religion created alliances between elites and peasants that resulted in successful rebellions. Distinct elite and peasant religions prevented such alliances in India, however, which undermined the rebellion.

Following the definitions of social classes outlined in Chapter 1 that underlie the book's central theory, the peasantry in the *bajío* region of Mexico, the site of the Cristero Rebellion, were landless workers on either ranches and farms or communally owned lands. Their counterparts in the Malabar region of India, where the Moplah Rebellion took place, were generally landless sharecroppers entitled to only one-third of what they produced for landlords called *janmi*, the group the colonial government recognized and supported as rightful owners of the land. Zimbabwean peasants were landless agricultural laborers or had land assigned to them by tribal chiefs.

The dissenting elites in Zimbabwe were Black professionals, such as lawyers and teachers, as well as independent farmers who owned small plots of land in areas assigned for Black ownership by the White-dominated government. The incumbent elites were the White farmers who controlled the most fertile and best-irrigated lands, backed by the minority-dominated government. In the Mexican *bajío*, the dissident elites were primarily cattle ranchers, urban professionals, and businessmen. Incumbent elites in this case were in the revolutionary government itself, which sought to control regional politics. The dissenting elites in the Malabar region of India, who could have collaborated with peasants, were the *kanam* who administered the *janmi* landlords' land and owned land themselves.

The studies of these classes show that shared grievances related to land, the primary resource in agrarian societies, cannot singly explain peasant participation. Specifically, they reveal that in the Moplah and Chimurenga rebellions, peasants' level of grievances vis-à-vis land rent and control was high; however, in the Cristero Rebellion, peasants participated despite enjoying freer access to land, which lowered grievances. Similarly, the effect of inequality on elite participation is inconclusive. Low inequality increased participation by elite classes in the Cristero Rebellion, and while high inequality coexisted with elite nonparticipation in the Moplah Rebellion, similar conditions encouraged elite participation in the Chimurenga rebellion. The only condition that varies and correlates with elite participation is shared religion. By fostering a collective identity with peasants and providing resources that reduced costs of participation for elites, shared religion induced elite participation.

Religion is a three-dimensional concept encompassing a set of ideas, a community of believers, and religious elites and organizations. Ideationally, it provides "beliefs and values concerning the ultimate origin, meaning, and purpose of life," which "find official expression in doctrine and dogmas" (Appleby 2000, 8). Thus, grievances related to religion either act alone or in conjunction with grievances arising from political and economic marginalization (Hasenclever and Rittberger 2003). Acting alone, religious grievances extend from demands against the state to freely practice a religion to claims that one particular religion dominates state institutions. Religion, in what Robert D. Benford and David A. Snow (2000, 615) characterize as diagnostic, prognostic, and prescriptive frames, can also be used, respectively, to create notions of injustice and tyranny; assign responsibility to groups and individuals for these problems; and provide resolutions such as rebelling to defend religious beliefs or capturing the state. In the selected cases, religious and material grievances could coincide, as in Zimbabwe's Chimurenga and India's Moplah Rebellion. Concomitantly, religious grievances may overwhelm material preferences, as in Mexico's Cristero Rebellion.

Religion's lived community is defined by shared rituals, such as prayers and devotions, and by following the "explicit moral norms governing the behavior" of those belonging to the religion (Appleby 2000, 9). The analysis of Mexico's Cristero Rebellion and Zimbabwe's Chimurenga show the existence of cross-class collective identities based on Catholicism and Shona indigenous religion, respectively. Conversely, elites and peasants did not share a religion in India's Moplah Rebellion: the peasants were Muslims, and the elites were Hindus.

The third dimension of religion is its organizations, such as churches and mosques, networks, and associated religious actors (Basedau and Vüllers 2010, 3), as well as leaders whose interests are distinct from those of believers (De Juan 2008; De Juan and Vüllers 2010, 7). Religious organizations and leaders provide tangible and intangible resources that facilitate the initiation and sustenance of conflicts (De Juan 2008). Religious organizations' role in overcoming barriers to collective action is highlighted in studies of peaceful mobilizations, such as that of the Black Church in the U.S. Civil Rights Movement (McAdam 1982; Morris 1984) and antiauthoritarian movements in other societies (Garcia and Parker 2011; Johnston and Figa 1988). In all three cases analyzed here, religious organizations supported rebelling peasants. However, separate religious identities, exemplified by the Moplah Rebellion, created exclusive groups within and between elites and peasants: under such conditions, provision of resources by religious organizations becomes ineffectual.

TABLE 2.1. CAUSES OF ELITE PARTICIPATION IN REBELLIONS				
Case	**Grievances: inequality**	**Political opportunities**	**Shared religion**	**Elite participation**
Cristero	Low	Moderate	Yes	Yes
Moplah	High	Moderate	No	No
Chimurenga	High	Moderate	Yes	Yes

Furthermore, it is important to note that spirit medium–based beliefs in Zimbabwe and Hinduism in India, as opposed to Catholicism in Mexico and Islam in India, are deeply polytheistic, locally heterogonous, and decentralized. Such characteristics, however, do not preclude Hinduism and the spirit medium–based religion from having the same mobilizing power for their adherents. The basic conception of what religion does for social mobilization—providing resources, ideologies, leadership, and organizations—is fulfilled by both centralized and decentralized religions. Thus, the compelling ideology in a spirit medium–based belief system is autochthony, a unifying belief of a community in their exclusive rights to a place. Whether such individual communities view themselves as explicitly national or not, spirit medium–based worship recognizes a broader community of belief with exclusivist claims to the soil. Therefore, it has the same potential to become a mobilizational ideology, paired with local leadership and organizations, as religions that are commonly understood as more organized and centralized.

Moreover, the perception of organized and centralized religion is a colonial artefact (Ellis and ter Haar 2004, 2007), and the distinction between localized practices and organized religion is often empirically unsupportable. In actual practice, even though Catholicism and Islam are viewed as centralized, they are embedded in the traditions and material realities of their communities of adherence. For example, the Day of the Dead (Día de los Muertos) in Mexico combines pre-Columbian beliefs into Catholicism and the shrines (*dargah*) built around the tombs of Muslim holy men (*peer*) in South Asia, frequented by both Hindus and Muslims.

Based on these definitions, Table 2.1 shows the role of the following elements in elite participation: initial grievances, initial opportunity structures, religious organizations' ability to foster a cross-class collective identity, and religious organizations' ability to resolve collective-action problems.

Analyzing the factors represented in Table 2.1, the chapter sections that follow present the studies of Mexico's Cristero, India's Moplah, and Zimbabwe's Chimurenga rebellions and conclude by summarizing the findings, explaining limitations, and suggesting future areas of research.

The Cristero Rebellion: Elite Commitment for Land and God

The Cristero Rebellion in the western-central states of Mexico—Jalisco, Aguascalientes, Guanajuato, Michoacán, and Queretaro—was unlike the country's contemporaneous rebellions. Beginning in 1926 and ending in 1929, the Cristero Rebellion occurred after the violent phase of the Mexican Revolution (between 1910 and 1920). More importantly, it was fought to defend the rights of the Catholic Church against the incumbent revolutionary regime and received support from both the elite classes and peasants. Thus, although nearly 60 percent of mobilizers were landless agricultural laborers and 15 percent rented their land, nearly 14 percent of Cristeros belonged to the rural middle class (Mabry 1978).

Despite extant grievances related to control and ownership of land, these were not apparently the pivotal factor for elite participation or peasant rebellion. The *bajío* region of Guanajuato, Michoacán, Queretaro, and Jalisco is covered with mountains interspersed with valleys. At the time of the Cristero Rebellion, it contained a large number of homesteads. This created an agrarian bourgeoisie and a small urban middle class directly and indirectly involved in commercial agriculture (Brading 1975, 131). In Michoacán, Jennie Purnell (1999) notes that the cattle-owning *ranchero* rural bourgeoisie existed in the "coastal highlands" and much farther inland near the "northwest highlands" around Lake Chalapa. In the highlands region of Jalisco, called Los Altos, the poor soil type was ideal for cattle ranching and attracted emigrants from Europe who maintained their lands and social ties by endogamy (Navarro 2000–2001, 1:30–31, 51–55). Alongside the rural and urban bourgeoisie, there also existed large hacienda-owning landlords, akin to the rest of Mexico (Brading 1975; Purnell 1999). However, despite the ethnic and economic differences within elites, prerevolutionary institutions had uniformly supported private ownership of land versus communal control of land, thus favoring the rural bourgeoisie and the landlords at the cost of surrounding indigenous villages (Hubert 1988).

Although the property-rights institutions supported elites, conditions for landless laborers and the indigenous peasant communities were also better than in other parts of Mexico (Susan Sanderson 1984, 33). In fact, where indigenous peasant communities felt deprived by local landlords, as in central and southern Jalisco, they fought against the Cristeros in order to gain the revolutionary government's support against landlords (Navarro 2000–2001, 2:21, 27, 38, 45).

Unlike inequality, changes in political-economic structures that threatened to deprive peasants of autonomy appear to have contributed to the rebellion. In this sense, it was the actual inability of the revolutionary government to repress local opposition (conditions of moderate repression), combined with the perceived threat of future repression, that propelled the rebellion. According to Jaime Tamayo (2008), the initial peasant uprisings were based on the realization that acceptance of land grants from the revolutionary government would mean surrendering their control over land. Such economic co-optation, it was further feared, would result in political subjugation to the revolutionary regime (Purnell 1999, 184–191).

The Liga de Comunidades Agrarias del Estado de Jalisco, for example, aimed to protect indigenous peasants from landlords and break up the large haciendas. Yet it was soon integrated into the Confederación Regional Obrera Mexicana (CROM), one of the official unions of the national regime (Tamayo 2008, 109–110). Furthermore, peasant beneficiaries in Aguascalientes were also forced to fight for the national government against the Cristeros (Fondo Genovevo de la O). Moisés Navarro (1985, 49) also notes that such forced conscription prevailed in most affected areas.

However, the critical factor that determined the participation of the elite classes was the Catholic Church, which provided a cross-class collective identity that increased trust among elites and peasants and provided leadership and finances that reduced participating elites' costs. The church was able to play this dual role because the Mexican church was a bi-layered institution: on the one hand, its central tenets and principles came from the Vatican and were imposed by a bureaucracy under bishoprics (Wilkie 1966); on the other hand, the laws and governance were instantiated in myriad small churches embedded in and responsive to regional villages and towns (M. Butler 2006). The centralized church bureaucracy propounded a cross-class ideology that the revolutionary regime was a threat to religious freedom (de Bonfil 1966; Jean Meyer 1974, 295, 303), while local church institutions enacted it by creating lay associations centered on religio-civic activities, such as the Liga Nacional para la Defensa de las Libertades Religiosas (LNDLR) and the Asociación Católica de la Juventud Mexicana (ACJM), which united bourgeois elites and increased interactions and trust between them and peasants (M. Butler 2004).

The Catholic Church's support of the rebellion was neither unprecedented nor altruistic. The church and the Mexican state had been opposed to each other since the mid-nineteenth century, when civil wars were fought in Mexico by pro-church conservatives and secular liberals (Bailey 1974; Jean Meyer 1974). The revolutionary government had always been aware of potential opposition from the Catholic Church, consequently forbidding the church from participating in politics and subjecting it to secular laws through Article 130 of the Mexican Constitution. Nevertheless, earlier postrevolutionary governments, under President Venustiano Carranza and President Álvaro Obregón, were unwilling and unable to enforce these laws (Tamayo 2008, 117–132). However, the more powerful revolutionary government under President Plutarco Elías Calles and its local representatives, such as Governor José Guadalupe Zuno in Jalisco, attempted to consolidate power by enforcing these laws (Aceves 2009). Given government repression and its social power, the church cemented a coalition between the elites, who provided leadership and finances along with the church, and the rebellious peasants (M. Butler 2006; Jean Meyer 1976).

The urban bourgeoisie participated in the rebellion by providing financial support and political leadership via the LNDLR and the ACJM (Bailey 1974, 304). Specifically, the LNDLR created a Special War Committee and attempted to manage the Cristero rebels (Bailey 1974, 114). Capistrán Garza of the LNDLR visited the United States on an unsuccessful mission to garner financial and political support for the rebels (Bailey 1974, 122). Elites in other, similar organizations, such as the Union Popular, provided urban hideouts for the rural rebels (Jean Meyer 1976, 128), collected money, provided supplies, and propagated the Cristero ideology (Purnell 1999, 101), while women who belonged to the Brigadas Femininas smuggled ammunition to the rebels (Miller 1984, 315–316).

In the rural battlefields, peasants were led by *ranchero* political bosses such as Ladislao Molina, who were once powerful all over Mexico. For warlords like Molina, religion functioned as both a means and a performance of their dominance over the local political economy (M. Butler 1999). Akin to the peasants' fear of loss of political autonomy, the revolutionary regime's land-redistribution policies and the introduction of peasant collectives connected to the regime also threatened the power of the bosses. Thus, they participated in a rebellion of landless and smallholding peasants (Ankerson 1984, 122–123).

Participation by members of the urban and rural bourgeoisie and the church created a rebellion that was pacified only via negotiations in 1929. The elite classes and the church acquired major concessions from the government. They were permitted political representation in a recognized party, which later developed into the Partido Acción Nacional (Jean Meyer 1976, 67–75). The revolutionary regime recognized the church's position in Mexico via the Modus Vivendi pact of 1929 (Reich 1997). To mollify peasants, the revolutionary government increased land redistribution during the rebellion and after it ended (Susan Sanderson 1984, fig. 5.3). However, the simultaneous introduction of peasant collectives, called *ejidos*, also co-opted peasants into the revolutionary regime (Ankerson 1985; de Bonfil 1966; Fábregas 1977).

The Moplah Rebellion: Divided Religions and Elite Opposition

Although motivated by religion, the Moplah Rebellion of 1921–1922, in the coastal Malabar region of the southern Indian province of Madras, failed to attract support from elite classes and was subsequently crushed by the British. Unlike the Cristero Rebellion, the Moplah Rebellion had a background of peasant grievances regarding land rent paid to the government and landlords. However, similar to the political conditions in Mexico under which the Cristero Rebellion occurred, political-opportunity structures appeared to change with the first anticolonial mass mobilization. The rebellion nevertheless failed because religious organizations centered on Islam alienated elite classes: it attracted neither elite co-religionists nor Hindu elites.

The peasants' grievances arose from the structure of landownership and revenue collection. Land in the Malabar region was historically owned by upper-caste Hindus (generally Brahmin) called *janmi*, but cultivation and revenue collection were managed by Hindus from the Nair caste called *kanam*. The British recognized the *janmi* as the permanent leaseholder of land from the government: the *janmi* paid assessed revenue directly to the government; could sublet this property or "transfer it by gift, sale, or mortgage"; had the right to retain such land as long as the *janmi* paid the revenue; and could increase or decrease holdings or abandon them entirely (Mill 1859, 241). Peasant cultivators, by contrast, became entitled to one-third of the produce that their land yielded (Krishnan 1993, 110).

Because the British favored the "natural" rights of the *janmi* and *kanam* (Logan [1887] 2004, 608), the Malabar region became characterized by high land rents and conflictual relations between landlords and peasants (Francis 1908, 340). Inequality of wealth also increased as land became concentrated in the hands of the *janmi* and *kanam*. Conrad Wood (1987, 141) has compared the censuses of India from 1901 and 1911 to show that, whereas landlords constituted 5.7 percent of the population employed in agriculture in 1901, they made up 5.1 of this population in 1911 (United Kingdom, Government of India 1903, 231–233,1913, 140–142). During the same period, the percentage of agricultural laborers in the population was 61.8 percent and 60.7 percent, respectively. Thus, the relative concentration of landownership and resultant inequality remained acute. British administrators analyzing the causes of the rebellion noted the poverty that characterized the Moplah peasants' existence, but instead of considering the peasants' grievances, they claimed that poverty made the Moplah ignorant and manipulable by outside agitators (Hitchcock 1925, 9).

Simultaneously, the Malabar region witnessed changes in political opportunities at the local and national levels. Locally, there was conflict between the *kanam* and *janmi*; the *kanam* became members of the Congress Party to increase their control over land vis-à-vis the *janmi* (K. N. Panikkar 1978, 885–886). The Justice Party, heading an anti-Brahmin movement favored by the colonial government, which dominated provincial politics at the time, was led by the middle class (Gough 1981; Irschick 1969; Washbrook 1977). Their grievances centered on the disjuncture between their enhanced economic power and low social status (Barnett 1976, 15–31).

At the national level, the first Gandhian mass mobilization arose in 1920. It was called the Non-Cooperation, or Khilafat, movement because it merged the mainstream anticolonial mobilization with the Islamic movement to restore the Ottoman caliph. Between June and August 1921, the Congress Party created local Khilafat committees to appeal directly to Moplah peasants' Islamic faith to start a movement to restore the caliph (Judith Brown 1972, 328). However, the control exerted by the Congress Party over recruits' activities was minimal, as "itinerant organizers would visit a *desam* (village), hold a meeting in the local mosque, collect subscriptions, appoint Khilafat officials, and pass on, hardly knowing who their new recruits were" (C. Wood 1987, 141). Although the Khilafat movement combined religious and political grievances, such appeals also tapped into preexisting pan-Islamic ideologies that had precipitated prior revolts led by local Muslim clerics (S. Alavi 2011; Dale 1977). The district magistrate of Malabar noted the involvement of senior Muslim clerics in Khilafat meetings and attempted to prevent further meetings from being held (Thomas [1921] 1923).

While pan-Islamism encouraged participation by Moplah peasants, it alienated possible elite-class supporters. The Islamic ideology spurring the rebellion centered on mosques' providing communication networks and local leadership via clerics (Hitchcock 1925, 3). Yet Islamic leaders also framed the conflict as a jihad against the British Empire and its local allies, the Hindu *janmi* and *kanam* (K. N. Panikkar 1989; Randathani 2007, 138–146). The divisions fostered by religion alienated Hindu elites. The effect of this was worsened because the wealthier landowning and middle-class Moplahs from northern Malabar also did not rebel (Hardgrave 1977, 97–98).

The unsuccessful peasant rebellion of 1921 was characterized by extreme violence. It led to the killings of British officials and soldiers, along with rapes and looting of Hindu property, the killing of Hindu landlords, and forcible conversion of Hindu peasants (Nair 1923, app., 52–72). However, it was crushed rapidly, and the peasants did not achieve their objectives of lower land rents and changing the system of landownership. Instead, the British passed the Malabar Tenancy Act, rewarding the middle classes for not participating by granting more rights to the *kanam* relative to the *janmi* and Moplah peasants (K. N. Panikkar 1978, 887). The middle classes continued in power via the Justice Party until the mid-1930s, followed by the Congress Party, both of whose primary function was to tap jobs and resources from the provincial government (Washbrook 1973, 525–527).

The Chimurenga Rebellion: Spirits of Elite Collaboration

The rebellion against White minority rule in Rhodesia—better known as the Second Chimurenga (the chiShona term for struggle) or the Rhodesian Bush War—began with the adoption of armed struggle by the Zimbabwe African People's Union (ZAPU) and subsequently by the Zimbabwe African National Union (ZANU). The two organizations had shared origins and characteristics: specifically, they were led by educated, socialist, urban leaders seeking to replace Rhodesia (the name the White minority regime used for Zimbabwe) with a regime that represented the Black African majority (Scarnecchia 2008). Yet, as the second part of the study shows, ZAPU used grievances centered on land dispossession and political repression to recruit members into its guerrilla wing, the Zimbabwe People's Revolutionary Army (ZIPRA). However, its initial attempts at insurgency failed due to dissension among the leaders, and ZIPRA subsequently created a conventional army in an unsuccessful attempt to control postcolonial politics. The study concludes by focusing on how ZANU conducted a successful peasant rebellion based on the same popular grievances as ZAPU. Although the core causes of the rebellion led by ZANU were also hunger for land and political marginalization, grievances and political opportunities and repression cannot fully explain the rebellion's success. Rather, as the study shows, the rebellion encompassed peasants and elite classes because of the role of the *mhondoro*—that is, Shona spirit mediums.

Although political repression played an important role in the Chimurenga, the racialized control by Whites over the most fertile agricultural lands, with its roots in the origin and development of the Rhodesian regime, was the most important source of grievance. The largest and most fertile tracts were occupied by a small minority of White settlers—approximately 5 percent at the regime's peak—via a series of laws and policies, most prominent of which were the Land Apportionment Act of 1930, the Land Husbandry Act of 1958, and the Land Tenure Act of 1962. In contrast, the Blacks who made up 95 percent of the population were permitted usufruct rights in small and less fertile communal reservations called Tribal Trust Lands (TTLs) or private ownership in African Purchase Areas (APAs).

In terms of political institutions, the British (White) settler colony of Southern Rhodesia was founded by the privately owned British South Africa

Company and achieved responsible government in 1923 under White minority rule; Britain retained certain reserve powers, including the right to protect "native" interests. Between 1953 and 1963, Southern Rhodesia unified with Northern Rhodesia (present-day Zambia) and Nyasaland (present-day Malawi) in an unsuccessful strategy to stave off Black majority rule (Franklin 1963). However, Britain's decision to retreat from empire in 1960 and grant African countries independence transformed the political equilibrium that underlay the Central African Federation, as the short-lived unified colony was called.

The Rhodesian Front (RF) headed by Winston Field and Ian Smith, a far-right party representing White settlers, won the elections in December 1962, which were dominated by White voters because of literacy and financial qualifications required for voting. Soon after its victory, the RF instigated the dissolution of the Central African Federation and attempted to declare independence from Britain under White minority rule. In line with its broader decolonization policy, Britain refused to grant Southern Rhodesia independence without the introduction of Black majority rule (United Kingdom 1963).

During this period of uncertainty, laws and regulations regarding politics and race relations initially remained undisturbed and later became more stringent (United Kingdom 1966). Consequently, Black Africans continued to be aggrieved about disenfranchisement and lack of land reforms (Meredith 1980, 91–106). Contemporary observers also noted that active repression of political opposition increased through the mid-1960s by way of a series of laws and regulations (Palley 1970). Yet the lack of change in political institutions and increasing repression did not immediately spur the rebellion.

The origins of violent Black opposition can be traced to the dissolution of the Central African Federation in 1963. Moderate Black opposition had been growing since the late 1950s, led by the Southern Rhodesian African National Congress (SRANC), founded in 1958. The SRANC peacefully protested discriminatory laws and regulations pertaining to the control and use of land and cattle, as well as the mistreatment of Blacks by the Native Affairs Department (Bhebe 1989, 66–67). Although the SRANC was banned and its leaders were detained by the government in 1959, the subsequently formed National Democratic Party (NDP) became even more radical, demanding universal suffrage, which implied Black majority rule. Combined with local frustration related to inadequate provision of public services and overcrowding in the segregated Black townships, these demands led to the Zhii riots in 1960 in Bulawayo, Rhodesia's commercial and industrial capital (Nehwati 1970). After several such incidents, including a general strike in July 1961 (Scarnecchia 2008, 106–107), the NDP was banned in December 1961.

However, the NDP leadership quickly reorganized under the ZAPU banner. The most salient difference between ZAPU and the earlier organizations was its willingness to use violence against the White settler regime. Although ZAPU began as an urban movement in 1961, it was truly cross-ethnic, with an array of Shona and Ndebele leaders in its National Executive. Prominent chiShona-speakers included Deputy President Samuel Tichafa Parirenyatwa, General Secretary Morton Malianga, Organizing Secretary Clement Muchachi, Information and Publicity Secretary Robert Mugabe, National Financial Secretary George Nyandoro, Deputy National Secretary Agrippa Mukahlera, and National Public Affairs Secretary James Chikerema. Important siNdebele speakers included President Joshua Nkomo, National Treasurer Jason Moyo, and Women's Affairs Secretary Jane Ngwenya. Further underscoring the cross-ethnic identity of ZAPU was the fact that some leaders were of mixed heritage—specifically, Youth Secretary Joseph Msika, who was of mixed Shona and Shangaan origin (Stauffer 2009, 155; Warner 1981, 27).

Furthermore, a quality of ZAPU that characterized its various splinter groups was the leaders' educated backgrounds and urban activism. Joshua Nkomo obtained a bachelor's degree before becoming a trade union leader. Jason Moyo, who attended vocational schools to train as a builder, was the only leader among those mentioned above who lacked a higher education degree. Among those who would lead the breakaway ZANU, Ndabaningi Sithole, its first leader, was an ordained United Methodist preacher with an advanced degree in theology from the Andover Theological School in the United States. Herbert Chitepo, who would lead ZANU from 1966 until his assassination in 1975, was the first Black barrister of Rhodesia. Finally, Robert Mugabe earned a bachelor's degree in history and English literature from Fort Hare College in South Africa and acquired other advanced degrees via correspondence courses with the University of South Africa and the University of London in economics and public administration.

The ZAPU leadership's initial political program centered on trade union politics–specifically, acquiring Black industrial workers' rights and linking trade unionism with a broader nationalist struggle. Union leaders such as Nkomo insisted on aligning nationalism with labor demands, while moderate leaders such as Reuben Jamela argued that labor's interests lay in supporting those of industry, which implied support for Whites (Mothibe 1996; Scarnecchia 2008, 111–116). However, these conflicts affected only the 16.6 percent of Black Africans who lived in urban areas in 1962 (Kay 1970, 64), not the vast majority in rural areas.

Nevertheless, ZAPU, too, had been banned by September 1962 in an unsuccessful attempt by the ruling United Federal Party to win over right-wing White supporters of the Rhodesian Front (West 2002, 228–229). After the RF's electoral victory in December 1962 on a clear platform of gaining independence from Britain under minority rule, the ZAPU leaders fled to Dar es Salaam, the capital of newly independent Tanganyika (present-day Tanzania), to seek support from President Julius Nyerere in forming a government in exile. However, Nyerere rejected the proposal and urged them to return to Rhodesia to lead the struggle (Scarnecchia 2008, 131).

Upon their return to Rhodesia, the ZAPU leadership became wracked with infighting, primarily over the leadership of Nkomo and on Ndebele-Shona ethnic lines, according to both historians (L. White 2003, 16–17) and contemporary observers (Brewer 1963). Leaders such as Sithole (1969, 35) also noted that the internecine conflict centered on ideological and strategic differences between a group led by Nkomo that sought to use violence as leverage for an ultimately negotiated transfer of power and another group, led by Sithole, that espoused radically redistributive political and economic goals, as well as a strategy of acquiring majority rule through total war.

The subsequent formation of ZANU, which broke away under the leadership of Sithole and was supported by Mugabe, led to serious violence in the Black township of Salisbury in early 1964. The resulting loss of life and property was exploited by the RF government in mid-1964 to justify the banning of both ZANU and ZAPU and the arrest of their leaders. Consequently, Nkomo, Sithole, and Mugabe spent the next decade in detention (L. White 2003, 16). The leaders who had escaped arrest in 1964 fled into exile in Tanzania or neighboring Zambia. This trend of exile persisted through the 1970s: after being released for a round of unsuccessful negotiations, Nkomo fled to Zambia in December 1974, and Mugabe left for Mozambique in 1975.

It is important to note here, however, that ZAPU remained a cross-ethnic national coalition even after ZANU broke away. At its founding in 1961, ZAPU had ten non–Ndebele speakers in the fourteen-member National Executive; after the split, it had ten non–Ndebele speakers in the reformed sixteen-member National Executive (Njekete 2014). Rather, ZANU's breakaway presaged the causes for the failure of the first wave of armed rebellion begun by ZAPU in 1966, which ultimately would lead to a further splintering of ZAPU in 1971 and its reshaping from a truly cross-ethnic organization to primarily an ethnic Ndebele one. Subsequently, ZAPU would rejoin the rebellion in the mid-1970s, but with an externally based conventional army and conducting an insurgency reduced to areas dominated by the minority Ndebele ethnic group.

Guerrilla operations by ZAPU peaked between 1966 and 1971. The ZIPRA forces' first engagement occurred in mid-1966 in northern Zimbabwe, but the guerrillas were neither properly trained nor equipped, resulting in massive casualties (Waldman 1975, 4). The Wankie (present-day Hwange) Battle of September 1967, in which eighty ZIPRA and allied African National Congress (ANC) guerrillas from South Africa fought the joint force of Rhodesian and apartheid South African military and paramilitary units, resulted in the death and capture of most guerrillas (Riley 1982, 43–44). However, the Zambezi escarpment battles of late 1967 and early 1968, between 150 guerrillas and Rhodesian security forces, lasted four months, indicating that the guerrillas had "gained the support and loyalty of some of the local population" (Riley 1982, 45–46). Throughout 1969, ZIPRA carried out smaller attacks and reconnaissance missions in the Wankie and Urungwe (present-day Hurungwe) districts. In 1970, one hundred ZIPRA guerrillas attacked the Victoria Falls airport and adjacent area and carried out minor operations in the Zambezi Valley region bordering Zambia (Riley 1982, 45–46; Waldman 1975, 5).

However, these guerrilla operations stopped abruptly in 1971 due to another major split within ZAPU, which irretrievably compromised its representativeness, military preparedness, and international alliances. In terms of its cross-ethnic makeup, the 1971 split resulted in the formation of a splinter group—the Front for the Liberation of Zimbabwe (FROLIZI)—by members of the Shona subethnic Zezuru group. Also, several highly trained and experienced Shona guerrilla leaders from ZIPRA, including Rex Nhongo, Thomas Nhari, and Robson Manyika, defected to ZANU. The departure of Manyika, ZIPRA's commander and primary liaison with the Frente de Libertação de Moçambique (FRELIMO), the Mozambican communist liberation movement that had captured the country's Tete province, also prevented ZIPRA from using Mozambique's shared border with Rhodesia, which was characterized by dense jungles that made it ideal for massive infiltration by guerrillas (Bhebe 1999, 34).

From 1971 onward, ZIPRA used land mines to retain the initiative in areas where it operated (Sibanda 2005, 165–166), which extended from the Mana Pools area to the vicinity of Chirundu, with the Otto Beit Bridge, which spans the Zambezi River and connects northern Zimbabwe with Zambia (Waldman 1975, 5–6). It is important to note that land mines are defensive area-denial weapons that prevent enemy forces from passing; they do not require active engagement with enemy forces and can be deployed with little manpower and thus somewhat overcame ZIPRA's organizational and leadership problems. Nevertheless, ZANU's guerrilla forces, the Zimbabwe African National Liberation Army (ZANLA), used the senior-level defectors from ZIPRA to establish new bases in Mozambique to begin the massive infiltration operations whose planning and coordination ZAPU had painstakingly undertaken (Sibanda 2005, 162–164).

ZIPRA's reentry into the rebellion in 1977 was distinct from its earlier strategy. Rhodesian intelligence estimated that the ZAPU had 16,000 trained guerrillas stationed in external bases and 4,055 deployed in Rhodesia. In stark contrast, ZANU had 3,500 trained guerrillas in external bases and 10,275 deployed in Rhodesia (Flower 1987, 248). The ZIPRA guerrillas operating within Rhodesia were trained by Cuba in Angola (Gleijeses 2013, 86–87).

More important, ZIPRA created conventional forces stationed in neighboring Zambia and relied primarily on Soviet weapons and advisers (Solodnikov [1998] 2013, 165). The Soviets provided heavy weapons such as T-34 and T-54 tanks, as well as 122-millimeter rocket launchers, armored personnel carriers, and large quantities of small weapons (Papp 1980, 11). The reluctance to deploy guerrillas in Rhodesia and the simultaneous acquisition of heavy weapons had two possible implications.

First, ZAPU was using its military strength to pressure the Rhodesians into delivering a mutually acceptable outcome via negotiations rather than having the outcome determined by an outright military victory, according to Christopher C. Chimhanda, ZAPU's director of information and publicity (quoted in Ndlovu 2003, 2–3). Indeed, since 1974, Nkomo had been conducting secret talks with Rhodesians for a transfer of power and even acceded to a temporary delay in the transition to majority rule (U.S. Department of State [1974] 2013). By 1976, Nkomo had become the accepted Black leader, and best possible future prime minister, by apartheid South Africa, Rhodesia's only external ally, and by the United States (U.S. National Security Adviser 1976). The explication of the transition to majority rule presented in Chapter 6 sheds further light on this aspect of Nkomo's role in the various negotiations through the 1970s until the British-mediated Lancaster House Agreement of 1979, as well as subsequent British efforts to forge an electoral coalition in 1980.

Second, ZAPU's strategy also indicated that it was preparing for a conventional war during the transition process to control or influence the postcolonial regime (Mutanda 2017, 146–147). Known as the "Turning Point" or "Zero Hour" strategy, it anticipated a "full-scale conflict in which [ZIPRA] would match the Smith regime's armour and air cover with armour and air cover of [its] own"; further, ZAPU's leadership "had requested the Soviet Union to accelerate the training of [ZIPRA] aircrews in that country" and provide "sophisticated modern aircraft [that] could strike on equal terms against Rhodesian strategic installations, communications and fuel supplies" (Nkomo 1984, 196). More covertly, in the event of a confrontation with ZANLA forces, the strategy even considered collaboration with Rhodesian forces in the effort (Onslow 2012).

As an important aside, there has been some recent controversy over whether the Turning Point strategy was actually achievable. In his work on ZAPU's role in the insurgency, Eliakim Sibanda (2005, 197–198) argues that given the ZIPRA guerrillas' intensive training and sophisticated weapons, such a strategy could have been carried out, especially with weakened Rhodesian forces and ZANLA. However, Darlington Mutanda (2017, 145–148) posits that the relative strength of the Rhodesian intelligence services and its air superiority would render the strategy ineffective.

Nevertheless, due to the uncertainties regarding belligerents' intentions and overall low information about their capacities imposed by the fog of war, British and U.S. policy makers feared a strategy that aimed to replicate that of the Soviet- and Cuban-backed People's Movement for the Liberation of Angola (MPLA) in neighboring Angola, which had captured power and pushed out two other Western-backed anticolonial groups right at the moment of decolonization in 1975 (Moyo 2017, 130–132).

However, the bringing down of Rhodesian civilian airliners in September 1978 and February 1979 with Soviet-supplied surface-to-air missiles removed any prospect of collaboration between ZAPU and the Rhodesians (Onslow 2009, 110–129). In retaliation, and given broader distrust of ZIPRA's intentions, Rhodesian forces conducted preemptive attacks on ZIPRA bases and Zambia's transportation infrastructure in November 1979 to thwart any planned invasion and steeply increase the costs to Zambia for continuing its support to ZAPU (Chongo 2015, 342–346).

The changing fortunes of ZAPU had a reverse effect on ZANU, which foreign sponsors such as the Organization of African Unity and the Soviet Union initially viewed as a splinter group that weakened the overall anticolonial struggle and that had acquired some international support only because of Tanzania's and Zambia's frustration with Nkomo's lack of commitment to armed struggle and willingness to compromise with Rhodesia (Reed 1993, 37–40). ZANU's initial attempts to conduct guerrilla warfare in 1965–1968 failed partly because of the guerrillas' lack of training and coordination. But most critically, peasants refused to join the rebellion, and their communities withheld support from rebels (Lohman and MacPherson 1983). The underlying problem for ZANU was its urbane leadership's inability to attract sympathy and support from the rural population—namely, the rural elites and peasants (Mazarire 2011). However, ZANU's decision to ally with Shona spirit mediums in the early 1970s catapulted it into becoming Rhodesia's primary guerrilla group and political opposition.

Broadly classified as *svikiro* (pl., *masvikiro*), usually men, the spirit mediums were the principal representatives of the Shona agro-cosmological religion, which sought to harmonize the rhythms of nature, human society, and the spirit world (Lan 1985; Schoffeleers 1978). Adherents believe that the real owners of the land are the autochthonous spirits "who intervene in the management and utilization of land" via mediums. The people govern that land only on behalf of the spirits, a connection instantiated by the overlapping agricultural and spiritual calendar (Sadomba 2013).

During the time of possession (but usually beyond that), spirit mediums are referred to as *mudzimu* (if they represent ancestral spirits) or *mhondoro* (if they channel spirits of ancient chiefs and heroic warriors). The process of recognizing a person as a *svikiro* involves acceptance and initiation by existing *mhondoro* and tribal elders. Once initiated, an individual *svikiro* may lose legitimacy with the public (Fry 1976). This study focuses on the *mhondoro* because they hold a higher position in the spiritual hierarchy.

Once accepted by elders, other mediums, and the public, a *mhondoro* provides authoritative opinions and judgments on matters that extend from familial disputes to political decisions. Most important, the *mhondoro* makes decisions regarding agriculture, such as when to plant and harvest, as well as whether it will rain (Bourdillon 1976). The ability of *mhondoro* to accomplish these tasks depends on their knowledge of local events and people. Consequently, divination frequently led to patients' being diagnosed as victims of witchcraft by their enemies or as having lost the protection of ancestral spirits (*mudzimu*) because of harming kith and kin (Fry 1976; Lan 1985).

While the colonial and White-controlled Rhodesian regimes co-opted the indigenous chiefs based on the broader imperial tactic of indirect control, the *mhondoro* remained an autonomous institution whose power was contingent on support from all segments of society (Fry 1976, 120). The ability of the *mhondoro* to deter dissent among the Shona and threaten collaborators with the Rhodesian regime made them attractive allies for the urban Shona leaders (Scarnecchia 2008). A *mhondoro*'s knowledge of local affairs and local legitimacy enabled him to punish dissenters and collaborators by labeling them witches, excommunicating them, and exacting fines (Latham 1986, 66–75). The *mhondoro* mediated relations between ZANLA and the rural populace by imposing restrictions on guerrillas regarding sexual relations with local women and helped guerrillas avoid detection by using their intimate knowledge of local terrain (Lan 1985, 164–165).

The demand for *mhondoro* services increased as ZANLA guerrillas advanced into, and the Rhodesian regime retreated from, rural areas, which threatened to fragment Shona society on lines of class, gender, and age. Poor peasants, youth, and women from ZANLA challenged the wealthy older men who held power (Kriger 1988). Given the shared background and ideology of the *mhondoro*, rural elites attended possession ceremonies with peasants and abided by strictures imposed on goods and services (Lan 1989). The *mhondoro* appealed to Shona landowners, who dominated politics in TTL and APA zones, because their ideology blamed the White-controlled regime for depriving them of land, rather than focusing on internal differences (Ranger 1985, 264–265, 269). Landowners' support was also incentivized because they expected future access to individual *mhondoro* if they were to become politically powerful and wealthy (Byers, Cunliffe, and Hudak 2001; Spierenburg 1995).

Familial ties between landowners and the *mhondoro* also engendered cooperation. Peter Fry notes that his assistant, who subsequently became a spirit medium among the Zezuru subethnic group of the Shona, belonged to a family who owned cattle and land in the TTL and an urban transportation business (Fry 1976, 68–106). Lan notes that the *mhondoro* among the Korekore subethnic group relied on intermediaries called *mutapi* from locally established families (Lan 1985, 6–62). As a result of these personal ties, the rural elites not only expected future benefits but also directly helped ZANLA guerrillas by providing them with food, clothing, blankets, and washing facilities (Machingura and Mozambican Information Agency 1977; Maxwell 1993, 368; Reid-Daly 1982, 325–327).

By the late 1970s, the tripartite alliance among the spirit mediums, ZANU, and local elites had transformed the small, disorganized, and easily defeated ZANLA of the mid-1960s into a guerrilla army firmly entrenched within the local population in areas dominated by the Shona. By the late 1970s, ZANLA guerrillas were using the local support to combat Rhodesian forces to the extent that large areas became "liberated zones" (Godwin and Hancock 1993, 245; Lohman and MacPherson 1983, 46–50). As Chapter 6 explains, these battlefield victories and negotiations mediated by Britain brought Black majority rule under ZANU, led by Robert Mugabe.

Conclusion

This chapter explains why elite classes participate in peasant rebellions motivated by religion by testing three major hypotheses on this topic: grievances related to inequality, political opportunities and repression, and shared religion. The findings demonstrate the salience of shared religious organizations with peasants in determining elite participation. In contrast, the findings regarding inequality are not sufficient to explain alliances between elites and non-elites: Inequality is high in the case of the failed Moplah alliance, high in the case of the successful Chimurenga alliance, and low in the case of the successful alliance in Mexico. Similarly, because repression was constant and moderate in all three cases, the political opportunities hypothesis does not explain variation in elite participation.

In addition to supporting the broader theses of this book regarding the participation of elites in peasant rebellions, this chapter also takes a first step toward creating a theory of elite participation in religiously motivated peasant rebellions. Consequently, future research can test and refine (or discard) the model presented here by applying it to comparable cases and broadening the theory by addressing associated concepts and addressing the limitations of this analysis.

In terms of broader comparative implications, this chapter's findings can be corroborated by at least three ongoing, religiously motivated rebellions in developing societies: the Moro Rebellion in the Philippines, the violent Boko Haram movement in Nigeria, and the Islamic militancy in Pakistan. Although grievances about economic and political exclusion are present in these cases, shared religious identity, as the following brief explications show, are more salient in generating popular support for these rebellions.

With regard to the Moro Rebellion, my theory accounts for Muslim Filipinos' grievances against political and economic marginalization by the Christian-dominated central government (Montiel and Macapagal 2006). Furthermore, my findings dovetail with Thomas McKenna's (1998) anthropological study highlighting the long-standing religious solidarity, centered on Islam, between local middle-class elites and poor citizens on the island of Mindanao.

Similarly, in Nigeria the latest insights suggest that the violent Boko Haram movement enjoys support from economically marginalized poor citizens and the local middle class, extending from professionals to businessmen (Agiboba 2013; Uadiale 2012). Despite grievances about marginalization by the Westernized elites who dominate the central government, Islamic revivalism has been central to the development of a collective identity between the Muslim middle classes and the poor (Abimbola 2010). Furthermore, there is evidence that a network of mosques in Nigeria is attracting funds from Saudi Arabian Salafi groups and indoctrinating refugee youth from neighboring Chad (Walker 2012, 3).

Regarding Pakistan, the theory presented here dovetails with both the bottom-up argument that political and economic marginalization of the rural populace by feudal landlords has increased popular support for Islamic militancy (Sareen 2010) and the top-down argument that sections of dissenting elites support the imposition of Islamic laws and regulations (Behuria 2010). Moreover, Islamic charities channel foreign funds to mosques that indoctrinate poor youth (del Cid Gómez 2010; J. Stern 2000). Based on this chapter's explanation, such a combination of factors can facilitate the formation of a revolutionary class coalition.

In terms of associated concepts, future research can consider the additive and interactive effects of ethnicity, nationalism, and religion (Hastings

1997; A. Smith 2003) in explaining class alliances. Furthermore, research in this vein can address the broader debate on whether popular movements for political representation and social justice are propelled by enlightened rationality or beliefs in universal natural rights (Kenny 2004; Ratzinger and Habermas 2007).

In terms of research design, the comparative study utilizes an elementary design that compares evidence regarding the existence of the posited causal factors on class coalitions between peasants and elites. The comparison shows why elite classes, regardless of whether they are bourgeoisie or landlords, ally with peasants. The next chapter, on the political and economic grievances that cause elite participation, therefore nuances the explanation presented here by focusing on competition among elite classes and the interests of different segments within each elite class. It studies the role of pro-British military servicemen with land grants in the northwestern colonial Indian province of Punjab, as well as the varieties of elites who led peasant rebellions in southwestern Mexico, from homesteading ranchers in Guerrero to landlords in Chiapas.

3

The Political and Economic Origins of Elite Participation

Peasant Rebellions in Colonial India and Revolutionary Mexico

This chapter evaluates four widely accepted factors believed to cause elites to participate in peasant rebellions: (1) political grievances; (2) economic grievances (Moore 1966; Popkin 1979); (3) political opportunities; and (4) inequality of wealth. By comparing peasant rebellions in central, southwestern, and southeastern Mexico from 1910 to the mid-1920s and in the eastern province of Bengal, southern provinces of Bombay and Madras, and northwestern province of Punjab, in India, from 1920 to the mid-1930s, I reveal that political and economic grievances are both equally important in determining elite participation. In contrast, the findings do not support changes in political opportunities (D. Meyer 2004; Tarrow 1998) due to dissension among ruling elites, institutional apertures via elections, state weakness caused by economic crises, or low levels of inequality (Acemoglu and Robinson 2006) as causes for elite participation.

In central Mexico, the incumbent elites were owners of large commercial haciendas. The primarily indigenous and mestizo peasants owned small plots of land, used communally owned land, or were landless agricultural laborers. The rural bourgeoisie from the same ethnic background consisted of cowboys and muleteers working for the haciendas, as well as village shopkeepers and itinerant merchants. The peasantry in southeastern Mexico exhibited similar characteristics, but the landlords controlled large commercial plantations producing cash crops for export and associated local industries, and the minuscule bourgeoisie was dependent on landlords. The peasants in southwestern Mexico exhibited characteristics similar to those of their central and southeastern counterparts, and the landlords were similar to the hacienda owners of central Mexico. However, in southwestern Mexico a significant class of rural bourgeoisie owned their own farmsteads and ranches or were small merchants and professionals such as teachers and lawyers.

The three regions of India exhibited greater diversity in the different classes' characteristics. Peasants in eastern and southern India were landless or tenant farmers, but their counterparts in northwestern India owned lands granted to them for military service, as well as incomes from such service and pensions. The incumbent elites of eastern India were landlords who owned or leased vast lands as tax farmers, and below them was a more numerous layer of subleasing landlords. The region also had British-owned cash crop plantations and collieries whose interests allied with those of the landlords. The dissenting elites of eastern India were urban professionals, such as lawyers and teachers, and wealthy peasants who owned land that they cultivated themselves, lent money, undertook small trading, and owned processing facilities such as rice mills. In peninsular southern India, in contrast, the incumbent elites owned land but were generally professionals or held positions within the colonial administration. The elites who allied with the peasants, however, were landowning farmers who were officially recognized as leaseholders by the government; in turn, they hired laborers and collected rents. In northwestern India, the British established an authoritarian, paternalistic administrative system that prevented the rise of autonomous agrarian elites. The elites who unsuccessfully sought to create a peasant uprising there were urban merchants and moneylenders.

The two very different comparisons of central Mexico with eastern India and southwestern Mexico with eastern India, derived from the studies of successful peasant rebellions in the three regions, affirm that both economic and political grievances were necessary for elite participation and, consequently, successful rebellions. However, the two comparisons also provide conflicting results on the effects of inequality and political opportunities. On the one hand, the comparison of central Mexico and eastern India affirms the validity of high inequality as a cause for elite participation. On the other hand, the comparison of southwestern Mexico and eastern India affirms the validity of political opportunities. The findings from the comparison of the two cases of successful rebellion in central and southwestern Mexico with eastern India's successful rebellion are illustrated in Tables 3.1 and 3.2.

The conflicting results arising from these comparisons regarding the effects of inequality and political opportunities on elite participation are addressed by comparing all four posited causal factors via within-case studies of three regions in each country. The findings from these comparisons reveal

TABLE 3.1. SUCCESSFUL REBELLIONS IN CENTRAL MEXICO AND EASTERN INDIA

Region	Economic grievances	Political grievances	Inequality	Political opportunity	Elite participation
Central Mexico	Yes	Yes	High	No	Yes
Eastern India	Yes	Yes	High	Yes	Yes

TABLE 3.2. SUCCESSFUL REBELLIONS IN SOUTHWESTERN MEXICO AND EASTERN INDIA

Region	Economic grievances	Political grievances	Inequality	Political opportunity	Elite participation
Southwestern Mexico	Yes	Yes	Low	Yes	Yes
Eastern India	Yes	Yes	High	Yes	Yes

that elite participation is contingent on the combined presence of political and economic grievances—that is, while the presence of each type of grievance is necessary, the grievances propel elite participation only when they are all present. Inequality of wealth and political opportunities, however, were found not to motivate elite participation.

Despite grievances related to political marginalization and outright repression by prerevolutionary and revolutionary leaders, the regional elites in central, southwestern, and southeastern Mexico from 1910 to 1915 participated in rebellions only when economic grievances accompanied political grievances. Political grievances were present in all three regions of Mexico, regardless of whether they experienced rebellions, suggesting that such grievances were a constant. Furthermore, although economic grievances were pivotal for elite participation, the nature of the grievances varied. In central Mexico, elite participation was caused by the decline of the traditional social and economic structures and relationships due to increasing control of land through principles of private property rights and new technology introduced by the prerevolutionary regime. In contrast, elite participation in rebellions in southwestern Mexico was caused by grievances against revolutionary changes in property rights and political institutions that threatened to restrict available economic opportunities. The absence of political and economic grievances explains why southwestern Mexico, unlike the other regions, remained at peace, despite a history of indigenous peasant

TABLE 3.3. REGIONAL REBELLIONS OF MEXICO

Region	Economic grievances	Political grievances	Inequality	Political opportunity	Elite participation
Central Mexico	Yes	Yes	High	No	Yes
Southeastern Mexico	No	Yes	High	No	No
Southwestern Mexico	Yes	Yes	Low	Yes	Yes

TABLE 3.4. REGIONAL REBELLIONS IN BRITISH INDIA

Region	Economic grievances	Political grievances	Inequality	Political opportunity	Elite participation
Northwestern India	Yes	No	Low	No	No
Eastern India	Yes	Yes	High	Yes	Yes
Peninsular India	No	No	Low	Yes	No

rebellions against hacienda owners, which were collectively called the caste war (Guerra de las Castas), through the second half of the nineteenth century. The findings of the comparative analysis are summarized in Table 3.3.

Similarly, the comparison of eastern, southern, and northwestern India from 1920 until the mid-1930s shows that elites participated only when political grievances were accompanied by economic grievances. The effects of economic grievances in and of themselves are inconclusive; they were present in northwestern India and absent in southern India, which did not witness successful rebellions. In contrast, the presence of both political and economic grievances centered on restrictive electoral institutions and a property rights system that favored landlords, underlay the successful rebellion in eastern India. It is important to mention, however, that a combination of military land-grant institutions and rebels' inability to acquire peasant and elite support across religious and urban divides accounts partly for why attempted rebellions in Punjab failed. The failures were also caused by significant political concessions made by the British (albeit accompanied by episodic repression) because the province supplied recruits to the colonial army. The findings from the comparative analysis are shown in Table 3.4.

The chapter sections that follow first present the studies of three Mexican and Indian regions to demonstrate the role of economic and political grievances in driving elite participation in peasant rebellions, based on the factors shown in Tables 3.1–3.4. After brief descriptions of the regions' social and political history, each study investigates whether and how grievances, levels of inequality, and changes in regional structures of political opportunity caused elite collaboration in rebellions, which determined the success of these insurrections. In the same manner, if the elites did not participate in or opposed rebellions, their reasons for doing so are explicated. The conclusion provides a summary discussion of the chapter's findings and avenues for further comparative research.

Central Mexico: Zapatismo and the Rural Bourgeoisie

The study of the Zapatista rebellions in central Mexico from 1910 to 1919 demonstrates that its underlying causes were political and economic grievances that revolved around the introduction of capitalist economic relations backed by legal changes. Divisions within the peasantry led to participation by members of the rural bourgeoisie, and the resources they delivered allowed the peasants to rebel under the titular leadership of Emiliano Zapata. Yet even before the rebellions ended, peasants became divided along the lines of those who had acquired land and those who remained landless, a cleavage exploited by their elite allies to retain power locally and in the evolving national regime.

The Zapatista rebellions affected the central Mexican states of Morelos, Hidalgo, Mexico, Puebla, and Tlaxcala, as well as the Federal District surrounding Mexico City, the national capital. The region is characterized by mountains, such as the southern Sierra Madre in Morelos and Puebla and the eastern Sierra Madre in Hidalgo. The mountains are interspersed with densely populated, fertile valleys where various cash crops were cultivated during the period under study, most prominently sugarcane in Morelos and maguey in Mexico.

The high population density, fertile soil, and ease of irrigation combined with the prerevolutionary government's push to commercialize the agricultural sector to bring about the highest level of inequality in landownership in the country (Susan Sanderson 1984, 15). Contemporary analysis showed that the largest percentage of the population were poor and landless peasants living in free agricultural villages: 93 percent in the Federal District, 82 percent in the state of Mexico, 78 percent in Hidalgo, 77 percent in Puebla, 74 percent in Morelos, and 65 percent in Tlaxcala (Tannenbaum 1929, 31–32).

The scarcity of land for such free agriculturalists was acute because they had been squeezed out economically by the new commercial haciendas and disfavored by a new legal system that elevated private-property rights over traditional communally owned property. Both changes were introduced by the prerevolutionary regime of Porfirio Díaz in its effort to develop Mexico along capitalist lines by integrating it with international markets and rewarding domestic owners of private property (Tutino 1990). Furthermore, the new cash-crop haciendas that produced sugar, for example, were more capital-intensive than their traditional counterparts, which reduced the need for peasant workers. Thus, the effects of land scarcity were exacerbated by a transforming relationship between haciendas and the peasantry that threatened the subsistence economy that until then had been sustained by precapitalist relationships of reciprocity between hacienda owners and peasants (R. Waterbury 1975, 438).

Nevertheless, although they held shared grievances, peasants remained divided based on their access to resources and relationships with hacienda owners. Peasant communities had been fighting over village boundaries and water resources, sometimes for centuries (Estado de México n.d.). The village of Teotipilco in Puebla requested the restitution of its common lands, waters, and pastures granted by the colonial authorities (Huerta and Macario 1916). Indigenous leaders from the village of Tlaxcalancingo in Tlaxcala were informed about a local commission that would help in the restitution of the village's common lands (Itzcoatl and Mixcoatl 1915).

Relationships with hacienda owners also divided peasant society hierarchically. Fixed tenants and hacienda administrators constituted the top layer; tenants and temporary laborers were in the middle; and temporary and indebted tenants and sharecroppers constituted the bottom layer (Katz 1976). The grievances of the peasants in the bottom layer, driven from their lands and without prospects for gainful employment, became causes for rebellion because the Porifirian institutions were unable to channel their centuries-old conflicts with landlords, which hitherto had been addressed through judicial and administrative channels. For example, two localities in the state of Mexico had such conflicts institutionally arbitrated, if not settled, in proceedings that extended from 1802 to 1936 (Santiago Zula, Municipio Tamamatla) and 1716 to 1956 (San Andrés de los Gama, Municipio Temascaltepec).

Although the small size and relative freedom within free agricultural communities provided both information networks and capacities to monitor and enforce peasant participation in rebellions (Chevalier 1960), local elites played a crucial role by providing leadership and organizational skills to create and sustain the rebellions. The rural petit bourgeoisie, classified as *pequeña burguesia* (Hart 1987) or *serrano* (Knight 1986), were integral members of such communities. They extended from cowboys and muleteers to schoolmasters, small village shopkeepers, and traveling merchants (González 1980)—people whose origins and occupations were much more intertwined with villagers' quotidian lives. Indeed, the most prominent regional rebellion began in Morelos under the leadership of a small merchant selected by his community because of his literacy, military training, and proven organizational capabilities: Emiliano Zapata (Womack 1969).

The Zapatistas confiscated hacienda lands and recognized the rights of indigenous communities over communal lands called *ejidos*, wherein the claims on lands were based on community or village rights (Warman 2004, 302–304) rather than on individually owned private property desired by northern Mexican rebels. Also, in contrast to their northern counterparts' gradualist approach of buying hacienda land before redistribution, the Zapatistas confiscated land and rapidly redistributed it to peasants (Associated Press 1914). When the northern revolutionary generals subsequently arrived to pacify the region, they recognized the peasants' demands and attempted to further address their grievances by abolishing debt bondage of peasants and imposing an eight-hour limit on daily work hours (LaFrance 2007, 353).

Nevertheless, despite their local support, the Zapatistas had insufficient economic strength and social networks to create a cohesive regionwide peasant rebellion (LaFrance 2007, 353). Paradoxically, the communal bases that strengthened the local efficacy of the Zapatistas in Morelos prevented their territorial expansion because the monitoring, punishment, and rewarding mechanisms needed to enforce participation were unavailable outside the state (Millon 1969). The Zapatista leaders also realized the need for finances to provision rebel troops and administer areas under their control. Thus, they unsuccessfully attempted to restart the sugar plantation–based economy by taking over defunct plantations and refinancing them via the public Banco Nacional de Crédito Rural (Warman 2004, 289–305). Nevertheless, as a result of such problems, smaller, unconnected regional rebellions arose that exhibited the same strengths and weaknesses. Domingo Arenas in Tlaxcala, for example, successfully fought for redistribution of land to peasants, yet he was unable to make headway in broader regional politics and fended off regional contenders by frequently switching sides between the Zapatistas and the northern Sonorans (Buve 2004, 306–335).

A crucial difference between northern and central Mexico was that urban labor and the middle classes did not participate in the central Mexican rebellions. Members of the organized labor movements centered in the textile industry, especially in Puebla, refrained from joining peasant rebellions for several reasons. First, their livelihood was contingent on the availability of cotton from northern Mexico; they therefore did not depend on the regional agricultural sector. Second, despite disputes with owners, urban laborers were paid more than their rural counterparts (Katz 1974, 28–29). Moreover, as northern revolutionary forces led by Sonoran generals arrived to pacify the region, they favored the urban labor movement to prevent coalitions between the laborers and peasants (Bortz 2003, 179–180). The urban bourgeoisie also did not participate in the rebellions because they were either minuscule, as in Tlaxcala, or dependent on the plantation economy, as in Morelos. Where an urban bourgeoisie may have developed, elite entrepreneurs did not spread technical skills or economic opportunities because they feared economic and political competition (Riguzzi 1999, 66).

Despite their subsequent military defeat by revolutionary forces from northern Mexico, the Zapatista and allied rebellions in central Mexico succeeded in redistributing land to peasants. The region made 868 solicitations for land grants between 1915 and 1920, the highest number of solicitations for land grants during that period and more than the combined solicitations from northern and western Mexico (Tobler 1988, 500–501). The average number of solicitations regional states made for land grants was 144.66, nearly double the combined total of 76.38 from the southeastern and southwestern regions (Tobler 1988, 500–501).

Most of the redistributed land remained with the peasants (Susan Sanderson 1984, 88–90), despite efforts by the Sonoran revolutionary regime based in Mexico City to return land to hacienda owners. In response to the presidential decree of September 19, 1916, annulling the authority of the governors and military commanders to hand over land to villagers who demanded it, and giving this power instead to the president, Arenistas in Tlaxcala—then local allies of the Sonorans—dated the registrations of their land transfer acts to before September 19, 1916 (Buve 2004, 319).

However, mirroring past divisions, peasants soon fragmented due to the uneven redistribution of land acquired from the haciendas (Tutino 1990). To protect land from being further subdivided, the controlling interests in the *ejidal* sector began to behave like the hacienda owners they had replaced: Zapata's son became a private landholder and represented landed interests (Knight 1986, 469). According to Raymond Buve (2004, 306–335), a three-tiered hierarchy developed in areas of Tlaxcala that were formerly controlled by haciendas, the lowest level occupied by landless laborers, peasant beneficiaries of Arenista land reforms, and former hacienda workers; the middle consisting of village-level politicians, politically connected businessmen, and hacienda managers; and the highest level comprising municipal council members, rebel military commanders, and political leaders directly involved in commerce or patronizing businessmen.

Rebels who replaced the first generation of leaders, including Zapata and Arenas, exploited the disintegration of the peasants' interests. Popular local leaders such as Priscilliano Ruiz (Contreras and Duran 1916) organized indigenous groups against hacienda owners (Ruiz 1915) to enrich themselves and consolidate their hold over local politics (LaFrance 2007, 83). Some leaders sought to leverage their control of the regional peasantry to attain membership in the evolving national coalition dominated by the Sonoran rebels from northern Mexico. Gildardo Magaña, who headed the Zapatista movement after Sonorans assassinated Zapata, fought against the Sonorans until they split between the faction led by Venustiano Carranza and the one led by Álvaro Obregón in 1920. Magaña subsequently allied with the Obregón faction (Secretaria de la Camara de Senadores del Congreso de la Union 1925) and embedded himself within the evolving national regime as chief of the military colonies in 1921; he first organized agricultural colonies for discharged soldiers and then the Confederación Nacional Agraria in 1923 for smallholding and indigenous farmers, and finally attained gubernatorial positions in the 1930s (Secretaría de Educación Pública 2014, 600–602).

The need to provision their troops and simple greed also soon made the Sonoran-backed national government's military commanders who had been sent to pacify the region turn to supporting the interests of the haciendas and of traditional indigenous leaders who were trying to retain their power. A letter, possibly from a Sonoran spy, talks about maladministration by Pablo González Garza, the governor of Puebla, and his lieutenants. It also provides information about the officers from the prerevolutionary regime's army who were occupying positions in the regional armed forces ("Oficina Secreta de Información de la Ciudad de Queretaro" n.d. [circa 1916]). One such general based in eastern Puebla, Pedro Villaseñor, confiscated land previously granted to mestizo and indigenous peasants after accusing them of being Zapatista sympathizers (Batista and Martinez 1916; Pacheco et al. 1916) even as he was supporting anti-Sonoran groups (LaFrance 2007, 83).

In conclusion, the study of eastern Mexico reveals that, because of their fragmentation, peasants' capacity to rebel became contingent on local elite allies. Furthermore, intra-peasant divisions reappeared soon after the rebellion began, centered on the uneven effects of land reform. Peasants consequently became vulnerable to co-option by local revolutionary leaders seeking to leverage their support to maintain power and become integrated within the evolving national regime. Although peasants gained some land, a result of their inability to unite was that the primary economic and political beneficiaries of the rebellions in eastern Mexico were the rebelling elites.

Southeastern Mexico: The Absence of Rebellions

Unlike their counterparts in northern and eastern Mexico, the four political entities in southeastern Mexico—the states of Campeche, Tabasco, and Yucatán and what was then the territory of Quintana Roo—did not witness significant peasant rebellions. This is even more intriguing because the indigenous Mayas who formed a large part of the population in the region had a history of rebellion, which included the Caste Wars of 1847–1910, that led to the formation of the independent state of Chan Santa Cruz, with which Great Britain even maintained treaty relations.

Although no rebellions of significance occurred, the study reveals an important facet of the overall explanation for elite participation: they are caused by the presence of both political and economic grievances. Despite political grievances, the retention of the prerevolutionary plantation economy in southeastern Mexico and the small number of elites meant that no groups of dissenting elites with economic grievances emerged. The region's high level of inequality of wealth perhaps also prevented elites from participating in rebellion, as did the absence of political opportunities, because the northern revolutionary forces simultaneously supported the plantation owners and sought to integrate peasants within the new revolutionary institutions.

Gilbert Joseph and Allen Wells (1990, 123) argue that, unlike northern Mexico, where middle-class leaders seeking political representation led and organized rebellions, the plantation economies of southern states such as Yucatán prevented the rise of a similar class. So great was their grip over local politics that when the new revolutionary regime attempted to consolidate its power in 1914–1915, the plantation owners funded an armed sovereignty movement (Joseph 1982, 7–8).

Indeed, owners of mahogany and banana plantations from the state of Tabasco, who were strong supporters of the prerevolutionary regime, survived almost intact until 1920 (Ridgeway 2001). During Tomás Garrido Canabal's governorship (1920–1934), Tabasco underwent a strict program of social modernization and persecution of the Catholic Church and its clergy and the creation of a proto-fascist political organization (Kirshner 1976). Yet land redistribution to peasants did not occur during Garrido Canabal's tenure (Steven Sanderson 1981, 100). The rationales and dynamics of such a process, in which the veneer of revolution was used to maintain the prerevolutionary social order, however, is most noticeable in neighboring Yucatán.

As the military commander representing the national regime nominally controlled by Sonorans, Salvador Alvarado defeated the sovereignty movement in the state. When he became the provincial governor, Alvarado aimed to separate peasants' interests from those of the hacienda owners but simultaneously co-opt both groups into the Sonoran-dominated national regime. Specifically, his goals were to increase agricultural output by introducing modern technology, improve the working conditions of agricultural laborers by organizing them, and redistribute haciendas' unused land to landless peasants to create a new set of smallholders loyal to the national regime (Ley

Agraria Complementaria del Estado de Yucatán 1916, chap. 1, art. 1–2; Joseph 1982, 129). Yet certain aspects of the new pro-peasant laws and policies actually undermined peasants' ability to organize rebellions. On the one hand, the new laws made the granting of land an administrative issue and introduced state-owned banks that could provide credit to peasants (Ley Agraria Complementaria del Estado de Yucatán 1916, chap. 4). On the other hand, such state-controlled institutions were used as instruments to control peasants.

The ideological motivation behind freeing peasants from domination by plantation owners but embedding them within new, elite-controlled state structures is outlined in a letter by President Carranza, which explains the Yucatecan laws of 1916 by citing Alvarado's views on the relationship among local, state, and national governments (Carranza n.d.[b]). Specifically, Alvarado justified the new laws to create independent municipal government based on the contention of the Swiss political scientist Johann Bluntschli that the state represents the will of the nation; thus, distinct state institutions should perform their functions in a hierarchical fashion. By this logic, a municipal government is an outgrowth of the family. Its goal is not directly political but economic and cultural; it stands between the individual and the state, between the private and public spheres (Bluntschli 1892). Therefore, peasants' liberation from plantation owners did not imply local autonomy in which peasants became capable of asserting their agency. Rather, such liberation meant fuller integration into new institutions and subservience to revolutionary leaders in charge of state institutions. Despite such efforts, however, Alvarado's inability to comprehend local cultural symbols and traditions undermined his ability to construct an institutional framework that channeled and addressed peasants' demands (Roggero 1997, 342–346). Yucatecan peasants thus remained subjugated and alienated.

Alvarado attempted to placate plantation owners by not abrogating their rights to own land, akin to the Zapatistas in central Mexico. Rather, he created a system in which communally owned land—implying land held by indigenous peasant villages—would exist parallel to private property (Ley Agraria Complementaria del Estado de Yucatán 1916, chap. 1, art. 1). Alvarado also created a state marketing board that sought to increase the price of henequen in international markets by removing American companies that hitherto had acted as middlemen (Younkin 1916). The policy and its ramifications for the formation of the postrevolutionary national regime itself are further explicated in Chapter 4. In addition to helping the Sonoran government in Mexico City, taxes on henequen were used to finance schools, public libraries, and public works projects (Knight 1986, 250), signaling the implicit acceptance of the regional plantation owners within the postrevolutionary political and economic system.

In conclusion, although southeastern Mexico did not witness the peasant rebellions that characterized Mexico from 1910 to 1920, the study of the region underscores the importance of the conditions under which elite participation was possible. Elites did not have economic grievances, although they had been politically disempowered. The authoritarian rule of local plantation owners allied with the prerevolutionary regime was replaced by that of representatives of the new regime, but the plantation-based economic structure remained intact. Consequently, the lack of elite support led to the failure of peasant rebellions, nay, even attempts to rebel.

Southwestern Mexico: Distinct Rebellions with Shared Causes

The peasant rebellions in Mexico's southwestern states of Guerrero, Oaxaca, and Chiapas arose from alliances between local elites and peasant groups. Despite declared differences in ideology, the causes for elite participation were both economic and political marginalization, although the former predominated among rebels allied with the national-level Zapatista cause. In Guerrero, these were sometimes private homestead–owning *rancheros*; in Chiapas, the owners of small plantations led the *mapache* rebellion; in Guerrero and Oaxaca, prerevolutionary political leaders also switched to rebelling. Furthermore, local rebels within and across the three states tactically allied with or opposed extra-regional revolutionary leaders, whether Madero and Huerta or Carranza, Zapata, and Villa. Nevertheless, the formation and success of these rebel groups centered on opportunities presented by the rise and fall of these extra-regional movements.

Jaime Salazar Adame (2011, 219–220) notes the existence of twenty-three separate bands of rebels around 1911, divided along geographical lines and represented by leaders from different classes: Ambrosio Figueroa, a wealthy rancher, dominated northern Guerrero; land and mine owners Ladislao Álavarez and Jesús H. Salgado rebelled in the Tierra Caliente area; Julián Blanco fought in the mainly indigenous central areas; Eucaria Apreza, a wealthy landlord, dominated Chilapa; Enrique and Pantaleón Añorve, from the mestizo smallholder population, fought in the Costa Chica area; and Tomás Gómez and the former schoolmaster Silvestre G. Mariscal fought in the Costa Grande region. Mariscal best highlights these tendencies: a prerevolutionary political leader and subsequent rebel, he was the only Guerrero rebel leader to ally with Huerta during the counterrevolutionary period, and who also refused to repress local Zapatista movements (Knight 1986, 61–62).

Peasants in coastal and central Guerrero generally belonged to indigenous groups who were in near-constant competition and occasional conflict with haciendas that began to surround and swallow their communally owned lands (Norberto 1998, 51–80). Zapatista rebellions allied to those in central Mexico arose in these areas, headed by Jesús Salgado and Julián Blanco (Jacobs 1982, 103, 128–129). Initially, the rebels defeated the counterrevolutionary federal army headed by General Huerta by capturing the heavily defended Chilpancingo in early 1914 under the combined leadership of Salgado and Zapata (Knight 1986, 149). Subsequently, Salgado led efforts to issue silver coinage under Zapata called "pesos zapatistas," to financially support their army and stabilize the local economy (González 1980, 24–42). However, the Zapatista forces became internally divided during the Carranza presidency: Salgado abandoned the Zapatistas in early 1918, although he continued fighting, but his subordinates, like General Amelia Robles, recognized the Carranza government in November, even joining efforts to pacify the state (O. Cárdenas 2000).

In northern Guerrero—el Norte and Tierra Caliente—the predominant mode of property rights was private ownership represented by small ranches (Carranza n.d.[a]). The rebellions in these areas were led by the rural bourgeois *rancheros* headed by Ambrosio Figueroa (Womack 1969, 80–84) in order to acquire political democracy and equitable taxation favoring the middle classes rather than the wealthy (F. Figueroa 1965). This latter rebellion initially allied with the northern Villista leaders and sidelined the indigenous Zapatista sympathizers. After the Villista faction's eclipse, the northern Sonoran faction, then led by President Carranza, continued to support Figueroa for two reasons: (1) because of Guerrero's strategic position, specifically port facilities and access to states controlled by Zapatistas, whom they were fighting, and (2) because of their inability to impose their own candidate owing to Guerrero's inaccessibility (Jacobs 1982).

In 1914, rebels in Chiapas began to fight against major landowners—from Tuxtla Gutiérrez, Cintalpa, Jiquipilas, and Ocoxocoautla—allied with the local representatives of the revolutionary government led by General Jesús Agustín Castro (Benjamin [1989] 1996, 188). However, the *mapaches*—which means "raccoons" in Spanish because of the rebels' ability to hide, hunt, and survive on corn—were not peasants. The movement was headed by two landowners from different parts of the state: Tiburcio Fernández Ruiz from Tuxtla Gutiérrez, who rebelled against the Sonoran-backed state government in December 1914, and Alberto Pineda Ogarrio from San Cristóbal, who joined the rebellion in 1916. The officers of the Mapachista movement were owners of small estates and ranches on the frontiers, in areas that remained underdeveloped during the prerevolutionary phase of modernization. The soldiers were ranch foremen, cowboys, ex-soldiers, loyal peons, and laborers (Benjamin 2004, 189).

The primary causes for the rebellion were political grievances related to the imposition of military governors by the revolutionary national government under President Carranza and allied major, generally coffee, plantation owners leveraging their economic power with the revolutionary regime in order to retain their lands (Benjamin 2004). In 1912, two years before the rebellion started, the revolutionary authorities garnered support from local elites, who created a state-supported militia called the "Hijos de Tuxtla" (Vázquez 1912), to put down a Mayan indigenous rebellion led by Jacinto Pérez, also known as "Pajarito" (Pastrana 1972), backed by elites from the old state capital of San Cristóbal (Maldonado 1912), although rumors about the Catholic church's support (Gamboa 1912) were unfounded (Benjamin 1980, 90). Later, the local elites also supported the counterrevolutionary national regime led by General Huerta without reservations (López Gutiérrez [1932] 1939, 115–116).

However, in September 1914, the revolutionary General Castro, appointed as military commander and governor by President Carranza, adopted a strategy similar to that of his counterpart Salvador Alvarado in Yucatán: undermining peasant support for local landed elites and simultaneously coopting peasants into the revolutionary government. Thus, he abolished debt peonage and promulgated the Ley de Obreros that prohibited child labor, fixed work hours, introduced minimum wages, and specified work conditions and certain perquisites for agricultural laborers (Benjamin 2004, 187–188). Nevertheless, the revolutionary soldiers' disregard for local customs, pillaging, rape, and attempts to despoil and destroy church property also made them unpopular (Benjamin 2004, 187–188).

The official declaration of the Mapache rebellion, loosely allied with the national-level movement by Pancho Villa, was the Acta de Canguí of December 1914, which stated: the rebellion is being fought against "the acts of vandalism that the Chiapan family has come to suffer due to the odious armed group that had invaded Chiapan soil, sent by the Carranza government without any reason other than to crush our political institutions, the basis of our sovereignty and declare itself the possessor of honor, lives and haciendas, planting pain and misery everywhere and attacking that which is most sacred to a man, the home" (Casahonda Castillo 1963, 34–35)—thus not only clarifying the political grievances but also slighting the economic transformations that Castro sought to introduce by freeing and empowering the peons.

As implied above, remedying economic inequality was not the primary motivator for the rebellion. The *mapaches* sought neither the redistribution of land from haciendas into communal or private properties nor the betterment of peasants (Ramos 1992, 41–65). In fact, the *mapaches* fought against the Zapatistas in Chiapas who wanted to redistribute land and politically empower peasant communities (Benjamin 1983, 600–601). Rather, the economic grievances were related to the elites' inability to continue with coercive labor practices vis-à-vis the generally indigenous peasantry, which elites publicly justified on racist lines (Núñez Rodríguez 2004, 38–39, extract from *Vida Nueva* 1914).

The rebellion initially took advantage of the weakening of the national government's control of Chiapas owing to the postrevolutionary civil war between Constitutionalists led by President Carranza and Conventionalists led by Pancho Villa and Emiliano Zapata, which allowed the rebels to form a loose alliance with Villa (García de León 1994, 257–259). Although they were unable to defeat the Carranza forces, the internecine conflict between revolutionary factions ultimately created an opportunity for them to ally with the Alvaro Obregon–led group and embed themselves within the coalescing postrevolutionary regime (Benjamin 2004, 187–188), while regaining their prerevolutionary economic dominance by crippling land reform (Lewis 2005, 17–19).

Elite participation in rebellions in the neighboring southeastern state of Oaxaca also showed similar causes: intertwined political and economic grievances. However, such grievances were not aimed at the prerevolutionary government and reactionary elites—after all, Porfirio Díaz had been a proud son of Oaxaca. Rather, they targeted the revolutionary government and openly expressed their satisfaction at the assassination of President Madero in demonstrations and newspapers (Silva 1991, 98–99). In contrast, there was latent support for the restoration of the prerevolutionary regime under the leadership of Porfirio Díaz's nephew Felix Díaz ("Oficina Secreta de Información de la Ciudad de Queretaro" n.d. [circa 1916]), who met with local political and business leaders (Pacheco et al. 1916) in order to start an unsuccessful rebellion. It was indeed the events revolving around the national-level political instability that spurred rebellions in Oaxaca.

The popular loyalty toward the prerevolutionary regime perhaps originated in Oaxaca, being the native state of Porfirio Díaz; however, more substantively, prerevolutionary Oaxacan elites retained power partially because peasants remained divided by geography and culture. The indigenous communities of Oaxaca inhabited valleys that contained most of the 10 percent of arable lands (Chance 1978, 9–29). Intercommunity collaboration was stifled by the physical barriers of intervening mountains, the cultural and linguistic differences between ethnic groups that dated back to the precolonial period, and the effects of colonial institutions that granted extensive autonomy to the indigenous communities (Taylor 1972, 25 [map]). These divisions were apparent in persistent conflicts between villages over land and resources, some of which originated in disputes dating back to the colonial period (Chichicastepec, Municipio Mixitlán n.d.; San Juan Lalana, Jurisdicción Villa Alta de San Ildefonso n.d.; San Juan Nochistlán, Municipio Tequixtepec n.d.; see also Chassen-López 2004, 443–444).

Given the problems in creating and maintaining horizontal linkages, local political leaders remained critical in deciding whether particular villages and communities would side with one political faction or another (Chassen-López 2004, 433–436). These leaders were usually small-business owners, merchants, and professionals, such as lawyers who were against joining any of the revolutionary forces led by Carranza, Villa, and Zapata (Garner 1985). For this reason, military commanders and political representatives sent by the revolutionary national government to govern Oaxaca sought the dissolution of the prerevolutionary political position of *jefes politicos*, which remained popular (Tejeda 1915).

In terms of grievances, there was considerable discontent regarding high levels of taxation imposed by the revolutionary national government of President Madero and near-famine conditions created by nationwide rebellions and the civil war fomented by the counter-revolutionary government of General Huerta (Garner 1990, 171). However, inequality of landholdings was low, relative to other parts of Mexico (Vásquez 1985, 194). Only 8.1 percent of the state's land was controlled by haciendas, as compared to 38.5 percent in Morelos in central Mexico (R. Waterbury 1975, 417). To qualify as a hacienda owner, one needed only 200 hectares; those considered large haciendas were between 3,000 and 5,000 hectares, and despite three or four that covered between 40,000 and 77,000 hectares, the common hacienda controlled less than 5,000 hectares (Chassen 2005, 28; Silva 1984).

Due to these grievances, two major rebellions occurred in the state. In 1911, an indigenous lawyer and *cacique* connected to the prerevolutionary regime, Che Gómez, fomented a rebellion among indigenous peasants against the Madero government (Chassen-López 2004, 434). Although the declared cause was that the Isthmus of Tehuantepec wanted to secede from Oaxaca and form its own state, Che Gómez intended to retain local political power against leaders being imposed by the governor backed by Madero (Ristow 2008, 136–154). Later, with increasing dissatisfaction at the series of state governments imposed by the Madero, Huerta, and Carranza regimes in Mexico City, the province as a whole attempted to secede in June 1915 in a movement termed as Soberanía (Garner 1990, 168). Again, the movement was headed by elites from the Vallistocracia, so-called because they came from the capital and the Valles Centrales area of the state and belonged to prestigious families established during the prerevolutionary period. Yet there was little ideological consensus between these elites other than to retake provincial power from the various leaders sent by Mexico City (Herrera Cruz 2011, 234).

Eastern India: From Political Awareness to Rebellion

The peasant rebellions that affected the eastern Indian province of Bengal from 1920 into the mid-1930s were caused by economic and political grievances that encouraged elite participation. Long-term grievances, in turn, originated in inequitable colonial institutions that determined control of, and rents derived from, land. More immediate grievances revolved around the issues of political participation and religious identity, which reflected deeper socioeconomic cleavages. However, the high level of inequality did not cause peasant rebellions in and of itself. Whereas during 1905–1911 elites failed to initiate peasant rebellions, they succeeded in the 1920s and 1930s under broadly similar conditions. Also, political opportunities did not provide a major impetus for such rebellions. British military power remained unchallenged throughout the 1930s, until it was threatened by the Japanese in the early 1940s. The national-level anticolonial movement led by the Congress Party was insufficient to motivate peasants to rebel in the 1920s, requiring the Muslim League's Khilafat Movement to do so. Moreover, both parties were challenged by the popularity of the Krishak Praja Party (KPP), which was dominated by the rural bourgeoisie and identified the parties with landlords and allied elites.

India's eastern region was dominated by Bengal, the largest, richest, and most highly populated province.[1] Colonial Bengal centered on three riverine plains: that of the Ganges, which flowed from northern India; that of the Brahmaputra, which flowed from the northeast; and that around the Padma River, which arose from the merger of the Ganges and Brahmaputra and drained into the Bay of Bengal through a vast delta. Alluvial soil, tropical climate, and plentiful water made agriculture central to the provincial economy. During the period under study, approximately 77.3 percent of Bengal's population depended directly and indirectly on agriculture (United Kingdom, Government of India 1923, 377). The climate and soil type were especially suitable for intensive biannual (autumn and winter) cultivation of rice as the major food crop. Commercial agriculture in the same areas centered

1. The other provinces generally excluded from the study are Bihar, Orissa, and Assam. Although this study makes minor comparative references to Assam, similar comparisons are made with Bihar in the study of northern India in Chapter 1 because of its shared social and economic characteristics.

on the production of jute, a hemp-like fiber valued for its high tensile strength. Tea plantations were located in the foothills of the Himalayas in northern and eastern Bengal. The output of both tea and jute increased between 1920 and 1936, although jute yields per acre began to stagnate and decline by the end of this period (Islam 1978, 93, 100).

The political-economic institutions that shaped Bengali society centered on the property-rights system, specifically regarding the ownership, renting, and use of land. Rent on agricultural land centered on the Permanent Settlement Act of 1793, which was introduced to raise the East India Company's revenue from an agricultural sector then characterized by scarcity of labor; abundance of land; and a precolonial system of overlapping layers of taxation, usage, and ownership (Bolt 1771, 163). To resolve these problems, the act aimed to create a simplified—if possible, single—layer of large landlords, or *zamindars*, with power to control the peasantry and collect rent (Wright 1954, 212–213). Moreover, akin to other colonial administrative institutions, the *zamindari* system was imposed because of its prevalence in the precolonial era and consequent popular familiarity (Raychaudhuri 1983, 13).

The Permanent Settlement Act created a set of *zamindars* who fixed the rent payable by peasants and paid a prearranged share of it to the government. Although essentially tax farmers, *zamindars* could sell, buy, rent, and inherit such land (Kuhnen 1982, 61), which could be auctioned by the government only upon nonpayment of the required rents (B. Chaudhuri [1983] 2005, 41). However, the *zamindar* rarely collected rent directly from individual peasants. Rather, the basic unit of taxation was the village (*mouza*) level, where headmen from groups or families with higher socioeconomic status negotiated with peasants and collected taxes on the *zamindars'* behalf, and frequently took advantage of such intermediation for personal benefit (B. Chaudhuri [1983] 2005, 135).

The *zamindari* system, however, had major inadvertent effects on the province's socioeconomic and administrative structures. It transformed the make-up of the local elites, immiserated peasants, and hamstrung the colonial government with regard to revenue collection—both setting the course for grievances and creating the belligerent classes that fought for political dominance from the mid-nineteenth century onward. Specifically in terms of peasant rebellions, evidence shows that peasants' grievances were caused by unequal landownership and control based on colonial institutions. However, the same institutions also created a landed peasantry who acted as a rural bourgeoisie, occupying the stratum between peasants and large landlords.

Responsibility for paying the government punctually destroyed the massive feudal landed estates of the precolonial era (Eric Stokes [1983] 2005, 41) and replaced them with smaller estates controlled by moneylenders, merchants, and locals connected with the colonial administration (B. Chaudhuri [1983] 2005, 109–118). However, the new *zamindars* undercut possible increases in government revenues. Whereas the *zamindari* system was expected to increase the government's share of land rent to 90 percent, while allowing landlords to retain 10 percent, by 1919 approximately 76.67 percent of the rent paid by peasants was being appropriated by *zamindars* and multiple layers of intermediary rent collectors (Chatterjee 1982, 120).

The immiserating effects of the *zamindari* system in the eastern district of Bakargunj can be demonstrated by comparing official colonial accounts from two time periods. William Hunter, a member of the Indian Civil Service and the first editor of the *Imperial Gazetteer of India*, writing in the mid-1870s, stated that the "material condition of the people is good. With scarcely a single exception, every man . . . is a small holder, and cultivates sufficient rice and other necessities for the support of his family" (W. W. Hunter 1877, 201–202, 205). The situation was entirely reversed in the next few decades, as *zamindars* added layers of intermediaries. The system, known as rack-renting, consisted of at least three layers in which *zamindars* sublet their land to *taluqdars*, who then sublet their land to *haoladars*. In 1909, colonial officials noted the process and logic of the system as it applied to Bakarganj: "The landlord's favorite method of raising money [is] to create an intermediate tenure between himself and the . . . tenure-holder immediately subordinate to him, at a rent slightly lower than he has been receiving, the premium paid to him being equivalent to the capitalized value of the reduction in rent" (Gait, Allen, and Howard 1909, 358–359). Most telling, the section of the same monograph evaluating the area of Assam on the far eastern side of Bengal—later made into a separate province—notes that a labor shortage made the tenants and even landless laborers wealthier than their counterparts in the rest of Bengal (Gait, Allen, and Howard 1909, 126). Despite such impoverishment, most peasants in Bengal rationally overcame the inelastic supply of land that prevented them from increasing total acreage under cultivation by maximizing gains from cultivating high-yield or high-value crops (Islam 1978, 201).

Alongside such coping strategies, the peasants' growing poverty and indebtedness led to a series of unsuccessful attempts at rebellion during the 1870s (Sengupta 1972). Although the colonial administration violently repressed peasant rebellions, it also attempted to constrain the *zamindars* and protect peasants via the Bengal Rent Act of 1859 and the Bengal Tenancy Act of 1885 to prevent further rebellions (D. Rothermund 1967, 90). The new laws created three classifications of peasants and institutionalized their rights vis-à-vis landlords: those who owned heritable leases on land at fixed rates, those who had twelve-year leases at variable rents, and those who were agricultural laborers (Chakrabarty 1985, 5).

These laws were significant because they changed the nature of the relationship between peasants and the colonial government and created a new class of peasants. Specifically, peasants recognized that, perhaps ironically, colonial institutions would protect them from depredations of native landlords (Chakrabarty 1985, 5). Furthermore, although they had existed as a liminal segment of the peasantry during the precolonial and early colonial period (Buchanan 1833, 235–236), a new class arose from the peasantry called *jotedars* because their rights had been defined as distinct from those of both *zamindars* and the landless agricultural laborers (Ray and Ray 1975). As "rich peasants who also engaged in money-lending and grain trading, and often also in small agricultural processing industries, such as rice mills" (Chatterjee 1986, 178), the *jotedars* thus became Bengal's rural bourgeoisie. In the northeastern district of Mymensingh, official records note, peasants with occupancy rights were wealthier and carried less debt because a large number of them were *jotedars* (Sachse 1917, 65, 68–70). Official records similarly note that *jotedars* formed a sizable segment of the peasantry in the northern district of Rangpur (Vas 1911, 79). Their relative wealth and grievances against landlords thus made the *jotedars* potentially the most critical class in provincial politics, which subsequent events would actually confirm (Hashmi 1992, 3).

The peasant and *jotedar* classes' role in provincial politics was made more prominent because they lacked counterparts in the urban-industrial economy and the commercial-agricultural sector. Although Bengal was colonial India's most industrialized province, industrial development and its consequent social transformation were retarded by the lopsided consumption of locally available coal by British-owned railway companies with government protection, precapitalist labor relations, and ethnically exclusive business and financial networks. Commercial agriculture of jute and tea, moreover, was primarily controlled by British companies, while indigenous ownership was restricted to certain ethnic groups.

The vast coal reserves in parts of Bengal and the neighboring province of Bihar did not foster coal-based industrialization. First, 30.9 percent of the domestic coal was owned and consumed by railway companies (United Kingdom, Government of India 1917, 1). The quantity of coal consumed by the railways increased through the 1920s and 1930s and remained higher than that directed toward the iron, steel, and engineering industries, as well as that consumed by the cotton, jute, and paper industries (Simmons 1981, 750). Moreover, the railway company that controlled access to the major coal-producing areas charged high rates for transportation, while other railways charged high rates for human carriage, which combined to make domestic-level industrialization prohibitively expensive (Hurd [1983] 2005, 758).

Although indigenous entrepreneurs had entered the coal-mining industry by 1920 (Simmons 1976), the relationship between colliery owners and laborers remained precapitalist, wherein wages were supplemented with land grants for subsistence. The *Investors India Year Book* (1914, 241) notes that "the Bengal miner is primarily an agriculturalist[,] and this large area of non-coal bearing land [30,000 acres] has been acquired by the [Bengal Coal] Company in order to secure their laborers their own land and so lessen the labor difficulties which are so marked a feature of the Bengal collieries." Similarly, the two major steelmaking companies in Bengal and Bihar had little positive effect on the surrounding countryside, functioning instead as isolated industrial enclaves (Krishnamurty [1983] 2005, 549).

Commercial agriculture also did not create a domestic bourgeoisie interested in forging alliances with peasants, because the two major industries—tea and jute production—were owned by British companies allied with the colonial government. English companies owned most of the tea estates (Griffiths 1967; B. Gupta 1997), and English and Scottish companies controlled jute production (K. Chaudhuri [1983] 2005, 853). Although indigenous capital entered jute production after 1920, entrepreneurs could not broaden their economic stratum because their financial and ownership networks relied on belonging to the northern Indian émigré Marwari community (Goswami 1987).

Despite the conditions these factors generated, the waves of peasant rebellions led by the *jotedars* did not appear to center on economic grievances. Rather, they most apparently centered on caste and religious identities, which overlapped with economic status and consequent grievances. However, although the generally peaceful and intermittently violent rebellions that took place from the 1920s on appeared as religious confrontations, the alliances among large portions of the Muslim community and lower-caste Hindus during the period revealed the political and economic causes that were propelling them. In contrast, while language had the potential for similar politicization, the cleavage never appeared because the rationales behind such politicization appealed to neither the peasants nor the *jotedars*.

There were four major lower-caste groups in the region: the Rajbansi, Namasudra, Kurmi, and Bagdi. Colonial officials noted social and economic discrimination by upper castes against all of these groups (Risely and Gait 1903, 218); only the Namasudras organized, however, forming the Bengal Namasudra Association to distinguish their aims from those of upper-caste Hindus (Broomfield 1968, 158–159). In terms of religion, the Hindus made up a demographic majority until 1872, when they numbered 18 million, compared with 17.5 million Muslims (Beverly 1874, 85). Subsequently, the Hindus became a minority (Murshid 1995, 28). The fear of religious domination was soon politicized by segments of the anticolonial movement dominated by the Hindu elite (Southard 1980) and exploited by colonial policy such as the Communal Awards, which created separate electoral constituencies on the bases of caste and religion (Chakrabarty 1989).

However, these religious and caste identities overlapped with class positions. Landlords were generally upper-caste Hindus, while the peasantry, including most *jotedars*, identified as Muslim and lower caste (J. Chatterji 1994). The Census of India noted that among Muslims, the proportion of actual cultivators was 7,316 in 10,000, while the proportion for Hindus was 5,555 in 10,000 (Risely and Gait 1903, 484). Furthermore, the level of urbanization was higher among Hindus than Muslims (Gait 1902, 208, subsidiary table 6).

While caste and religious identities differed, all of the groups in the province accepted Bengali as a common language by the mid-nineteenth century (Broomfield 1968, 10). This linguistic hegemony was undisputed after the Hindi-speaking western and Oriya-speaking southeastern areas of the province separated to create, respectively, the provinces of Bihar in 1912 and Orissa in 1913. Nevertheless, it is important to note that, like most Sanskrit-based languages, Bengali had a formal, or written, form, called *shadhubhasa*, and a spoken form, called *chalitobhasa*, which varied widely across different regions of the province (Haldar 1986). Whereas the written language was highly Hinduized because of its nearness to Sanskrit through a series of nineteenth-century "purifications" conducted by upper-caste Hindu scholars, the spoken language also became dominated by the dialect spoken by Hindus in the western districts of the province (Acharya 1986). As a result, Muslim-educated elites disliked the official language, but it also handicapped upper-class Hindu leaders' ability to mobilize peasants across Bengal (Acharya 1989; Bhattacharya 1987).

Ironically, the source of peasant rebellions lay in an elite rebellion primarily of Hindu landlords and the dependent urban middle classes against colonial rule. It failed to gain popular support because it became evident that the rebellion sought to protect landlords' political and economic dominance. Although the elites acquired certain concessions from the British, their inadvertent achievement was the politicization of the peasantry and rural bourgeoisie, who became aware of their own potential for political power.

Primarily high-caste Hindu professionals and landowners (Broomfield 1968, 5–12), collectively called the *bhadralok*, led the rebellion against the partition of the province in 1905 by the British, who, the *bhadralok* claimed, sought to divide Bengalis along religious lines. Importantly, significant numbers of the allied urban professionals and small-business owners were actually absentee landlords themselves, with portions of their incomes derived from renting out agricultural land via intermediary shares in various *zamindari* estates (Chatterjee 1982, 121). Landlords were also some of the primary backers of the rebellion because of their fear that tenancy legislation in the new province of East Bengal would economically undercut them (De 1977, 27). Due to their privileged social position, the *bhadralok* remained unconcerned about—indeed, unaware of—the economic repression peasants faced (S. Sarkar 1973, 515).

The attempted rebellion's central strategy was to boycott colonial institutions—extending from courts to colleges—as well as British products to fight economic domination (Chand 1983, 338–339). The boycott of British products and their replacement with Indian ones, however, adversely affected peasants, who could not afford to buy the more expensive domestic products, as well as rural shopkeepers and merchants selling these imported products (S. Sarkar 1973). In East Bengal, these deleterious effects were worsened by floods in 1905 that caused partial crop failures in 1906 and 1907 (S. Ahmed 1974, 123). Consequently, the boycott of British goods failed. In fact, aggregate data show that consumption of foreign goods steadily increased during the ostensible boycott (Biswas 1995).

Despite its failure, the elite rebellion had three long-term effects. First, it exacerbated the grievances of peasants and the rural bourgeoisie against the Hindu landlords and dependent urban bourgeoisie who attempted to coercively impose the observance of the boycott (Lahiri 1991, 72–73). Second, the *bhadralok* both lost British support by supporting urban terrorism and failed to garner necessary support from the rural classes in order to successfully rebel (Southard 1980). Finally, the British attempts to placate the *bhadralok* by creating a provincial legislature dominated by landlords (Simon 1930, 191–193) and the abrogation of the partition in 1911 further antagonized Muslim leaders seeking to dominate the erstwhile province, as evidenced by their concern about establishing a public university for East Bengal (S. Ahmed 1974, 301–304).

The *bhadralok* again attempted to start a rebellion revolving around the 1920 national-level Non-Cooperation Movement led by Mahatma Gandhi. Urban *bhadralok* leaders such as Chitta Ranjan Das, like members of the Indian National Congress Party led by Gandhi, sought to leverage labor unrest in tea plantations in the neighboring province of Assam (Behal 1985). According to the official report, they fomented a series of strikes and economic stoppages in eastern Bengal and Assam (Bamford 1925, 60–62).

Concomitant to this attempt by the *bhadralok*, the rural Muslim peasantry first joined politics through the Khilafat Movement in 1920–1922, which began in tandem with the Non-Cooperation Movement but sought to restore the Ottoman emperor and Islamic caliph, who had been deposed after losing World War I (Momen 1972, 88–89). This movement was led by Muslim landlords and urban professionals who had grievances arising from the mid-nineteenth-century evaluation by the British that they were severely underrepresented in urban professions such as medicine and law, as well as in the bureaucracy (W. W. Hunter 1876). Despite their ongoing tactical alliance with the Congress Party, the Muslim upper classes had successfully attempted to ameliorate their marginalization through administrative reforms in education (S. Ahmed 1974, 18–20).

After the conclusion of the Non-Cooperation and Khilafat movements in 1922, the Bengal Pact of 1923 between the *bhadralok* leader Chitta Ranjan Das of the Congress Party and the Muslim League politician Fazlul Huq allocated seats in elected municipal bodies in proportion to the size of the local religious communities—sixty and forty for the majority and minority, respectively—and guaranteed Muslims 80 percent of new government appointments until they had 55 percent of all positions (Sartori 2014, 159–160). Consequently, that year the Swarajya Party, led by C. R. Das and comprising Congress Party leaders running for provincial election, also became the single largest in the provincial Legislative Council, winning forty-seven out of 139 seats, of which it allocated twenty-one seats to Muslim candidates (Sartori 2014, 159).

Nevertheless, the *bhadralok* so opposed the pact's concessions that if the pact had preceded the elections instead of following them, colonial reports stated, the Swarajya Party would not have won such a victory (L. Williams 1924, 260). Hindu-Muslim comity did not last long, because the Swarajya Party was beholden to the Hindu *bhadralok* and would not countenance any agrarian-reform legislation; their attacks on the introduction of the pro-peasant Bengal Tenancy Act (Amendment) Bill in 1925 and the Royal Commission on Agriculture yet again exposed the *bhadralok* as anti-peasant and pro-landlord (Hashmi 1988, 176). The provincial Bangla Congress also rejected the Bengal Pact in 1926, and it was immediately rejected by the national-level Congress Party in 1923. However, the grievances of Muslim elites were also alien to the existential grievances faced by the peasantry, especially regarding excessive rents and the quotidian oppression by landlords (De 1995, 18–19). As a result, the peasants allied with the rural bourgeois *jotedar* class, who were primarily Muslim and identified with the peasants' anti-landlord sentiments (C. Sarkar 1991, 71).

Rural bourgeois participation in peasant rebellions occurred as grievances peaked after 1930 due to the precipitous collapse of the price of jute, which was mainly produced by *jotedars* (Gallagher 1973, 612). The falling prices for food and cash crops caused by the Great Depression impoverished peasants and economically weakened landlords but strengthened the rural bourgeoisie (Mukherji 1986). Their power became evident when they began a "no-rent" campaign during the 1930s, which simultaneously fought the colonial authorities and anticolonial Hindu landlords and dependent provincial Congress Party backed by the urban bourgeoisie (Hashmi 1992, 190–191). Azizul Huque, a senior Muslim provincial politician, articulated the cause of popular grievances, demanded redress, and implied such concessions' advantages to the British: although Muslims were a demographic majority, he argued, the property qualifications for voting restricted their number to a minority of 38 percent of eligible voters for the provincial legislature (Huque 1931, 11–16). In other words, widening the franchise would channel the rebellious Muslim majority into colonial-representative institutions.

The colonial administration conceded to the demands of the no-rent campaign, especially because doing so would co-opt the bulk of the peasantry and its leaders within established representative institutions, as well as further undermine the *bhadralok*. The first concession was the Communal Award of 1932 that created separate electorates for Muslims; subsequently, the Government of India Act of 1935 lowered the property requirements and tax qualifications for eligibility to vote (J. Chatterji 1994, 68–69). The increase of Muslim representatives in the provincial legislature from 18 percent to 47 percent (Chakrabarty 1989, 499, table 2) successfully legitimized colonial rule and marginalized the *bhadralok*.

The peasant rebellions through the 1930s subsequently were channeled into the institutionalized politics of the provincial legislature by the successful KPP, formed in 1936–1937 by *jotedar* politicians led by Fazlul Huq (Momen 1972; Shila Sen 1976).[2] The rural origins of the KPP's leadership is confirmed by Myron Weiner's tabulation of the urban-versus-rural origins of political leaders in West Bengal, which demonstrates that the number of rural leaders increased throughout this period (Weiner 1959, 280, table 1).

The KPP also distanced itself from the national-level Muslim League, whose members were landlords and urban professionals (Murshid 1995, 170–171). Its local-level *praja samitis* (peasant committees) had even mobilized voters against Muslim League candidates in the 1937 election (Bose 1986, 202). In a testament to its ideology, the KPP-controlled legislature pushed through pro-peasant laws that further undermined the landlords' economic position. They included the Bengal Tenancy (Amendment) Act of

---

2. "Krishak Praja Party" translates as the Farmer Subject Party. Whereas "Krishak" signifies farmers, "Praja" implies peasants who were tenants or landless. Thus, the party represents both *jotedars* and peasants on *zamindari* estates.

1938, the Agricultural Debtors (Second Amendment) Act of 1940, the Bengal Money-Lenders Act of 1940, and the Bengal Secondary Education Bill of 1940 (Broomfield 1968, 291–295; Jalal 1985, 152). In 1938, an official investigative commission's report advised that the *zamindari* system itself should be changed because of the multiple layers of rent-collecting intermediaries and consequent rural poverty (Floud 1941, 35–36, 41–42). The recommendation was not implemented due to the influence of the *bhadralok* on British provincial administrators and the governor (Ahmad 1970, 154–193; Cooper 1988, 50–62).

Unfortunately, the economic battles were soon expressed via political competition along the lines of religious identities. In different parts of Bengal, the strength of the anticolonial movement and ethnoreligious movements became contingent on whether specific areas were dominated by Hindu *zamindars* and *bhadralok* or the Muslim *jotedars* (Ray and Ray 1975, 101–102). To shore up their popular support, the *zamindars* and broader *bhadralok* segment used shared religious identity to ally with low-caste Hindu peasant communities, such as *namasudras* in eastern Bengal and *rajbanshis* in northern Bengal, whose demands they had ignored and even opposed in the past (Bandyopadhyay 1990, 1998). The Hindu Mahasabha, a religious chauvinist party backed by the *bhadralok*, gained popularity in the province and managed to enter the ruling coalition in the 1940s (J. Chatterji 1994, 249–250).

Similarly, the Muslim landlord and *jotedar* interests used Muslim identity politics to paper over their differences, which permitted the Muslim League to increase its presence since becoming all but irrelevant in the early 1930s (Ispahani 1976, 14). A paradoxical outcome of this alliance was that the landlord-based provincial wing of the Muslim League began supporting the KPP, ultimately merging with it at the provincial level, although leaders from the two parties continued to disagree on the pivotal question of land reform (Islam 1978, 197–198). Nevertheless, the provincial Muslim League government's crushing of the violent Communist Party–backed Tebhaga rebellion of sharecropping tenants against *jotedars* and *zamindars* in 1946–1947 revealed that neither the established nor the new Muslim elites favored unlimited land reforms and peasants' emancipation (Bhattacharya 1978, 615–617).

Peninsular Southern India: Peasant Inclusion without Rebellions

Peninsular southern India was territorially and demographically dominated by the province of the Bombay Presidency on the western side and the Madras Presidency on the southern and southeastern side. In the 1920s and 1930s, the region did not face the widespread and sustained peasant rebellions targeting landlords and their British patrons that characterized contemporaneous northern and eastern India. The analysis presented here reveals that the absence of such rebellions resulted from a combination of economic and political factors that simultaneously reduced economic inequalities and encouraged local representation through political institutions. Specifically, peasants' and elites' economic grievances were low because of changes in institutions controlling land that, unlike in northern and eastern India, replaced large landlords with a landed peasantry that soon became a rural bourgeoisie. Political grievances were not salient in fomenting elite participation because the rural bourgeoisie were already participating in the provincial-level representative institutions, unlike their counterparts in northern and eastern India. Moreover, such preexisting access to political institutions and elite representation highlight that apertures in local institutions and elite coalitions could not encourage elite participation. More intriguingly, when lower levels of inequality interacted with cross-class caste and language cleavages in regional society to attract elite participants in the Vaikom Satyagraha in the Madras Presidency and the Mulshi Satyagraha in the Bombay Presidency, class and caste divisions undermined peasant support for these movements.

The two major subnational entities of peninsular southern India, the Bombay and Madras Presidencies, had predominantly agricultural economies. Even in 1931, approximately 86.3 percent of the population of the Madras Presidency lived in villages, while the province had only four towns with populations of more than 100,000 (Baker 1976, 5). Although the urban-rural statistics in the Bombay Presidency could be skewed by the presence of the city of Bombay, with its one-million-plus inhabitants, as well as large cities such as Karachi, Ahmedabad, and Poona, the presidency had seven towns with populations of more than 100,000 (United Kingdom, Government of India 1933). Including the four largest cities, however, only 20.9 percent of the population lived in towns of more than five thousand, and if the four largest cities were excluded, only 13.9 percent lived in such towns (Haynes 2012, 109).

The land-revenue and property-rights systems in the region differed from those of its northern, northwestern, and eastern Indian counterparts (Banerjee and Iyer 2005). The land-revenue system introduced between 1818 and 1828 was called *ryotwari*. In this system, the government owned the land and directly taxed peasants, or *ryots*, who held *pattas*, or leases, that specified "the area held, type of land, land revenue payable, and the installments" in which it was to be paid, as well as other payable taxes, such as for roads, and restrictions, such as mining rights (D. Kumar 1975, 230). In the Bombay Presidency, the *ryotwari* villages covered 28,475,016 acres of revenue-paying land, compared with 3,857,686 acres of all other forms of revenue-paying land (Baden-Powell 1892b, 251). In the Madras Presidency, such villages covered 19,084,677 of revenue-paying land, compared with 18,087,620 acres of all other forms of revenue-paying land (Baden-Powell 1892b, 142). The other types of land revenue systems that existed in both the Bombay and Madras Presidencies were the Wanta, Mewasi, and Maliki tenure systems in the northern Gujarat region of the Bombay Presidency; the Khoti, Shilotri, and Izafat tenures of the Konkan region of the Bombay Presidency; and the Kanara tenure system in the Madras Presidency (Baden-Powell 1892b, 250).

In contrast to the Bombay Presidency, which was almost completely under the *ryotwari* system (United Kingdom, House of Commons 1903, 150), two other systems of landownership were present in the Madras Presidency that shaped its politics in ways that were distinct from those under the *ryotwari* system. First, between one-third and one-fifth of the Madras Presidency was under the Permanent Settlement, or *zamindari*, system, akin to Bengal (Baden-Powell 1892b, 23–34). The British used the *zamindari* system to co-opt the *poligars*, the large feudal-military landlords from the precolonial era (United Kingdom, Government of India 1893, 70). Unlike in Bengal, where the system devastated precolonial landlords, the British managed to retain and neutralize *poligars* as conflicting local political actors (Baden-Powell 1892b, 18–22). Second, the Malabar areas on the western coast of the Madras Presidency had a system that resembled the *ryotwari* but in reality was closed to a *zamindari* system centered on precolonial landed upper castes called *janmis* (Krishnan 1993, 11). This system and its effects on the Moplah peasant rebellion were discussed in Chapter 2.

Although the *ryotwari* system was more equitable than the *zamindari* system, the method of its imposition and its practices stratified local societies. Initially, the British imposed and attempted to efficiently extract high land rents in *ryotwari* areas because they could not comprehend that comparably high precolonial rates factored in losses due to rent intermediaries and evasion (Raghavaiyangar 1893, 26). As a result, the *ryotwari* system created a set of landholding farmers, officially recognized as *ryots*, who employed landless laborers, sharecroppers, and tenant farmers on their land (Kumar [1983] 2005, 237–238). The Madras peasants' responsiveness to price changes for cash crops prevented merchants from buying in-country crops cheaply and selling them for high profits in regional markets (Parikh 1972). A new set of *ryots* developed who controlled numerous such *pattas* and leveraged market access for food and cash crops such as groundnuts and cotton to create inordinate wealth; consequently, they employed and dominated large numbers of landless peasants (Washbrook 1973, 487). These *ryots* also gave poor tenant farmers loans so they could meet rent obligations to the government (Bruce 1983, 69–70). In addition, the colonial government of the

Bombay Presidency gave *ryots* relief from moneylenders intent on acquiring agricultural land by passing the Deccan Agriculturalists Relief Act of 1879 (Fukazawa [1983] 2005, 196).

The establishment of landed farmers profitably involved in the cash economy, however, did not create inequities and popular grievances similar to those of the *zamindari* and associated landlord-dominated land-tenure and revenue systems in northern and eastern India. Indeed, that neither eastern (D. Kumar 1975) nor western (Fukazawa [1983] 2005, 206) peninsular southern India was characterized by major concentrations of land and consequent rural impoverishment has sometimes confounded scholars. For example, Shri Krishan (2005, 111–112) explains that the rural bourgeois leaders of the Congress Party were integrated into peasant communities and thus mediated between landlords and peasants to create unified rebellions—albeit peaceful ones—against the British. Yet his own records show that those he classifies as landlords controlled 9.28 percent of land that provided government revenue; peasant proprietors controlled 78.22 percent of such land; and 12.34 percent of the land was held in perpetual, or lifetime, revenue-free grants (S. Krishan 2005, 49). Thus, even if individuals who owned revenue-free land were to be classified as landlords, the relative equality of landholdings and predominance of peasant proprietors become clearly evident.

Whereas lower levels of inequality in landholdings created and sustained by more peasant-friendly colonial institutions lowered political and economic grievances, crosscutting cleavages centered on geographic and cultural differences increased barriers to collective action to mount rebellions. Culturally, the coastal plains of the Western Ghats and the northwestern part of the Deccan Plateau of peninsular southern India, both located in the Bombay Presidency, were influenced by the shared history of the precolonial Maratha Empire, which fostered a strong Marathi identity (C. Bayly 2001, 21) and displaced competing subregional identity narratives (Hansen 2001, 20–36). It is important to note that the Maratha Empire was connected via both competition and alliances with the precolonial Mughal Empire, which spanned northern, eastern, and northwestern India and deepened its identification with northern political trends and aspirations. The other political culture, located in the southern part of the peninsula spanning both the Eastern and Western Ghats, originated in the precolonial Vijayanagara Empire and the smaller Nayaka Kingdoms that had bequeathed the military-feudal *poligars* (Seylon 2004, 248–249).

Two other factors further divided regional politics: language and caste. Political cleavages revolving around language appeared during the nineteenth-century revival and politicization of Marathi (Solomon 1994) and

Tamil identities (Rajendran 1994). During the early twentieth century, language interacted with caste and ethnic identities, and even class solidarity, to increase friction among some groups and cohesion within others (Baker 1984). Regional-caste identity became somewhat contingent on groups' class and political power (Upadhya 1997) and, consequently, more malleable and fluid in practice than widely recognized (S. Bayly 1999).

Although these characteristics initially increased collaboration among different religious, ethnic, and class groups, they also ultimately undermined such coalitions. The Vaikom Satyagraha in 1924, carried out by the upwardly mobile and better-educated lower-caste Ezhava (Sanoo 1978, 176) against upper-caste discrimination centered on a Hindu temple in a native princely state adjoining the Madras Presidency, attracted help from local Christian and upper-caste supporters. Yet upper-caste leaders counseled by Gandhi—who also asked non-Hindus and lower castes to refrain from participating—subsequently compromised with temple authorities and undermined the movement's goals (King 2015).

Similarly, the Mulshi Satyagraha from 1920 to 1924 against a dam being built by the Tata Company in the Bombay Presidency met with sustained opposition from urban, middle-class, upper-caste leaders and local peasants (Vora 2009). Yet lower castes from other parts of the province refrained from participating because they were being aided by traditional leaders, such as the maharajahs of Kolhapur, in fighting through courts and seeking reservations in the new electoral institutions (I. Rothermund 1999, 78). Due to the lack of support, the peaceful rebellion eventually failed, and its leaders were imprisoned after resorting to violence.

Instead of rebellion, however, greater social mobility and crosscutting cleavages facilitated the entry of peasants into the nascent provincial representative institutions. Most prominently, the rural bourgeoisie of the Madras Presidency allied with peasants against the upper-caste Brahmins, whose political power stemmed from occupying positions in the colonial bureaucracy. The Justice Party, formed in 1920, therefore was led by the rural bourgeoisie, whose grievances stemmed from their enhanced economic power but continued low social status (Barnett 1976, 15–31). Although it was initially victorious in the provincial elections, the party had collapsed by the 1930s because it could not sustain the patronage networks available from access to local government funds and jobs (Washbrook 1973, 525). The Congress Party, which won against the Justice Party in the provincial elections of 1937, used defecting leaders from the Justice Party to create its own regional coalition based on the same method of acquiring and disbursing resources (Washbrook 1973, 526–527).

Although colonial representative institutions were not preferred sites of popular expression in the Bombay Presidency, mutually beneficial collaboration between peasants and the rural bourgeoisie was targeted at neither the other indigenous elites nor the British. The popular Congress Party was led by the rural bourgeoisie, whose local power rested on the control of land (Omvedt 1976, 171–206), as well as their pivotal role in colonial military-recruitment strategies (Deshpande 2004). During the 1920s and 1930s, the commercialization of agriculture and access to rural credit further facilitated the rural bourgeoisie's untrammeled control of provincial politics (Catanach 1970).

In summary, the study of peninsular southern India confirms this chapter's theses, regardless of certain subregional variations. The notable exception, presented in Chapter 2, was the Malabar area in the eastern Madras Presidency, which was characterized by unequal landholding patterns, poverty, and political exclusion reminiscent of northern and eastern India. The study of the failed Moplah Rebellion demonstrates that religious differences overlapping with class divisions prevented elite participation: Muslim Moplah peasants attacked Hindu landlords and administrators instead of seeking them as local elite allies. Nevertheless, the role of political and economic grievances presented in the broader regional study here and that of the Moplah Rebellion complement each other. The absence of shared religious identities in the context of an economically stratified society consequently prevented peasant-elite alliances and doomed the Moplahs. Elites throughout the peninsula lacked the economic and political grievances that could encourage collaboration with peasants. Shared cultural identity such as caste and religion stimulated initial elite participation, but their fluid and crosscutting nature also facilitated elite and peasant withdrawal.

The Stable Northwest: The Military-Political Reasons for Peaceful Authoritarianism

This study first presents the economic and political institutions of the northwestern colonial Indian province of Punjab. The economic institutions arose in order to achieve the colonial regime's goal to encourage the cultivation of cash and food crops and to recruit and maintain a loyal Indian Army. The accompanying political institutions, rather than relying on landlords or being institutionalized, were more intrusive and arbitrary. The study thereafter flows into analyzing the province's distinct social structure dominated by a class of landed farmers who depended on the colonial government for their land, access to water, and employment; the British prevented the development of an independent bourgeoisie by legally protecting farmers from moneylenders investing in land, and military recruiting strategies divided the farmers based on religious identity.

The analysis of the various attempts at rebellions shows how these social and institutional characteristics of Punjabi society undermined them. It reveals that rebellions neither arose from nor were sustained by coalitions among urban elites and peasants. Furthermore, British repression of attempted rebellions was nearly always followed by concessions. These factors combined to prevent the type of province-wide rebellions witnessed in contemporaneous northern and eastern India. Thus, despite grievances against taxation and political repression, the urban bourgeoisie were unable to create rebellious coalitions with any of the rural classes.

Northwestern India had an agrarian economy centered on a system of canals constructed by the British that irrigated 10 million acres of what was until then semi-arid land. Approximately 500,000 acres of fertile and irrigated land in what were called the "Canal Colonies" were granted to former military personnel from the British Indian Army (Ali 1987). The irrigation and land-grant system indicated the extent to which the colonial institutions shaped the provincial socioeconomic structure, from geography to governance (Ali 1988). According to the geographer Gopal Krishan, the Canal Colonies developed a five-tiered landholding structure (G. Krishan 2004, 81): the biggest landholdings were larger than 125 acres; a second set of holdings was between 75 and 125 acres; a third set was between 12.5 and 50 acres; a fourth set was reserved for retired military and police personnel, with the size of land grants contingent on rank; and the fifth set ranged from 12.5 to 25 acres granted to displaced people.

Despite these variations, the landholding structure was not as unequal as in Bengal or the United Provinces. Instead, it resembled the homesteading and ranching systems of southwestern Mexico. Of the 56.86 percent of the provincial population who were wholly and partially supported by agriculture, 96.66 percent were classified as "peasant proprietors"—landholders and tenants—while noncultivating rent receivers (prevalent in Bengal and the United Provinces) constituted only 1.32 percent (Rose and Thompson 1908, 59). In addition to the distribution of land, two further factors accounted for the relatively egalitarian landownership structure. First, there existed overlapping layers of tenants, owner cultivators, and landlords (Fox 1985, 73). Second, though favoring landed farmers, the land-revenue collection system encouraged cooperation between rural classes (Banerjee and Iyer 2005, 1193). The prevalent *mahalwari* system classified individual villages as collective landowners, and a village notable called the *lambardar* was assigned to collect the rent (Kuhnen 1982, 63–65).

Although the Canal Colonies relieved pressures on land, some parts of Punjab, such as the Salt Range area, remained unsuitable for agriculture because of a combination of aridity, infertile soil, and uneven topography. Official records regarding the Khuddar area, the Phaphra Circle, and the Thal Circle in the district of Jhelum attest to this (W. Talbot 1901, 20–25). Consequently, Punjabis from these areas used jobs in the colonial Indian Army to supplement their agricultural income (Yong 2005, 80–85). The link between wealth and power and loyalty to the British was exemplified by the Tiwana family, who leveraged their personal service and recruitment capabilities for the colonial army to increase their wealth and influence from the mid-nineteenth century onward, reaching their apogee under Khizr Tiwana, who headed the dominant political party in the province during the 1920s and 1930s (I. Talbot 1996).

As implied by this evidence, the colonial government wanted a revenue and property-rights policy that secured it a steady stream of recruits for the Indian Army. In fact, 75,000 men from the 141,000-member Indian Army came from Punjab (Yong 2005, 68). The dependence of the British on Punjabi recruits forced them to artificially insulate the agricultural sector of Punjab from economic changes, a strategy that first became manifest in the Land Alienation Act of 1900, which debarred selling and mortgaging of land to "non-agriculturalists." More significant, the act recognized Punjabi society and landownership itself as contingent on ethnic identity—specifically, tribal identity. It obstructed the entry of new economic players both from within (land could be sold and mortgaged to members of the landowner's own "statutorily recognized" agricultural tribe) and outside the agricultural sector—that is, from non-members of agricultural tribes (Rose and Thompson 1908, 114). This was followed by the Court of Wards Act of 1903, which "gave the government the right to place any insolvent aristocratic families under an official court of wards without prior consent of the family" (Barrier 1967b, 355).

Although such laws saved landed farmers from impoverishment, they also prevented the rise of new classes such as bourgeois moneylenders, who until then were acquiring increasing amounts of lands by forfeiture of mortgages (Dewey 1972), creating a military-feudal social structure wherein landownership and wealth became contingent on loyalty to the British government (I. Talbot 2007, 8). The new electoral laws emanating from the Montague-Chelmsford Reforms of 1919 politically institutionalized the domination of such landowners by stating that only members of agricultural tribes, as specified by the Land Alienation Act of 1900, could become candidates from rural constituencies (I. Talbot 1996, 57–58).

Along with preventing economic transformation, colonial policies classifying religious, caste, and tribal groups reified differences among these identities while ignoring overlaps in ethnoreligious identities and cross-religious issues of inequality of wealth (Bhagat 2001, 4353–4354). The province had a slim majority of Muslims, at 57.1 percent of the population, followed by Hindus, at 27.8 percent, and Sikhs, at 13.2 percent (Ambedkar 1946, 429). Military recruitment and training procedures based on ascriptive identities reinforced these religious divisions so that regiments from one group could be used to quell uprisings by another group (K. Singh 2004, 112–113). Administrative policies based on recognizing such differences made social and economic mobility contingent on religious identities, which further increased competition along these lines (Hasan 1980, 1395–1406).

As a result, by the early 1900s political competition among elites came to revolve around religious differences (Reinhardt 1972, 116–139), which, as evidence marshalled here shows, overlapped with economic and urban-rural social cleavages. The wealthy Muslims and Sikhs generally lived in the rural areas and were agriculturalists, while the wealthy Hindus primarily lived in urban areas and dominated finance and urban professions such as law and medicine (R. Stern 2001, 56). However, given that 11.4 percent of the total population lived in towns (Risely and Gait 1903, 26), and because speculation in land was precluded by law, the geography of the Hindu elites' economic dominance was limited.

Akin to the agricultural sector, the colonial administration of law and order in Punjab was more authoritarian and paternalistic than its counterparts in the rest of India. Called the "Punjab School," the administrative apparatus relied on direct interventions by British officers at the district level into the minutiae of rural life. A former British officer provided the best explanation of how the quotidian administration of Punjab functioned compared with Bengal in the mid-nineteenth century, an administrative mind-set that continued through the years:

> When a case arose, [Bengal officials] consulted their law-books, found the law that applied, passed orders in accordance therewith, and troubled themselves no further. In the Panjab, on the contrary, when a case arose, as there were no laws to go by, each officer had to think the matter over and determine the best course of action. He had to do it promptly, too, for there was no time for prolonged reflexion or hesitation, and having issued his order, he had to personally see it carried out and ensure that it worked satisfactorily. He had often to get on his horse, ride to the place concerned and in person see to the execution of his order. In Bengal such a thing was unheard of. An order once passed was made over to the proper native officer to be carried out,

> and any further instructions that might be required were applied for and given in writing. In Bengal before you could issue an order you had to find a section of an Act or Regulation empowering you to do so. In the Panjab, you did so, because you thought it was the proper thing to do. (Beames [1867] 1961, 129–130)

There were two long-term effects of this form of paternalist governance: personalist rule and its complementary lack of institutionalization. The opinions and commands of colonial administrators from the district collector upward therefore become critical to the functioning of rural Punjab rather than laws and regulations, as was the case in the rest of India. Furthermore, as demonstrated by the study of failed rebellions below, the precedent of using discretionary powers allowed colonial officials to become more actively involved with, and thus more responsive to, local collaborators than their counterparts in Bengal or the United Provinces. Thus, the combination of elite support and involvement made local administrators similar to the *jefes politicos* of prerevolutionary Mexican states such as Oaxaca, which were intimately connected to the prerevolutionary regime.

The first attempted peasant rebellion, euphemistically called the Disturbances of 1907, was caused by grievances against increases in land rents from peasants in the Canal Colonies and the retroactive change of contractual conditions between the government and recipients of canal lands (Barrier 1967b, 171). In particular, the government unilaterally declared that the colonists were "tenants at will," increased the oversight and enforcement powers of officials over such land, and "specified that their decisions could not be challenged in court" (Cell 1992, 33). Protests and demonstrations leading to anticolonial speeches spread from the major cities of Lahore and Amritsar to smaller Canal Colony towns such as Lyallpur, which were attended by soldiers regardless of religion (Cell 1992, 34). According to Tan Tai Yong (2005, 95), the British unsuccessfully attempted to repress the Disturbances by banning public meetings in affected areas and dispersing those that took place, charging supportive newspapers with sedition, and arresting and deporting the leaders Lajpat Rai and Ajit Singh. Nevertheless, riots occurred in Amritsar, Lahore, and Rawalpindi; agitation spread to Manjha District, the central recruiting area for Sikhs in the army; and soldiers were suspected of fomenting mutiny within the ranks (Yong 2005, 95).

Although the urban leaders attempted to convert the Disturbances into a broader anticolonial struggle, the rebellion failed, by Lajpat Rai's (1908, x–xi) own admission, because the British had successfully divided the provincial class interests of agriculturalists and the urban bourgeoisie via the Punjab Land Alienation Act of 1900. Moreover, Rai belonged to the Arya Samaj

(Aryan Society), a Hindu-revivalist organization that espoused positions against Muslims, who were the predominant religious group in the rural areas (Barrier 1967a, 376–377). Rai had been a member of the organization since he was eighteen and frequently used organizational networks and related social connections for anticolonial activities (Rai 1915, xxii–xxiii). Ajit Singh, a Sikh leader, also appealed to fellow Sikhs, not Muslim peasants. Most important, after a few weeks the British managed to rescind the offending laws and regulations (Barrier 1967a, 369–372) because, unlike in other Indian provinces, the British were more concerned about military recruitment and the spread of disaffection to serving soldiers from these communities (Barrier 1967b, 363–379).

A decade later, in 1919, the existing social and institutional structures faced discontented former soldiers, who had returned to the province after being demobilized following World War I. The former soldiers' grievances centered on their inability to acquire land grants after being discharged (Ali 1988, 117) and the sudden increase in the cost of basic commodities (United Kingdom, House of Commons 1918, 72, 126). Although food prices increased because of the war, the availability of cultivable land had decreased over a longer period of time as a result of the province's steadily increasing population pressures. Gopal Krishan (2004, 79) shows that, from 1881 to 1921, the provincial population grew at 0.47 percent annually, after which the rate increased to 1.57 percent from 1921 to 1941. Prior to this, moreover, the availability of cultivable land had been shrinking. Total cultivated land increased from 35,423 acres in 1888 to 42,312 acres in 1903–1904. More important, the amount of "cultivable but not cultivated land" decreased from 34,515 acres in 1888 to 26,373 acres in 1903–1904 (Rose and Thompson 1908, 154). Consequently, the price of cultivable land rose from 81 rupees per acre in 1901 to 392 rupees per acre in 1931 (United Kingdom, Government of India 1937a, supp. 52).

Simultaneously, the urban bourgeoisie was aggrieved due to the sudden increase in taxes on small businesses and general income taxes, as well as the increased efficiency of the provincial revenue services in collecting them (W. H. Hunter 1920b, 100). The Super Tax of 1917, the increased Income Tax of 1918, and the Excess Profits Tax were possibly forced by expenses incurred during World War I. The extension of wartime laws permitting arbitrary arrests, extrajudicial trials, and press censorship through the Rowlatt Act, however, became the more immediate catalysts for the urban bourgeoisie to begin agitating against the government (Yong 1994, 835). Provincial leaders of the Congress Party attempted to use these grievances to garner support for the nationwide Non-Cooperation Movement started by Gandhi, and in its annual meeting in Amritsar recognized these laws as the central cause of discontent (Mittra 1921, 16).

The grievances led to a series of violent attacks against government property and sites of colonial power, such as police and railway stations, as well as post and telegraph offices in the urban areas of Punjab. The relatively urbanized districts surrounding the cities of Amritsar, Lahore, Lyallpur, Gujranwala, and Gujrat suffered high numbers of attacks on government property, especially the telegraph service, railways, and revenue-collector's office (W. H. Hunter 1920a: app. 1, 237–266). These cities also suffered the greatest amount of property damage: Amritsar, 1,697,511 rupees; Lahore, 144,568 rupees; Lyallpur, 52,900 rupees; and Gujrat, 29,000 rupees (W. H. Hunter 1920a: app. 3, 270–275). A significant share of the leaders were urban professionals, particularly lawyers; there were eleven recorded instances of members of the legal profession becoming involved in the movement (W. H. Hunter 1920a, 237–266). Moreover, the leaders attempted to foster Hindu-Muslim cooperation in the urban areas. Twenty meetings urging Hindu-Muslim unity were held at various places, five of them at Islamic houses of worship (Sunni mosques and Shia imambaras). Three were held on the Hindu holy day of Ram Navami, and one was held on the holy day of Rath Yatra (W. H. Hunter 1920a, 237–266).

However, the rural Muslims and Sikhs did not participate in these events because the local institutions, such as the District Soldiers' Boards, were manipulated to control their activities (Yong 1994). The broader Non-Cooperation Movement, in which these incidents were being contextualized by political leaders, also collapsed because it relied on urban bourgeois leaders who failed to mobilize the agricultural classes (Yong 2005, 261). The provincial administrators also responded with overwhelming military force, leading up to the Jallianwallah Bagh Massacre, in which British Indian Army Troops shot 379 unarmed Indian protestors. Finally, realizing that the massacre was undermining British legitimacy and control over Punjab and other provinces (Irish 2009, 22–33), and with declining violent opposition (Collett 2005, 219), Britain repealed the Rowlatt Act in March 1922.

Parallel to this event, a rebellion called the Gurdwara Reform, or Akali, Movement was started by fundamentalist Sikhs from rural communities who intended to wrest control over their places of worship, called Gurdwaras, from Hinduized priests called *mahants* (Yong 1995). The underlying reason for the movement was that control over Gurdwaras brought with it control over vast lands and wealth that they owned (Fox 1985, 86). A massacre in 1921 of Sikhs attempting to take over a shrine in the town of Nankana by the Mahant's hired Muslim Pashtun goons and similar incidents of lesser magnitude in Guru-ka-Bagh in 1922 and Jaito in 1924 created widespread support among Sikhs and support from Gandhi, who unsuccessfully attempted to frame the events in terms of anticolonialism (N. Singh 2003). The British conceded to the Sikhs' demands in 1925 with the Sikh Gurdwaras Act, which abolished the hereditary position of the *mahant* and accepted the demands to create an elected administrative committee for the shrines called the Shiromani Gurdwara Prabandhak Committee in 1925 (Mazumder 2003, 230). Ironically, British concessions were based on the assumption that the rebellion's demands and fulfilment were religious; thus, the Sikhs' acceptance of such concessions post facto characterized the movement as a religious rebellion without political or economic goals (Mandair 2015, 125–126).

Moreover, the British had used the Montagu-Chelmsford Reforms of 1919, the first electoral step to eventual self-government, to introduce electoral institutions in Punjab that enfranchised rural landowners who paid more than 25 rupees in land revenue, local officials including 58,000 *lambardars,* and 160,000 former soldiers (Jalal and Seal 1981, 425). Given these institutional incentives, a pro–British landowners' party called the Punjab Unionist Party formed in 1923. The Unionists controlled provincial politics from then until after the legislative elections of 1937, which were based on an enlarged franchise and new rules of the Government of India Act of 1935. Headed by both Hindu and Muslim leaders (Sir Chhotu Ram and Sir Fazl-i-Husain, respectively), the party relied on rural patron-client networks to retain power (Dewey 1993, 185–187). The party also maintained equal distance from the Congress Party and the Muslim League, although it acted as the latter's provincial representative (Jalal and Seal 1981, 425). The rural patronage networks and the Unionist Party's official stance of rejecting the nationwide parties consequently marginalized the urban bourgeoisie in provincial politics and sustained a quiescent coalition of landed farmers in power.

Conclusion

The two types of comparisons of the six regional studies presented here show that elites collaborate with peasants to create successful rebellions when they have political and economic grievances. The two very different comparisons of eastern India with central and southwestern Mexico, respectively, show the validity of political and economic grievances, but they also provide conflicting findings regarding the role of inequality and political opportunity in propelling elite participation. Specifically, the comparison between eastern India and central Mexico shows that elite participation is contingent not just on the presence of political and economic grievances but also on the presence of high levels of inequality in a society. The comparison of eastern India with southwestern Mexico shows that, along with political and economic grievances, political opportunities cause elite participation.

Nevertheless, the within-case comparison of eastern, southern, and northwestern India affirms that political grievances accompanied by economic ones cause elite participation, while the effects of inequality and political opportunities are inconclusive. The within-case comparison of central, southwestern, and southeastern Mexico similarly affirms the role of political and economic grievances while showing that the effects of inequality and political opportunities are inconclusive. Although political grievances are present in all three regional Mexican studies, it appears that political grievances are not in and of themselves capable of causing elite participation; they do so only in combination with economic grievances. This further confirms the general theory, if only in Mexico, that elite participation is caused by the presence of both political and economic grievances.

The studies presented in this chapter as a whole confirm that political and economic grievances cause elite participation in rebellions and that, in turn, elite collaboration is necessary to overcome the collective-action barriers to successful rebellion imposed by peasants' large population size and poverty. By doing so, the chapter extends research on peasant rebellions, which either ignores the role of elites (Scott 2009) or assumes their opposition to rebellions seeking redistribution of wealth (Boix 2003). Nevertheless, the studies do not undermine the notion of peasant rebellions per se; rather, they reveal the role of dissenting elites in fomenting or sustaining them.

Dissenting elites' political and economic grievances have affected more contemporary rebellions in agrarian societies. In the South Asian nation of Sri Lanka during the 1970s and 1980s, two distinct rebellions arose: the Janata Vimukhti Peramuna (People's Liberation Front; JVP) and the Liberation Tigers of Tamil Eelam (LTTE). The JVP was a Marxist-Leninist organization that led rebellions in 1971 and 1987–1989 by "underprivileged rural youth . . . the children of small or middle-level farmers from . . . geographically, economically, and psychologically" peripheral areas, which targeted landed and bourgeois elites backed by the government (Venugopal 2010, 601–602). Both rebellions were rapidly crushed, their leaders and senior cadres summarily executed at the end of the second rebellion in 1989. Centered on Tamil ethnonationalism, the LTTE rebellion, initiated in 1983, was backed by middle-class Tamils angry about their increasing marginalization from government jobs and higher-education opportunities by pro-Sinhalese exclusionary policies imposed by the Sri Lankan government (DeVotta 2000). The LTTE was funded by a broad diaspora of émigré Tamils in North America and Western

Europe (Fair 2005; Human Rights Watch 2006). Until its eventual defeat in 2009, the LTTE enjoyed considerable success, even forcing the Sri Lankan government to sign a peace treaty in 2002 that recognized LTTE control of northern and eastern Sri Lanka.

The involvement of the Nicaraguan bourgeoisie, extending from big-business owners to small merchants and professionals, was similarly critical to the successful outcome of the Sandinista Rebellion in 1979. The Frente Sandinista de Liberación Nacional (FSLN) was established in 1961 by university students engaged in organizing peasant rebellions following Marxist-Leninist ideology but remained unable to threaten the urban centers and the overall regime through the 1960s (S. Palmer 1988, 97; Zimmerman 2000, 96–122). The FSLN's fate changed when it was joined by senior academics, professionals, clerics, and business owners epitomized by the exiled Los Doce in 1977 (Everingham 1996, 134–135). It finally defeated the regime of Anastasio Somoza in 1979 with support from the middle classes, especially business owners frustrated with official corruption and nepotism. That frustration reached its nadir when the mismanagement of international aid following the 1972 earthquake became an entrenched obstacle to economic recovery (Everingham 1996, 110–176), thus granting substantial political and economic power to business elites after the revolution (Sholk 1984).

Beyond the broad insights that elite participation is necessary for the success of the peasant rebellions, and the role of economic and political grievances in propelling such elite involvement, the subnational comparisons presented here endeavor to reveal how local conditions shape elite and peasant preferences in superficially dissimilar but at base similar ways. In its efforts, the chapter used sources for empirical data, such as censuses and official gazettes, that can facilitate future quantitative research using cross-country and even subnational statistical comparisons across these societies. Yet the studies' use of historiographical, sociological, and anthropological insights also indicates how research on elites, whether they oppose or support such rebellions, must account for local cultural, economic, and institutional histories and realities that may not seem to fit comfortably within elegant social science models, thus implying the necessity of agnosticism regarding methods in conducting comparative historical research of elite participation in peasant rebellions.

4

The Economic Origins of Warlord Support for Peace

Postrevolutionary Mexico

The Mexican state, which the first revolutionary president, Francisco Madero, inherited from the prerevolutionary era, began crumbling due to the rebellions unleashed by his deposal and assassination in 1913. Until the late 1920s, Mexico was characterized by a series of unstable coalitions between warlords who fought one another even as state institutions utterly collapsed. When postrevolutionary institutions formed, however, they revealed that warlords' willingness to make peace was caused by two individually necessary and jointly sufficient circumstances: (1) the economic elites underwriting the warlords' political and military organizations desired peace and (2) the costs and risks of continued conflict became intolerable for the warlords.

This study's findings reaffirm the book's broader theory that foreign economic elites who control fixed assets, such as land or natural resources, support warlords and sustain or exacerbate conflicts because new state institutions can heavily tax or nationalize their properties. In contrast, domestic elites who control similar fixed assets prefer nationwide peace agreements, contingent on such agreements' predicted effects on their local assets—that is, whether the agreements and subsequent institutions secure or expropriate their assets. Finally, domestic and foreign elites who control mobile assets, such as financiers and bankers, favor peace agreements that encourage macroeconomic stability, which benefit their investments.

In postrevolutionary Mexico, foreign-owned petroleum companies backed regional warlords and political leaders, undermining national stability, until the companies were expropriated by the revolutionary government. Large domestic landowners also backed the warlords before switching their support to the national government, which protected their assets. The cases of financial and industrial elites show that they supported warlords. However, the analysis shows that they supported warlords who aspired to create a national government and sought to create new institutions in banking and currency. To clarify the terms used in the broader theory as they apply to Mexico in the early twentieth century, the concepts of intertwined state institutions and elites, warlords, and peace agreements are contextualized below.

The state is defined as a political-legal entity exercising a monopoly of legitimate coercion over a population in a given territory (Weber [1922] 1978, 54). However, in addition to providing public goods, such as security and infrastructure, incumbent leaders rely on revenue generated through taxes and tariffs to garner support and pay state administrators (Migdal [2001] 2004). Consequently, in the context of poor agrarian societies with narrow tax bases, domestic and international elites become inordinately influential (Rueschemeyer, Stephens, and Stephens 1992).

In prerevolutionary Mexico, which provides the backdrop to the following section, popular legitimacy centered on localized loyalties (*la patria chica*), local leaders, and elite factions (Falcón 1998, 14–15). Consequently, the national government under Porfirio Díaz relied on shifting alliances among local political leaders and factions (Vanderwood 1981). District prefects appointed by Díaz, called *jefes politicos*, used direct payoffs and permitted local allies to exploit their power to gain wealth. To deter and quell rebellions, the Porfirian state used various security forces, from federal army and rural constabulary and semiprivate guards at haciendas to deputized rangers from the U.S. border states of Texas, Arizona, and New Mexico guarding American-owned properties (Joseph and Buchenau 2013, 22–23). In terms of its relationship with elites, the Porfirian strategy sought to start economic development and industrialization by cooperating with a narrow group of domestic and international economic interests, while large segments of Mexican society remained agrarian and poor (Haber, Razo, and Maurer 2003). Moreover, these linkages between political leaders and economic elites were based on personal friendships and family ties rather than institutionalized relationships and centered on regional, *not* national, political power (Cozzi 2010; Shafer 1973).

In the absence of a state that performs its core function of providing security, armed groups arise controlled by warlords (Keen 2012) to provide this service. In turn, warlords lead armed groups to control "small pieces of territory using a combination of force and patronage," thus becoming "lords (essentially, feudal landlords) who threaten to use war (violence unleashed by their militias) to retain power" (Marten 2012, 2). This was the case in revolutionary Mexico, the period covered in the next section. As noted by the historian Friedrich Katz (1998, 730), prerevolutionary political leaders and their personal networks; institutions of political power, from *jefes politicos* to judges and policemen; and the federal army all disappeared and were replaced by local authorities who refused to submit to centralized control, along with an enormous army that frequently was loyal to regional warlords. Political parties and military organizations centered on a warlord's patronage network made that warlord "master of his army, and through his army, of the land that he occupied" (Rouquie 1987, 202). Consequently, the area controlled by a warlord "resembled a mini-state where his personal opinion and judgement were as good as written law" (Quintana 2010, 2).

As an aside, the warlords who came to control Mexico's political and physical landscape, were called "caudillos." Although the terms "caudillo" and "cacique" can be used interchangeably (Joseph 1980, 201; Knight 1997), recent research does distinguish them: the historian Alan Knight notes that Mexican "emic usage" considers caudillos "praetorian" figures, whereas *caciques* were political bosses or brokers between the state and the local populace (Knight 2005). Alejandro Quintana, another historian, supports this dichotomy, saying that *caciques* presided over constructed local kinship networks (*compadrazgo*), while caudillos controlled larger areas and broader networks (Quintana 2010, 3).

The penultimate section of the chapter focuses on a variety of peace agreements that were written and unwritten. They were institutionalized and informal and were made across different economic and political dimensions by caudillos, their financial backers, and the political-military organizations they controlled. As the analysis shows, when the costs of continued conflict became intolerable for the caudillos, such mutually reinforcing interactions and agreements reduced mistrust engendered by lack of information about one another's intentions and capabilities and dissuaded cheating on agreements—that is, they lowered information asymmetry and commitment problems (Hoddie and Hartzell 2005; Kirschner 2010, 745–770) and increased the mutual benefits of sharing power and participating in multiple dimensions of cooperation, including political, territorial, military, and economic cooperation (Hartzell and Hoddie 2007). The new official political party formed in 1929 thus both reflected and contained such interactions.

Warlord Organizations in Revolutionary Mexico and the High Costs of Conflict

After attaining power via armed rebellions, caudillos relied on the rural masses for popular and military support. Specifically, upon achieving control over a territory, caudillos prevented internal opposition and defended against external challenges by creating standing armies, filling government positions with loyalists, and creating parties and organizations to channel political participation. Economic elites, whose relationships with caudillos began with brigandage and looting, subsequently became key actors because they provided resources necessary for caudillos' popular and military survival.

After several rounds of conflicts that began in 1910 ending around 1915, central authority in Mexico collapsed. The caudillos who came to control Mexican politics initially refused to join national coalitions to share power, rejecting proposals in 1919 to create a national party consisting of incumbent caudillos (Garrido 1986, 54–55). Instead, they relied on local popular support to retain power. Powerful caudillos such as Saturnino Cedillo, from the state of San Luis Potosí, retained popularity by combining land redistribution with the need for a standing army by creating military agrarian colonies that supplied *agrarista* recruits (Ankerson 1985). Cedillo's strategic disbursal of government positions to clients further increased his control. He removed all existing officials in the state, extending from town councils and local legislatures to bureaucrats, with the sole exception of the judiciary, to replace them with loyalists (Lerner 1980, 413). However, even Cedillo was forced to accept the autonomy of minor caudillos who enjoyed considerable popularity, such as Gonzalo Santos of the state's La Huasteca region (Falcón 1988, 284).

Similarly, other caudillos created mass organizations that channeled popular support, repressed internal opposition, and fought external threats. Southern caudillos, such as Tomás Garrido Canabal in the state of Tabasco and Felipe Carrillo Puerto in the state of Yucatán, created Ligas de Resistencia to recruit the local peasantry. Adalberto Tejada of the eastern-central state of Veracruz established the Liga de Comunidades Agrarias y Sindicatos Campesinos del Estado de Veracruz, with similar membership and the aim to retain power. Tejada, like Cedillo, used the acquiescent municipal governments and a pliable state bureaucracy to redistribute land differentially to loyal peasants to cement his popularity (Ginzberg 2000). According to a leading figure of the organization in its early years, the caudillo of the western state of Michoacán (and future Mexican president) Lázaro Cárdenas created the Confederación Revolucionario Michoacana del Trabajo during his tenure as the state's governor (Martínez 1982, 130).

Some caudillos also created political parties that enjoyed support not merely from the rural poor but also from urban labor and sections of the rural and urban middle classes. They included the Partido Socialista de la Frontera, centered on Emilio Portes Gil, in the northeastern state of Tamaulipas; the Partido Socialista del Sureste, led by Felipe Carrillo Puerto, in the southern state of Yucatán; and the Gran Partido Revolucionario de Jalisco, backed by Margarito Ramírez, in the western state of Jalisco.

The ostensible national government in Mexico City, controlled by a group of caudillos from the state of Sonora, attempted unsuccessfully to create similar organizations at the national level to co-opt the local caudillos' followers. The most prominent was the industrial labor–based Confederación Regional Obrera Mexicana (CROM), led by Luis Morones and backed by the Sonoran caudillo Plutarco Elías Calles, which fought against other caudillos' armies (Aceves 2009, 101–102). However, such national organizations lacked steady presence in rural areas—which covered the vast majority of territory and contained the majority of the population—that were dominated by regional organizations controlled by local caudillos who opposed recruitment by national organizations (Juan Meyer 1971).

Like regional caudillos, the Sonorans eliminated independent parties that did not center on them and sought to unify agrarian interests across Mexico. The Partido Nacional Agrarista, led by Antonio Díaz Soto y Gama (a former Zapatista), was unable to compete with its local caudillo-sponsored counterparts or with the national parties backed by Sonoran caudillos (Weyl and Weyl 1955, 228). Ultimately, Díaz Soto y Gama was co-opted by the Sonorans and backed by their local ally Saturnino Cedillo for a seat in the Camara de Diputados, the lower house of the Mexican legislature (Castro 2002).

Consequently, as indicated above, the Sonorans—headed by Álvaro Obregón and then Plutarco Elías Calles—could neither politically control regional caudillos nor protect allied caudillos against challengers (Knight 2005). The underlying reasons for their powerlessness were both economic and political. Economic scarcity hindered the government from acquiring weapons and materiel (Merchant 2002). Politically, the federal army was especially prone to rebellion and desertion because it was an agglomeration of local forces whose commanders (either caudillos or aspirants) and soldiers shared territorially specific grievances and loyalties that were distinct from, and sometimes opposed to, the national government (Brewster 2005, 118–119; Carriedo 2005, 63–64).

In the absence of a stable national government, caudillos' imperatives to maintain popular organizations and military strength became reliant on resources provided by economic elites at the regional and national level. During the 1920s, caudillos and regional economic elites shared a symbiotic relationship: while economic elites sought protection of their lives and assets, the caudillos looked to domestic economic elites (sometimes backed by foreign companies) to finance the popular and military organizations that secured their power.

The relationship between caudillos and the economic elites began as simple extortion during the 1910s, both to provision troops and to enrich the caudillos (Hostetter 1913a, 1913b, 1913c; Katz 1998, 596). With the passage of time and continued collapse of state authority, such relationships became regularized to an extent at which companies reported such extortion as taxes or levies to their shareholders. In the August 22 issue of the *Engineering and Mining Journal*, a "Mr. Main" wrote that "forces of Constitutionalist Party entered El Oro [in the state of Mexico] on Aug. 7, after evacuation of town by Federal troops, but except for levy of various companies operating, under which this company was assessed 200,000 pesos, peace of camp was not disturbed" ("The Mining News" 1914, 764). Between 1917 and 1920, when the Sonoran caudillo-backed national government led by President Carranza was unable to pay soldiers and purchase war materiel due to the U.S. embargo and other adverse economic conditions, such relationships between the Sonoran caudillos and economic elites became institutionalized (Chávez 1984).

The major exceptions to these relationships were in eastern Mexico, where international petroleum interests officially participated in Mexican politics through domestic legal counsel and direct foreign political pressure. A letter from the Mexican representative of a petroleum company informed President Carranza that the official gazette of Yucatán had published a financial law that established an excise duty on the possessions, products, and salable goods brought into the state; the legal representative considered the law anticonstitutional and asked the president to block its application (Representante de la Compañía Mexicana de Petroleo el Aguila, S.A., 1916). For similar reasons, U.S. Secretary of State Robert Lansing (1916) wrote to seek protection for the property and workers of the petroleum companies that dominated the economy of the state of Veracruz. The petroleum interests also backed the largest Gulf Coast caudillo, Manuel Peláez. After Peláez fell, they supported the Sonoran caudillo-backed national regime. Finally, they backed the Sonoran Adolfo de la Huerta in 1923 in his unsuccessful rebellion against the other Sonorans (Jonathan Brown 1993).

In terms of popular challenges, the petroleum interests did not face violent uprisings from the laborers. First, a significant segment of skilled laborers and managers were foreigners who had come to work in the higher positions of the petroleum industry and thus were uninterested in mobilizing (Hall and Carver 1984, 229–230). Second, wages in the petroleum sector were much higher than those in the surrounding rural areas (Secret Agent n.d.), which discouraged laborers from rebelling (Salamini 1978). Although workers initially organized in sporadic labor militancy and unionized, they also cooperated with oil companies to keep oil wells functional against depredations by armed groups (Jonathan Brown 1993, 307–366).

Despite their frequent political shifts, however, the underlying theme from 1917 onward was the petroleum companies' opposition to Article 27 of the 1917 Constitution, which vested subsoil rights in the Mexican government (Jonathan Brown 1993; L. Hall 1995) and consequently meant that the ownership of oil wells could become illegal if contracts were not renegotiated with the federal government. However, the petroleum companies' support for de la Huerta, accompanied by fewer discoveries of new oil fields and declining production levels (R. Arnold 1921, 21), led to their demise.

Specifically, declining oil production reduced tax revenues, which simultaneously decreased the oil companies' incentives to pressure the national government even as it increased the government's incentives to enhance revenues by directly taking over operations (Haber, Razo, and Maurer 2003, 190–235). Consequently, by the time the post-Sonoran national government took power in 1938, the oil companies had ceased to be effective political players (Haber, Razo, and Maurer 2003, 190–235).

In southern Mexico, owners of henequen plantations in Yucatán, who also held stakes in the state's railway system (Wells 1992), supported various local caudillos. The U.S. companies International Harvester and Plymouth Cordage (U.S. Senate 1919, 1221–1224), the former of which consumed more than 60 percent of Mexico's henequen exports until 1940, backed the henequen plantations (Joseph and Wells 1982). They were therefore not expropriated, despite the creation of a state marketing board and even after the planters launched a failed secessionist movement against the Sonoran-controlled federal government (U.S. Senate 1919, 1716–1727). Instead, the victorious Sonorans' local political-military representative, the caudillo Salvador Alvarado, was asked by Finance Minister Luis Cabrera (at the instruction of Sonoran-backed President Carranza) to impose a special contribution of one gold centavo for each kilogram of henequen produced in the state to guarantee obligations contracted by Yucatán (Carranza 1916).

In the state of Tabasco, similar relationships existed between local caudillos and the banana plantation owners, who were connected to the U.S.-based Standard Fruit Company, now known as Dole (Ridgeway 2001). Although the local caudillo Tomás Garrido Canabal created corporatist peasant and labor organizations, as well as curtailed the Catholic Church's privileges and expropriated its assets, he refused to antagonize the plantation owners (Kirshner 1976; De la Peña Marshall 2005; Vera 2005).

Finally, coffee plantation owners in Chiapas also supported the local caudillo, Tiburcio Fernández Ruiz, who allied himself with the Sonoran caudillos in matters of national politics (Lewis 2005, 19). Ruiz attempted to abrogate revolutionary social changes by reinstating prerevolutionary policies vis-à-vis land ownership (J. Figueroa 2002, 52–54; Ramos 1992, 48–50). However, as international prices fell in the 1930s and the local regime under Fernández Ruiz crumbled, the central government expropriated the plantations and redistributed the land to agricultural laborers (Lewis 2005, 19). This, like the case of the petroleum interests in Veracruz, reveals the interdependent nature of caudillos and business owners.

In northern Mexico, the major economic actors were industrialists and financiers—specifically, banking interests—because bills of exchange issued by banks were the central characteristic of the Porfirian (pre-1910) currency. Before the beginning of conflict and state collapse, Mexico contained banks of two types: national and regional. The two national banks, Banco Nacional de México and the Banco de Londres y México, maintained branches across Mexico. Although regional banks were initially permitted by the Profirian government to lend within specific states, the Banco Central was established in 1897 as a clearinghouse and lender of last resort, thus giving the regional banks access to cross-regional transactions (Merchant 2002, 31–43).

The private banks, however, did not function within a regulated environment in which credit was given to qualified applicants. Rather, credit was based on familial and social networks or personal connections centered on reciprocity (Cerutti 2000). Although such lending methods reduced risks for lenders, this also meant that lending was restricted to an exclusive, interconnected group. Consequently, the Terrazas-Creel family, who owned vast tracts of land in Mexico, also controlled mines and banks (Wasserman 1993, 10–11).

As the state began to collapse from 1910 onward, the same informal banking networks that obviated the need for formal regulations and oversight deepened the crisis (Kaminsky and Reinhart 1999, 496). By 1914, Mexico's financial and monetary systems had finally shattered, due to a combination of extortion by caudillos of banks and the uncertain political-security environment that rendered lending too risky (Reyes 2006, 140–144). The paper currency dissolved into various types of local paper monies issued by whichever caudillo controlled a region (Merchant 2002, 55).

Although certain industries survived and flourished (Haber and Varela 1993), the links between industries provided by banking and finance—both undergirded by a common currency—disappeared. This financial vacuum was filled partially by a set of intermediary institutions called "unchartered banks" that developed in 1914 (Gómez-Galvarriato and Recio 2007). However, political instability and security threats made these banks prone to "constant frauds, falsifications, and panics" (Gómez-Galvarriato and Recio 2007, 102). Consequently, their longevity and credibility became contingent on political patronage (and protection) from local caudillos.

Official documents regarding the financing firm Lacaud y Hijo exemplify this system. The owner, Jules Lacaud, speculated in various foreign and domestic currencies (Secretario de Hacienda 1916a). His company collapsed when the Sonoran caudillo-controlled central government nullified Veracruz's paper currency (Secretario de Hacienda 1916b). Nevertheless, as noted by Luis Merchant (2002, 118–119), despite the company's liquidation and Lacaud's exile from Mexico, his relationship with the Sonoran caudillo Álvaro Obregón allowed his other business interests to survive through the 1920s.

Due to the political and security uncertainties, however, the public refused to accept the various paper monies, thus reducing the incentive to save and invest (Merchant 2002, 118–119). Official documents noted that the consequent hyperinflation adversely affected the agricultural sector (Rebolledo 1915), causing a series of nationwide strikes of industrial workers, including electricians and miners (Semo 2006, 186). Unable to purchase food because they had not received acceptable currency, people in small towns even petitioned President Carranza for help, threatening to undertake banditry to provide for their families (Montes de Oca and Rebolledo n.d.).

To stabilize the economy, the Carranza government—supported by the Sonoran caudillos—initially opposed private banks and tried to impose a government-controlled single paper currency based on a bimetallic (gold and silver) standard or a gold standard (Reyes 2006). Consequently, it nationalized the private banking industry in 1916 and introduced a paper currency called *infalsificables*. Continued political instability, however, led the currency to lose most of its value within a few months (Sanchez 2006, 208). In 1919, the government tried to create a central bank but failed because Finance Minister Rafael Nieto was unable to acquire sufficient loans from foreign creditors (Zebadúa 1995, 72). The government was unable to access foreign credit until 1922 because of its unwillingness and inability to honor outstanding loans (Sanchez 2006, 308–310). The government subsequently decided to support private banking to placate foreign creditors (Gómez-Galvarriato and Recio 2007, 102). In 1924, a convention of Mexico's major bankers and government representatives led to an agreement.

The next year, the government attempted to create a unified banking and currency system by establishing the Banco de México. However, despite the Sonoran regime's efforts, the goal of a unified currency and financial stability remained unrealized through the 1920s. Given continued political instability and conflict, Mexicans nearly universally rejected the Banco de México's bills in preference of gold and silver (Cardero 1977, 1341–1342).

It is worth reiterating that such pushes for institutionalization centered on the Sonoran caudillos' informal alliances with northern business and financial elites. Most important, despite their enmity, the Sonorans collaborated with the Terrazas-Creel family, which owned the Banco Minero de Chihuahua. In fact, even during the 1924 convention between bankers and the government, official documents reveal, the Sonorans suspected the bank of trying to undermine them politically through debt contracted to the Banco Minero de Chihuahua by the Compañía Industrial Mexicana (Report n.d.). The demands made by Enrique Creel, who represented the bank at the convention, centered on maintaining a high reserve requirement for banks (Merchant 2002, 180–182), which could restrict new banks from entering the market and re-create the pre-1910 exclusivity of the banking sector.

Thus, although the process of integrating the economic elites was neither harmonious nor linear (Herrera 1996), the origins of Mexico's monetary and fiscal stability were these networks of caudillos and businessmen during the 1920s (Aguilar 2001). However, the stabilization of the financial system occurred only after political-military peace was ensured in 1929. The General Law of Credit Institutions of 1932, along with modifications introduced in 1941, provided the regulatory and institutional infrastructure that lasted until the monetary and fiscal crises of the 1970s and 1980s (Del Angel and Marichal 2003, 694).

A Country of Institutions: War and Party Formation

By the end of the 1920s, political instability and the consequent violence that resulted from the inability of the caudillos (as individuals and in coalitions) to capture the Mexican state in an outright victory or protect themselves from challengers had made the caudillo system unsustainable. This assertion dovetails with Jürgen Buchenau and William Beezley's (2009) finding based on the rapid turnover of state governors, a position that depended on the relative power of local caudillos. As this section of the chapter highlights, three rounds of violent conflict centered on capturing the presidency increased the economic costs and personal risks of retaining power for the caudillos. Specifically, the De la Huerta Rebellion (1923–1924), the Gómez-Serrano Rebellion (1928), and the Escobar Rebellion (1929) revealed that no caudillos were able to win an outright victory, singly or in coalition, and the costs of fighting continued to rise. It was in light of such instability and risks that caudillos agreed to join an official party comprising all of the incumbent political-military leaders, which would control the state in the name of the revolution. As the official party and state institutions strengthened, the caudillos lost power to political bosses called *caciques*, who initially acted as the caudillos' agents in the party and state institutions and subsequently became the purveyors of the party and state's dominance.

The De la Huerta Rebellion of 1923–1924, led by the disgruntled Sonoran former interim president Adolfo de la Huerta, was the most serious because it had the support of 40 percent of the federal troops and 20 percent of the officers' corps, which was composed of caudillos (Lieuwen 1968, 76). The most prominent of the regional caudillo generals were Guadalupe Sanchez, from the eastern state of Veracruz; Enrique Estrada, from the western state of Jalisco; Rómulo Figueroa, from the southwestern state of Guerrero; and Salvador Alvarado, from the southeastern state of Yucatán.

As a participant in the rebellion noted, however, the rebelling officers were unable to maintain a united front and soon confined their ambitions to restoring or maintaining power in their respective localities (Capetillo 1925). Taking advantage of these divisions—along with the support of allied regional caudillos and weapons and funding from the United States—the Sonorans defeated the rebellion (Machado 1972). However, regional caudillo allies of the Sonorans, such as Saturnino Cedillo, gained strength because their militias defended the government (Ankerson 1985). Nevertheless, the singular contribution of the rebellion was the exile or execution of a large number of caudillos who had commanded the rebelling federal army (Lozoya 1970, 45), thus both reducing the number of possible spoilers who could prevent future peace agreements and demonstrating the steep costs of continued conflict.

The subsequent Gómez-Serrano Rebellion of 1927 involved twenty caudillo generals and 20 percent of the standing army (Lieuwen 1968, 52–53). Yet again the rebellion resulted from the process of presidential succession that had begun in 1927. In this case, the rebellion was led by two caudillo generals of the federal army, Francisco Serrano and Arnulfo Gómez, who opposed the Sonoran caudillo and candidate Álvaro Obregón's presidential bid. Although General Serrano was arrested and shot almost immediately, General Gómez continued fighting in the state of Veracruz until November 1928 (De la Pedraja 2006, 294–295). Even though it failed, the rebellion weakened the central government's forces fighting the Cristiada (as the Cristero Rebellion was also known), a religious uprising in western-central Mexico backed by the Catholic Church, smallholders, and agricultural laborers (Purnell 1999, 86). When combined with the cost of containing the Cristiada, the rebellion more than halved the government's foreign currency reserves, from $39.8 million in May 1926 to $15 million in January 1927 (E. Cárdenas 1994, 28). The only positive aspect of the rebellion was the further reduction of the number of caudillos.

The Escobar Rebellion of 1929, the third such major rebellion, involved 34 percent of the federal army and affected the northern states of Sonora, Chihuahua, Coahuila, and Durango (Meyer, Segovia, and Lajous 1978, 68). The rebellion closely followed the creation of the official party, the Partido Nacional Revolucionario (National Revolutionary Party; PNR), created by the Sonoran caudillo and Mexican President Plutarco Elías Calles in that year. In the wake of President Obregón's assassination by a Catholic and another expected round of conflict—one that would pit Calles against Obregón's regional allies—Calles himself felt that such a party would prevent the recurring conflicts centered on presidential succession that were wracking Mexico every few years (Calles [1928] 2002).

Backed by the Sonoran caudillos, the PNR was supposed to include all of the incumbent caudillos in an elaborate power-sharing agreement. However, the rebelling caudillos, led by General José Gonzalo Escobar, felt that their own prospects for national power were thwarted by the newly formed party. As with the two previous rebellions, differences between rebelling caudillo generals arose almost immediately in the eastern state of Veracruz; caudillos from southern states—most notably, Oaxaca—refused to rebel (Dulles 1961, 441); and other caudillos loyally fought for the Sonoran-backed national government (Garrido 1986, 121). Despite the rebellion's failure, however, it cost the Mexican economy approximately 13,800,000 pesos (about $6.9 million), not including the 25 million pesos (about $12.5 million) that banks lost to looting by rebel caudillos (*Federal Reserve Bulletin* 1929, 35; Garrido 1986, 121). Nevertheless, the abortive rebellion created a consensus among caudillos regarding the unsustainability of continued political fragmentation and military competition (Un Observador 1929).

The peace agreement centered on the PNR, which aimed to "unify in the party all of the local parties, the majority of the existing labor groups and organizations and all of the dispersed/various forces that signified the various revolutionary forces" (Díaz Soto y Gama 1959, 29–36). After joining the PNR, caudillos began to rely on a new group of political intermediaries, who represented local (implicitly caudillo) interests to attract resources from the national government (Voss 1990). The caudillos' unwillingness to restart conflicts was demonstrated by their acquiescence to declines in the budget allocation for the federal military—effectively militias commanded by the caudillos—from 53 percent in 1929 to 30.9 percent in 1931 (Wilkie 1967, 102–103).

With the diminution of their military capabilities, the caudillos became incapable of opposing changes to the organization of the PNR undertaken by President Abelardo Rodríguez in 1932–1934. The most important of these changes was the PNR's transformation from a conglomeration of caudillo-controlled regional political organizations into a party based on individual membership. Combined with the preexisting prohibition of reelection for government offices—which made politicians dependent on local caudillos—this change made the new political intermediaries' seats in the national and provincial legislatures dependent on both the PNR and the caudillos (Nacif 2002; D. Smith 1974; Weldon 2003).

As a result, despite political instability in certain states, such as Chihuahua, Queretaro, and Colima, the PNR negotiated the installation of favored candidates as governors and state and national legislators (Mecham 1942, 256–280). Certain states, such as Zacatecas, which remained outside the PNR's control because of the exigencies imposed by the pro-Catholic Cristiada, came under control within a couple of years (Olague et al. 1996, 161–162). The increasing control of the PNR agreement was made further apparent by the increasing share of per capita revenue enjoyed by the federal government, instead of state and local governments, that were until recently, or still, controlled by the caudillos (Wilkie 1967, 19).

Conclusion

The study of postrevolutionary state formation in Mexico presented here takes a strategic-choice approach to a well-documented historical case. It demonstrates that Mexican caudillos joined peace agreements under two conditions: (1) when their economic backers incentivized such agreements and (2) when the costs and risks of competing to retain power became intolerable. By doing so, the chapter reveals a singular characteristic of bargains and competition between political leaders and economic elites: they occur simultaneously in distinct but interconnected arenas (Tsebelis 1991). The selection of particular political and economic institutions depends on the outcome of such bargains and competition. The process of state formation therefore reveals that national-level financial elites and their regional economic counterparts, represented by regional warlords, came to entrench themselves in Mexico's new state institutions.

However, the new state institutions were not entirely authoritarian. Although they excluded independent peasant interests from national power and co-opted them into the warlord organizations—and, subsequently, the official party—the new institutions also permitted limited contestation of power and mass participation.

The observable effects on popular participation of the elite bargains on state institutions were consequently twofold. On the one hand, the elite bargains led to the creation of a servile bureaucracy, which permitted leaders to differentially disburse public goods to benefit supporters and punish rivals

(Greene 2007, 39–42). Moreover, the regime continued to use repression as a last resort, as exemplified by the massacre of protesting students in Tlatelolco in 1968 (Gyula 1997). On the other hand, the state institutions lent themselves to corruption as the caudillos were replaced with the *caciques* who used their official positions for personal gain, thus making the system more permeable to local interests than later portrayed (Centeno 1994; Collier and Collier 1991). Furthermore, the regime was not averse to permitting leftist groups into mainstream politics in 1977 and granting amnesty to communist guerrillas in 1979 (Imaz 1981; Middlebrook 1981, 5–7).

5

Class, Religion, and Power

The Elite Origins of Postcolonial India

From 1920 into the early 1930s, Indian regional politics was characterized by peaceful and violent rural rebellions. Peasants refused to pay land rents, demanded tenure rights, marched, demonstrated, and destroyed local government and landlords' property. From landed farmers and small merchants to urban professionals, elite allies of peasants funded, led, and organized these rebellions through various political parties. Thus, the elite-dominated political parties came to control peasant rebellions, articulate peasants' demands, and manage peasants' political tactics and alliances.

This chapter explains the subsequent process of state formation, which began with the introduction of provincial-level elections in the mid-1930s. The study specifically centers on the questions of how competition and bargains among political parties, representing their constituent social groups, influenced the decolonization process. The findings reaffirm the book's broader theory that elites' greater resources and cohesion, which make them critical to the success of rebellions, also allow them to strategically select or capture institutions via inter-elite bargains.

The study of Indian politics right before and after the 1937 provincial elections, based on a significantly broadened franchise, reveals that colonial institutions initially appeared to have successfully channeled peasant grievances and bourgeois aspirations and to have safeguarded landlords' and broader colonial interests. The next section highlights the effects of the elections of 1937—specifically, victories for bourgeois-led peasant coalitions in all but the northwestern province of Punjab. The third section explicates the reaction to these elections by landlords who began supporting political competition based on religious cleavages to retain popular support. Nevertheless, the underlying pattern is one of competition shaped by the parameters of the 1937 electoral institutions. The fourth section investigates the origins of the indigenous businessmen and the reasons they began to support the Congress Party in the 1930s. The study shows that the Indian businessmen based in Bombay sought to displace foreign competitors who were based primarily in Calcutta and, consequently, sided with the rural bourgeoisie–based Congress Party to achieve their goals.

World War II, however, led to the collapse of the equilibrium of the mid-1930s and, ultimately, precipitated the partition of India. As the chapter's fifth section shows, the war weakened the colonial state. The cumulative nationwide effect of its political and economic dislocations, which arrived on the back of prior popular mobilizations that merged economic interests and religious identity, was massive religious conflict. Specifically, on the one hand, Britain's industrial demands precipitated an economic boom and rapid development in urban Bengal, primarily inhabited by the Hindu urban bourgeoisie and absentee landlords, while its defense requirements simultaneously precipitated a rural famine that generally affected the Muslim peasants and rural bourgeoisie. On the other hand, in the northwestern province of Punjab, the personnel needs of the British Indian Army shattered the pro-British rural coalition in the province along the lines of Sikh and Muslim religious identity. As a result, the Muslim landlords from northern India and their landed farmer-soldier counterparts of northwestern India exited the polity altogether to form the western half of Pakistan. Although the Hindu landlords and the dependent urban bourgeoisie centered in Calcutta remained in the rump province of West Bengal, their land was marooned in the more populous and larger Pakistani province of East Bengal.

The landlords' departure and destitution left the rural and urban bourgeoisie of northern and southern India, and the Congress Party that represented them, politically triumphant in independent India. As the sixth section explains, postcolonial land reforms and industrial policies of the Congress Party served their interests. In contrast, the poor peasants were given political rights but denied land redistribution. The conclusion summarizes the chapter and discusses how the findings respond to existing research on India's decolonization.

Controlling the Mobilizations: Bourgeois Triumph and Declining Landlords

Facing peaceful but persistent peasant rebellions throughout the 1920s, the British government in India made a series of institutional changes in the early

1930s. The Communal Award of 1932 and the Government of India Act of 1935 sought to accommodate the interests of mobilized peasants and their allied elites within new institutions. The British also aimed to use province-level electoral competition and the institutionalization of religious differences to prevent the disparate movements from uniting to challenge the British for national power. Given the trajectory of the regional rebellions, the elites, allied with peasants, used the 1937 elections, based on the new electoral rules, to gain control over provincial legislatures and politics. Thus, bourgeois elites came to control politics in northern, eastern, and southern India, while the landlords retained power only in northwestern India. However, the institutional recognition of religious differences facilitated the defeated landlords' support for ethnoreligious parties to protect their own interests, consequently setting the stage for postwar civil conflict.

The Government of India Act attempted to channel popular politics into provincial institutions. The year before its introduction, Chief Secretary G. T. H. Bracken, the highest bureaucratic official of the Madras Presidency, noted that the act would make the provinces the focal point of politics, thus weakening "the grip of any all-India movement"; consequently, further mass mobilizations would be "so localized" that it would be impossible for the Indian National Congress (INC) to organize a countrywide movement (D. Arnold 1977, 188). This objective was met by establishing two lists of subjects under the distinct jurisdictions of the viceroy reporting to the Secretary of State for India (United Kingdom, Government of India 1936, seventh schedule, list 1, federal legislative list) and the provinces governed by elected prime ministers with extraordinary powers for the British governors (United Kingdom, Government of India 1936, seventh schedule, list 2, provincial legislative list), as well as a third list over which the provinces and the central government shared jurisdiction (United Kingdom, Government of India 1936, seventh schedule, list 2, concurrent legislative list). The powers of the central and provincial governments were underwritten by distinct revenue streams (United Kingdom, Government of India 1936, seventh schedule, list 1, federal legislative list, list 2, provincial legislative list).

The two most important aspects of the distribution of responsibilities regarded control of land and commerce, which directly affected the Indian landlords and bourgeoisie. The provincial governments were given control over the subjects of land redistribution and land tenure, the central axes of peasant mobilization. However, the elected provincial legislature could make only marginal changes, because assent from the British provincial governors was required before any land could be expropriated (United Kingdom, Government of India 1936, pt. 12, miscellaneous and general, art. 3, sec. 299). In terms of commerce, the provincial government could legislate on intraprovincial trade, while imports, exports, and interprovincial trade remained under central control. More important, in terms of revenues, income taxes and company taxes remained under the central government.

The new institutions also attempted to use religion to fragment popular aspirations. This strategy was articulated in the Communal Award of 1932, which designated the percentage of legislative seats that would be allocated to the majority and minority religious groups in each province. The expected outcomes would not affect electoral results in provinces where either Hindus or Muslims were a predominant majority. The majority of the population of northern and southern Indian provinces identified as Hindu in the 1910s. Hindus made up 85.32 percent of the population in the United Provinces; 82.4 percent in Bihar; 88.9 percent in the Madras Presidency; and 76.02 percent in the Bombay Presidency (United Kingdom, Government of India 1916, 191). Even in the 1930s, Muslims constituted a majority in only the small northwestern province of Sindh, at 71.8 percent of the population (H. Alavi 1988, 71).

However, the Communal Awards had the potential to affect political outcomes in the provinces of Punjab and Bengal, where Muslims had a thin demographic majority of 52.3 percent and 54.5 percent, respectively (H. Alavi 1988, 71). In these provinces, the Communal Awards reserved 49 percent of the seats for Muslims in Punjab's provincial legislature and 48 percent of the seats in Bengal's provincial legislature (Jalal and Seal 1981). The British reasoned that because 45 percent of eligible Bengali voters and 44 percent of eligible Punjabi voters were Muslim, given property and educational qualifications required to vote, without such reservations the thin Muslim majorities in these provinces would translate into a minority of legislative seats (Simon 1932, 146–147).

The Government of India Act of 1935 added to the effects of the Communal Awards. It considerably increased the size of the electorate for provincial legislatures by lowering property and educational requirements. This resulted in an electorate of thirty million, or approximately one-fifth of the entire adult population (Bell 1948, 21). The combination of the ethnically based electoral rules and mass politics incentivized political parties to appeal to ethnoreligious loyalties to gain the reserved seats in the legislatures.

These British efforts had partial success. The outcomes of the 1937 elections repudiated religious politics but were determined by socioeconomic cleavages that propelled the provincial mobilizations. The electoral loss of the landlords in most provinces and the rural bourgeoisie's victories had two far-reaching effects: (1) they indicated that the future provincial and nationally dominant political class would be the regional bourgeoisie and (2) they signaled the end of landlords' dominance over provincial and Indian politics.

The success of provincial-level socioeconomic causes over ethnic cleavages is apparent in the victories of the secular provincial and national parties, such as the Unionist Party in Punjab, the Krishak Praja Party (KPP) in Bengal, the Azad Muslim Party (Free Muslims Party; AMP) in Sindh, and the Congress Party across all provinces. Election results reflected the failure of religious politics even in provinces with slim Muslim majorities. In the Muslim-majority province of Bengal, in eastern India, the secular KPP, dominated by the peasants and rural bourgeoisie, won thirty-six seats out of a total of 250. In turn, they allied with twenty-three independent lower-caste Hindus with similar socioeconomic interests (Bandyopadhyay 1994). The Congress Party, backed by the predominantly Hindu urban bourgeoisie and landlords, won fifty-two seats, and the Muslim ethnoreligious All-India Muslim League, backed by landlords and the urban bourgeoisie, won only thirty-nine seats (United Kingdom, Government of India 1937b).

In northwestern India, the defeat of ethnic politics was starker in Muslim-majority Punjab, where the secular landlord- and landed peasant–supported Unionist Party won ninety-one seats, while the urban bourgeoisie–backed Congress Party won nineteen seats, and the Muslim League won just one seat out of a total of 175 seats. In Muslim-majority Sindh, in northwestern India, the AMP, backed by landlords, won thirty-four seats, while the Congress Party won six seats among the urban bourgeoisie, and the Muslim League won no seats out of a total of sixty (United Kingdom, Government of India 1937b). The Hindu religious party Hindu Mahasabha also won no seats in these provinces.

There was a similar effect in the Hindu-majority provinces. In the Bombay Presidency, in southern India, the secular INC, backed by peasants and the urban and rural bourgeoisie, won eighty-five seats, while the Muslim League won eighteen seats, out of a total of 175 seats. In the Madras Presidency, also in southern India, the Congress Party's coalition of peasants and rural bourgeoisie won 159 seats, while the Muslim League won nine seats, out of 215 seats. In the United Provinces, in northern India, a similar social coalition led by the Congress Party won 134 seats, while the landlord- and urban bourgeoisie–backed Muslim League won twenty-six, out of a total of 228 seats. Again, in northern India, in the province of Bihar, an identical Congress Party coalition won ninety-two seats, while the Muslim League won no seats, out of a total of 162 seats (United Kingdom, Government of India 1937b). The Hindu religious party won three seats in all of the provincial assemblies combined, while minor Hindu parties won a combined thirty-three seats in all of the provinces (Chiriyankandath 2001, 76–77).

There were a few alliances of convenience between the victorious provincial elites and the Muslim League, because its overwhelming defeat in 1937 gave provincial parties more leverage than they would have had in the victorious non-religious INC. The most important of these occurred between the Unionist Party of Punjab and the Muslim League in 1937, which maintained the Unionist Party's supremacy in Punjab while accepting the League's leadership on national issues (I. Talbot 1996, 73–74). Similarly, the rural bourgeoisie of Bengal represented by the KPP also allied with the Muslim League in 1937 to get enough seats to form the provincial government (Jalal 1985, 40). Given the KPP's alliance of rural bourgeoisie and peasants and the Muslim League's backing by landlords and the urban bourgeoisie, they actually contested the elections as rival parties, and the subsequent alliance occurred only after the Congress Party turned down the KPP's offer (Chatterji 1994, 84–85).

As evidenced above, the 1937 elections revealed the political decline of the landlords and the triumph of the rural bourgeoisie. The rural bourgeoisie were further strengthened when the newly powerful urban bourgeoisie entered politics in the 1930s. In response, the landlords started to use British support and ethnoreligious politics to remake themselves as communal leaders in the eyes of the peasants, a strategy whose violent results were unknown at that time.

Knotting Religion with Land: The Landlords' Last Gambit

Facing defeat at the hands of the regional bourgeoisie, the landlords decided to use ethnic politics to cast themselves as leaders and protect their material interests. In their fight to retain power, the landlords were also aided by British policy and institutions. As an important aside, landlords could not follow such a strategy in southern India because their economic, and consequent political, power was minimized by the *ryotwari* system, which recognized peasant cultivators, not intermediaries, as responsible for paying land rents.

In northern India, the Hindu and Muslim landlords increased their support for ethnoreligious parties—specifically, the Hindu Mahasabha and the Muslim League (Reeves 1991, 218–219). The Muslim landlords in the United Provinces were aware that, demographically, the provincial Muslim population was too small to prevent the Congress Party from dominating. Consequently, they supported the national-level Muslim League to retain their economic dominance in the province (Brennan 1984). In 1946, a senior Muslim League leader and prominent landlord in the United Provinces expressed the underlying reason in a confidential meeting with the viceroy: landlordism and Islamic identity in the United Provinces were intertwined to such an extent that an attack on one could be construed as an attack on the other ("Meeting between Cabinet Delegation . . . 1946" 1980, 166).

Although the shift of Muslim landlords' loyalty to the Muslim League had begun even before the 1937 elections (Jalal 1985, 30), the trend accelerated throughout the late 1930s and early 1940s. In response, the League fought against the tenancy reform legislation of 1939: elected League legislators and allied landlords walked out of the provincial legislature during the voting (Reeves 1991, 272). Given such elite resources and support, an Islamic mobilization began in the late 1930s, which created an implicitly Hindu and Sikh counter-mobilization led by the provincial Congress Party (Kudaisya 2006, 274–275). Facing the imminent withdrawal of the British after 1945, these class tensions led to religious violence.

Similarly, in the eastern province of Bengal, it was the Hindu elites (especially landlords) who started supporting the Hindu Mahasabha during the late 1930s. Threatened by the growing popularity of the Mahasabha, the provincial Congress Party started to identify itself with Hindu landlords (J. Chatterji 1994). Even though a large section of the provincial Congress Party dissented, and then defected, in 1939 to form an anticolonial secular party called the Forward Bloc, they, too, sought top-down modernization and opposed land redistribution (Chakrabarty 1990). Despite the ostensibly secular aims of the Forward Bloc, the provincial Hindu Mahasabha drew support from the same segments of society (Broomfield 1968, 282–284). Given their growing economic strength and stakes in Bengal, the predominantly Hindu indigenous bourgeoisie also started to support the Hindu Mahasabha (J. Chatterji 1994, 236, 254–256). The support of 126 Hindu notables (including scientists, businessmen, and landlords) in a memorandum of protest against Muslim political domination—and, by implication, the one person, one vote democratic principle—reveals that the religious cleavage revolved around anxieties regarding the loss of their dominant economic and political status:

> Hindus of Bengal, though numerically a minority, are overwhelmingly superior culturally, consisting [of] as much as 64% of total literate population and more than 80% of school going population. Their economic preponderance is equally manifest in the spheres of the independent professions and commercial careers[,] making up nearly 87% of the Legal, 80% of the Medical and 83% of the Banking, Insurance, and Exchange business. . . . [They, consequently, protested] strongly against the unfair and unprecedented provision to protect a majority community by conferring upon it a position of permanent and statutory predominance in the legislature and making that position unalterable by any appeal to the electorate. (Hindus of Bengal 1936)

Landlords' interests also continued to receive support from British policies and institutions. Most important, the landlords were constitutionally protected by the non-elected British governors via Article 3(299) of the Government of India Act of 1935, which specified that no bills amending landownership, control, and revenue could be introduced in the national and provincial legislatures without the viceroy's and governor's assent, respectively (United Kingdom, Government of India 1936, pt. 12, sec. 299, art. 3). Moreover, the British directly aided the creation of landlord parties in the United Provinces and Punjab. Only in Bengal did the British not support landlords because they were backed by the provincial Congress Party against a generally pro-British rural bourgeoisie and peasant coalition headed by the KPP and the Muslim League (J. Chatterji 1994, 103–149).

In the United Provinces, the British attempted to replicate the National Agriculturalists Party of Agra and National Agriculturalists Party of Oudh as electorally oriented organizations. District-level officials attempted to intervene during the electoral campaigns on behalf of landlords and in opposition to the Congress Party because of its stance on land reforms (Bradley 1937). However, personal disagreements among large landlords and their inability to articulate a clear alternative to land reforms proposed by the Congress Party blocked their electoral success in 1937 (Reeves 1991, 214–217). The British also did not intervene in the design and ratification of the United Provinces Tenancy Act No. XVII of 1939 because the Congress Party government avoided attacking the landlords' proprietary rights and the land tenure and revenue systems (Crane 1951, 139, 143, 163).

In Punjab, a coalition made up of landlords and peasants succeeded under the Unionist Party because electoral institutions enfranchised former servicemen (United Kingdom, Government of India 1934, 358–366). Although enfranchisement applied to former servicemen in all of the provinces, soldiers were recruited in the largest numbers from Punjab and were connected to colonial land grants in the Canal Colonies. Consequently, the former servicemen's electoral support became a bulwark for landowners (Yong 2005, 276–277). Moreover, the electorate in Punjab was biased against the urban population: 143 seats out of 175 for the provincial assembly were from rural areas (Yong 2005, 176). As a result, pro-British landowners backed the Unionist Party to a victory in 1937 before switching to the Muslim League in the 1946 elections, which ensured their continued political and economic dominance (Yong 2005, 300).

Unlike the Congress Party government in the United Provinces or the Unionist Party government in Punjab, the rural bourgeoisie–backed KPP government in Bengal undertook a series of reforms on land occupancy and usufruct rights (Chatterjee 1982, 194). However, because the KPP had to ally with the landlord-dominated Muslim League to take power after the 1937 elections, the Permanent Settlement system could not be abolished. Historian Partha Chatterjee (1975, 80) states that the provincial Muslim League's leadership was an "almost exact replica of the Bengal provincial Congress leadership, which was intent on protecting landlords." In 1940, however, the report by the provincial government's appointed Land Revenue Commission asked for the abolition of the Permanent Settlement system, on which landlordism was based, and suggested the installation of the *ryotwari* system prevalent in the Madras and Bombay Presidencies instead (United Kingdom, Government of India, Government of Bengal 1940, 41, para. 94). Despite these efforts, landlords were expropriated and lands were redistributed to Bengali peasants only after decolonization. The Permanent Settlement Act was abolished under the post-independence East Bengal State Acquisition and Tenancy Act of 1950.

From Dependence to Opposition: The New Urban Bourgeoisie

Previously economically insignificant or dependent on their connections with British firms and the colonial government, domestic industrialists' growing economic strength and antagonistic British trade and tariff policies in the 1920s and 1930s made them enter Indian politics in alliance with the rural bourgeoisie–based Congress Party. After presenting the origins and characteristics of the new urban bourgeoisie, this section therefore explains how their alliance with the Congress Party contrasted with the decreasing influence of their foreign competitors.

The regionalized nature of the Indian economy created two separate urban bourgeois groups: the Indian bourgeoisie, centered in Bombay, and the British bourgeoisie in Calcutta (Markovits 1985, 17–26). The Indian businessmen in Bombay focused mainly on cotton and textile production (Bagchi 1972, 219–261), although the Tata Iron and Steel Company (TISCO), the first wholly Indian steel company, founded in 1907 by Jamshedji Tata, was also a part of this group. TISCO remained the only Indian-owned steel company until 1939, when the partially Indian-owned Indian Iron and Steel Company (IISCO) was founded in Calcutta. These Indian business interests were represented by the Federation of Indian Chambers of Industry and Commerce (FICCI), established in 1927.

In contrast, Calcutta was dominated by British managing agencies centered on the production of jute products, coal and iron mines, and tea gardens. Although Indians served on individual companies' Boards of Directors, these companies were controlled by London-based managing agencies that made the final business decisions (Brimmer 1955, 556) over interests ranging from collieries to tea estates (Bagchi 1972; Markovits 1985). The interests of the British bourgeoisie were represented by the Associated Chambers of Commerce of India and Ceylon, established in 1919, which in turn was dominated by the Bengal Chamber of Commerce headquartered in Calcutta.

Initially, the urban Indian bourgeoisie was generally pro-British. In Bombay, TISCO profited from British government contracts. During World War I, the British government bought more than 80 percent of the steel TISCO produced, though at below-market prices (Bagchi 1972, 304). The tariffs introduced in 1924 to protect the Indian steel industry directly prevented TISCO from being bankrupted (United Kingdom, Government of India 1924, 17, 80) by competition from Belgian steel (Wagle 1981, 123). The Marawari financiers from northern India moving into Calcutta, who were initially dependent on the British bourgeoisie, also provided short-term loans to British companies (Goswami 1989, 294), acted as intermediaries between British industries and rural producers in the case of jute (Timberg 1977, 190–191), and were distributors to in-country markets for products imported to India by British industries (Kochanek 1974, 21–22).

Thus, during the 1905–1906 agitations against the first partition of Bengal, these financiers opposed the boycott of imported products demanded by Bengali nationalists (Broomfield 1968, 33, 220). The Marwari Chamber of Commerce wrote to its counterpart in Manchester that the Bengalis' boycott of British goods was threatening the Marwari merchants with ruin and would make them incapable of making future contracts "unless the Secretary of State [for India] withdrew the Partition" and the boycott stopped (S. N. Sen 2006, 146). In short, the urban bourgeoisie remained uncommitted to anticolonial agitation, if not pro-British.

Their attitude changed when British tariff policy from the early 1920s began favoring the importing of British cotton goods to India because of pressure for preferential treatment from the Lancashire-based industry, which had fallen behind due to outdated technology and high labor costs that the late-developing Indian and Japanese textile industries did not encounter (Muldoon 2009, 153–186). The pro-British policy became apparent in the preferential tariffs given to Lancashire in the Cotton Industries Protection Bill of 1930, which adversely affected the Indian textile industry in the Bombay Presidency—specifically, in the cities of Bombay and Ahmadabad (Lockwood 2012, 113). As a result, industrialists based in Bombay started supporting the Congress Party–led boycott of foreign goods, especially British cloth, during the regional mass mobilizations during the 1920s (Markovits 1985, 70–71).

Urban bourgeois support for the Congress Party increased when indigenous financiers started attempting to control the Calcutta-based industries hitherto dominated by British interests (Goswami 1987, 172–196). Chief among these financiers was Ghanshyam Das Birla, who supported the Congress Party both directly and indirectly. These industrialists' actions toward industrial laborers, who were backed by the Congress Party, reveal this alliance. Rather than blaming the laborers backed by the Congress Party, Birla viewed strikes in 1929 at the textile mills in Bombay as the result of mill owners' intransigence, while another industrialist refused to blame local communists who were openly supporting the strike and instead accused mill owners of not responding to laborers' basic demands (Lieten 1982, 699).

Collaboration between the urban bourgeoisie and urban labor continued throughout the anticolonial movement, as evidenced by Birla's later permitting and paying laborers to leave work and join the anticolonial mass mobilization ("Birla Encourages Mill Laborers to Strike" 1942). Also, Walchand Hirachand and G. L. Mehta of the Scindia Steam Navigation Company financed political and industrial agitation in British-owned firms in Bengal because they thought the government had unfairly refused to sponsor their efforts at "automobile-and-aircraft manufacturing" ("Kiran Shankar Roy Is Reported to Have Accepted Rs. Two Lakh from CWC to Organize Disturbances" 1942).

However, the urban bourgeoisie were not passive supporters of the Congress Party. Rather, they pressured the party to tamp down its strategy of rural agitation and rebellion after 1931 and join constitutional channels provided by the negotiations that led to the Government of India Act of 1935 (B. Chatterji 1992, 324–325). They also argued that the budget allocation for provincial governments could increase if the central government lowered expenses incurred for the military-security apparatus (Birla 1955). This last matter had major ramifications for the landlords of Punjab, whose political and economic power depended on the maintenance of a large military-security apparatus (Yong 2005). Despite its acknowledged effects on the Punjabi economy, the Congress Party's position on the military came to reflect the revenue-expense logic expressed by the urban bourgeoisie. The leader of the backward and untouchable castes evaluated the military expenditures of India and the possible creation of Pakistan as a homeland for Indian Muslims, to demonstrate the preponderance of Punjabi Muslim soldiers in the army and the high costs of maintaining a large army (Ambedkar 1946, 51–87).

Unlike their indigenous counterparts, the British bourgeoisie based in Calcutta were unable to have an effect on mass politics because their method of influencing government policy was by directly approaching senior bureaucrats in India (Kochanek 1974, 113). This strategy worked admirably until the early twentieth century: between 1904 and 1913, 501 out of 528 (or 95 percent) of senior civil servants were British (Potter 1973, 49). Thus, they opposed opening positions in the higher administration to Indians (M. Misra 1999), which the urban professionals and university-educated members of the Congress Party strongly demanded (Banerjee 2010, 150–190; Rai 1916). K. M. Panikkar (1920, 30), then a scholar who would become a foreign policy bureaucrat in independent India, explicated the link between such obstructions and the Indian elites' grievances, writing, "There is a closed door in the *Administration* of India; there is a closed door in the *Government* of India also. The one excludes Indians from the most important places in the official hierarchy: the other excludes the people of India from political power. Each is a cause of Nationalism, and, of these two causes, the latter—the closed door in Government—is the more penetrating, and the more widely operative."

Conceding to such demands, the Islington Commission of 1912 proposed that the official ratio of Indians to Britons for the Indian civil service, the highest level of bureaucrats, should be increased to 25:75. The ratio was later increased to 33:67, with an increase of 1.5 percent each year, as proposed in the Montford Report of 1918. Finally, the Lee Commission of 1923 increased the ratio to 50:50 while promoting Indians from the provincial civil services to fill 20 percent of senior administrative positions at the national level. Nevertheless, in areas such as the diplomatic services, the quota remained unmet (Hogden 1981). In other areas, such as the Indian civil service itself, the quota was exceeded because of unavailability of British recruits from the 1920s onward (Beaglehole 1977; Potter 1973). The consequent increase in Indian candidates in higher bureaucratic positions through the 1920s and 1930s therefore decreased the bureaucratic avenues for British capitalists' influence over policy making.

Parallel to their influence over the government, the British bourgeoisie's economic strength declined because of the entry of indigenous capitalists in their sectors. Omkar Goswami (1989, 294) uses data from multiple sources to show how indigenous financers bought up shares of firms owned by British managing agencies in Calcutta during the 1920s and 1930s and joined the boards of directors. By the time India decolonized in 1947, indigenous interests succeeded in entering the jute and coal industries, although they failed to enter the tea industry (Kochanek 1974, 21–22).

The Effects of War: The Collapse of British Rule and the Partitions of Bengal and Punjab

This section shows how the interreligious violence that resulted in the partition of British India in 1947 was the cumulative outcome of the uneven economic effects of World War II and the landlords' continued support for politics centered on religious cleavages. In turn, the partition drastically affected the economic and political fates of the competing landlord and bourgeois elite classes. The exit of Muslim landlords from Punjab and the United Provinces, combined with the loss of land by their counterparts from Bengal, destroyed landlords as a political force in postcolonial India. As presaged by prior Congress Party victories in provincial elections, the partition and decolonization affirmed the triumph of the bourgeoisie in postcolonial India by removing landlords and their colonial backers.

To begin with, World War II transformed elites' attempts to foster ethnic politics as a mass phenomenon because its economic effects were felt differentially by religious communities due to their locational and economic characteristics. In the eastern province of Bengal, the Muslim rural bourgeoisie and peasants were most negatively affected, while the Hindu urban bourgeoisie based in Calcutta and landlords remained unaffected. In the northwestern province of Punjab, the Muslim landlords profited from the war, while the Hindu rural and urban bourgeoisie and Sikh peasants were economically and politically threatened. As British capacity to secure law and order collapsed after the war, elites used the coincidence of political-economic grievances with religious identities to foment religious violence.

In the rural areas of the eastern province of Bengal, crop failure and official policies led to a catastrophic famine that killed three million to four million people. Initiated by the failure of the rice crop from disease (Tauger 2009), the famine's effects were exacerbated by the British requisition of rice stocks and destruction of transportation networks to block a Japanese advance (J. Mukherjee 2015, 68, 116; A. Sen 1981, 195–216). In its official report on the famine, the government acknowledged such denial policies against a feared Japanese attack: boats capable of carrying ten or more passengers were requisitioned from "areas vulnerable to invasion" in the deltas, as was rice paddy land from the coastal districts of Khulna, Bakargunj, and Midnapore (Woodhead 1945, 25).

Paradoxically, the war also created an urban-industrial boom centered in Calcutta, where indigenous capitalists acquired large government contracts (D. Rothermund 1993, 116–118) as part of a broader cross-regional industrial boom (Morris 1983, 640–643) because competition from British and other European companies became physically impossible. Furthermore, in order not to disturb the war effort, Britain's provision of food focused on the greater Calcutta area, with its largely Hindu population. The diversion of food supplies created more shortages and higher prices for food (specifically rice) in the rural areas (Greenough 1982, 102–116; A. Sen 1981, 70–78). Thus, the predominantly Hindu absentee landlords and associated urban middle class in Calcutta were sheltered from the famine (Iqbal 2009, 1346–1351). Also, urban laborers in Calcutta were protected, while the famine was acutely felt by the rural poor (Woodhead 1945, 2), who were predominantly Muslim.

Immediately after the war, when bans on political activity were lifted and decolonization seemed imminent, provincial Muslim League politicians used these economic grievances to foment religious mobilizations against Hindus. There was no fundamental difference in the renewed mobilization based on religion and the prior rebellions based on economic grievances: it was targeted against landlords, led by the rural bourgeoisie, and supported by the peasants (S. Das 1990; Hashmi 1988). The critical difference was that the Muslim League controlled the provincial government after the provincial elections of 1946, but its majority in the legislature relied on KPP defectors or Muslims previously allied with the KPP. Thus, to shore up popular support, the League government aided and abetted the violence via both anti-Hindu propaganda and the obstruction of security and police personnel. The pro-Muslim bias of the elected government and its aid and abetment of rioting criminal gangs were accepted by the accounts of senior British (Moon 1998, 58) and Indian (Khosla 1989, 49–51) officials in the colonial bureaucracy.

Facing enormous violence throughout 1946 and 1947, especially in the districts of Noakhali and Tippera in eastern Bengal and the urban center of Calcutta, the fearful Hindu landlords and urban bourgeoisie—represented by both the religious fundamentalist Hindu Mahasabha and the Congress Party of Bengal—demanded the immediate division of Bengal into two provinces: a Hindu-majority West Bengal and a Muslim-majority East Bengal (Burrows 1980a, 1980b). Revealing the still existent secular strains of provincial politics, a small group of Hindu and Muslim elites, led by the Muslim League's provincial Premier Huseyn Suhrawardy (1980), attempted to maintain a united Bengal containing the Hindu-dominated economic center of Calcutta and West Bengal by creating a sovereign country (J. Chatterji 1994, 261–262). However, according to an opinion poll undertaken by the vernacular daily *Amrita Bazar Patrika* of Calcutta (Chakrabarty 2004, 146), the overwhelming majority of Bengali Hindu elites wished to partition the province, a sentiment shared by national-level Congress Party leaders such as Jawaharlal Nehru, who favored the scheme of allowing provincial minority-dominated areas to secede in order to join either India or Pakistan (Nehru 1980). Thus, West Bengal remained part of postcolonial India, while East Bengal joined Pakistan.

In the northwestern region, the war also created major social dislocations because the largest number of recruits into the British Indian Army came from the province of Punjab. At the beginning of the war, the dominant landlords effectively responded: recruitment drives were organized by landlords, and the number of recruits from the peasantry increased significantly (Yong 2005, 282–283). Overall, of the approximately 665,000 soldiers recruited from the start of the war in 1939 through 1941, the majority were soldiers from Punjab (Prasad 1956, 400–407). Moreover, the landlord and peasant coalition headed by the Unionist Party remained secular and even open to including members from the provincial Congress Party, if they agreed to support the war effort (Craik 1939).

However, through the war years the pro-British coalition of landed farmers started to face a number of strains. Steep increases in food prices caused by the government's acquisition of food for the military and to reduce the food deficit in provinces such as Bengal were the primary cause of grievances against the landowners (Fox 1985, 68, table 12). Although the colonial government imposed anti-inflationary measures (Secretary of State for India 1943a; Yong 2005, 292–293), soldiers recruited from the province sought pay increases to aid their families and/or wanted to return to cultivating to take advantage of the high food prices (Secretary of State for India 1943b, 11). Some Punjabi soldiers from peasant stock began to view landholders and the urban bourgeoisie as war profiteers benefiting from government contracts and titles, while they were sacrificing their men and facing economic instability (I. Talbot 1988, 151).

Sikh ethnic politicians representing rural interests, under the Akali Dal party, joined the secular Unionist Party government in 1939 to support the British war effort. However, the Sikh politicians started to fear Muslim political dominance after the Muslim League's declaration in 1940 (supported by the Unionist Party) that Punjab would become an independent Muslim state after decolonization (A. Singh 1987, 59–60). The Sikh leaders' fears increased after the Cripps Mission, a British commission sent in 1942, supported the notion that the provinces could secede to form independent countries in line with the Muslim League's declaration in 1940 (Secretary of State for India 1945).

Two further developments allowed the Sikh politicians to create an anti-Muslim mobilization among the peasants. The first consisted of grievances against provincial Muslims due to the Sikhs' declining recruitment in the British Indian Army, which, paradoxically, was caused by Sikhs' discontentment and several incidents of mutiny during the war (Yong 2005, 286–288). Despite the decline, Punjab supplied 50 percent of total troops for the Indian Army in 1942, with Sikhs providing 10 percent and Muslims supplying 35 percent of total troops (Viceroy of India 1942). In the second development, the hitherto apolitical Sikh princes, with a political-economic position akin to that of landlords in northern and eastern India, supported religious mobilizations to safeguard their legitimacy among Sikhs (Copland 2002).

Concomitantly, the predominantly Hindu urban bourgeoisie became antagonistic toward the Unionist Party as a result of a series of laws against moneylenders passed in 1938 (Oren 1974, 401). Their antagonism was shared by Sikhs who were increasingly wary of the Unionist Party because of its alliance with the Muslim League and that party's increasing appeals to religious identity to acquire popular support (Oren 1974). Consequently, the provincial wing of the Congress Party began to support the Sikh leadership, which allowed the creation of a Sikh-Hindu united front against the provincial Muslims (Grewal 1990, 178). Nevertheless, a senior official's memoirs reveal that, even in 1946, Sikh leaders feared both Hindu and Muslim domination. They had a clear preference structure: first, a united India with safeguards for Sikhs at the provincial level or, second, an independent Sikh state if India had to be divided (Menon 1957, 242–243). With the imminent creation of Pakistan, the Sikhs turned against Muslim domination in Punjab (United Kingdom, Government of India 1980b, 513). Thus, the Hindu-Sikh alliance's demands came to mirror the logic of ethnoreligious self-determination hitherto used by the Muslim League across India to demand the province's division.

Due to the demographic dominance of Muslims in Punjab, akin to that of Bengal, the Muslim landowners could continue their dominance based on Muslim support, albeit with a diminished majority. They finally abandoned the Unionist Party and directly joined the Muslim League (I. Talbot 1980, 71). The cross-religious ties also collapsed because the Muslim League's leaders used networks of Muslim holy men to garner popular support (Gilmartin 1998). The resulting consolidation centered on religious identity allowed the Muslim League to defeat the Unionist Party in the elections of 1946 and led to civil conflict in late 1946 and early 1947 based on religious animosities (Grewal 1990, 157–180), underlying which were long-running class cleavages (I. Talbot 1996, 111–116) and colonial policies (Yong 2005, 281–302).

The two factors that could have prevented the partition were the repression of violence and the agreement of national political leaders to enter united political institutions. However, in 1946–1947, the British were losing their grip on their primary instrument of control over India: the Indian armed forces (United Kingdom, Government of India 1946, 1; United Kingdom, Cabinet Secretary 1946). Concerns about the unreliability of the armed forces were related to their participation in the war itself. Small numbers of prisoners of war were defecting to the Germans and Italians and joining the Indian Legion, which fought with the Wehrmacht and then alongside the Waffen-SS. Similarly, prisoners of war in Japan joined the Indian National Army in the aftermath of the British collapse in Malaya, Singapore, and Burma (Bayly and Harper 2005). Immediately after the war, nearly twenty thousand sailors of the Royal Indian Navy mutinied with guidance from the Communist Party (Spector 1981; Spence 2015).

Sensing the end of colonial rule, as demanded by its Lahore Declaration of 1940, the Muslim League initially wanted the entirety of Punjab and Bengal but agreed to divide the province based on ethnic majorities. Mohammed Ali Jinnah, now the Muslim League's undisputed leader, "made it clear that he was willing that substantial Hindu areas in Bengal and the Punjab should go into Hindustan" (United Kingdom and Additional Secretary to the Cabinet 1946, 2). The Congress Party supported the Hindu and Sikh elites of Punjab, as well as the Hindu elites of Bengal (United Kingdom, Government of India 1980a, 70). Thus, the support from national-level leaders led to the provinces' division into a Hindu- and Sikh-majority East Punjab and a Muslim-dominated West Punjab, and a Hindu-dominated West Bengal and a Muslim-dominated East Bengal. The Muslim areas became part of Pakistan, while the non-Muslim areas remained part of India.

Postcolonial India: The Domestic Bourgeoisie's Fulfillment and the Peasants' Fall

This section explains how the urban and rural domestic bourgeoisie in India shaped new state institutions to serve their interests while ignoring the peasants. The analysis shows that, although the specific effects of the institutions varied regionally, the ruling Congress Party became allied to the new rural elites and the established domestic business houses. The section focuses first on the urban bourgeoisie who helped create institutions that protected them from external and internal competitors. It then explains how the rural bourgeoisie benefited from postcolonial land reforms at the cost of the peasants. And it concludes by showing how land redistribution to peasants was stymied by successive governments across the political spectrum through the 1970s.

The urban bourgeoisie from Bombay wanted to leverage their links to the Congress Party to influence postcolonial economic policies. In particular, they wanted protection from foreign rivals and new domestic competitors. Their intention is revealed in their collaborative publication of the so-called Bombay Plan, a two-volume study in which they asked for state intervention in the economy to increase investment in the urban-industrial and service sectors, as well as protection from foreign competitors (Thakurdas 1945). In their endeavor, the urban bourgeoisie also supported the rural bourgeoisie, as shown by the Bombay Plan's appreciation of the *ryotwari* system of the Bombay and Madras Presidencies and demand for the abolition of the *zamindari* system of Bengal, United Provinces, and Bihar (Thakurdas 1945, 2:14–16).

The Bombay Plan influenced postcolonial economic institutions. Consequently, the indigenous urban bourgeoisie from Bombay made significant gains via their political influence. Although there are two interpretations of the need for, and ultimate effects of, the plan, they agree that it benefited Indian industrialists and the urban bourgeoisie in general. On the one hand, Vivek Chibber argues that the Bombay Plan was a defensive maneuver against rising leftist attitudes among Congress Party leaders by setting the agenda of the debate on the role of state and private entrepreneurs in postcolonial development (Chibber 2003, 89, 94–95). Thus, the industrialists opposed the five-year plans because the Bombay Plan's conception of government intervention was different from what they had envisaged (Chibber 2003, 127–158). On the other hand, Amal Sanyal (2010) argues that the content of at least the next three five-year plans reflected the Bombay Plan's demands. The latter position is supported by economists who demonstrate that the postcolonial governments discouraged foreign investment and created regulations to protect the politically connected indigenous urban bourgeoisie from both foreign competitors and new domestic entrepreneurs (Bhagwati 1985, 37; J. Waterbury 1993, 191). The most convincing evidence of the Bombay Plan's effect on postcolonial economic policy, however, was the acknowledgment made in 2004 by the prime minister and former finance minister of India himself (M. Singh 2004).

The close cooperation between the state institutions and the urban bourgeoisie led to the inclusion of trade and industry organizations in major government councils. They included the Advisory Council on Trade, the Board of Trade, Customs, and the Central Excise Authority (Kochanek 1971, 874). The extent to which postcolonial government regulations succeeded in protecting the urban bourgeoisie is revealed by data showing that the top-twenty large indigenous business enterprises had remained almost the same since the early twentieth century (India, Ministry of Law and Company Affairs 1979, 248–250).

Despite the overall beneficial effects of the new institutions, however, there was some opposition to the postcolonial economic policies from business houses. Most significant among them was Tata, which suffered the nationalization of its domestic and international aviation business in 1953 and insurance company in 1956 but managed nevertheless to recoup its losses and diversify into making heavy vehicles, chemicals, and even cosmetics (Piramal 1998, 482–483). As a result, Tata (Piramal 1998, 494) and a few other business houses turned to supporting free market–oriented parties in the 1960s, such as the Jan Sangh and the Swatantra Party (Erdman 1967, 172–174).

Similarly, the rural bourgeoisie gained economically from the redistribution of land, while landlords lost their dominant economic position. In East

Punjab, which remained in India, landlords lost their influence due to a variety of political and economic pressures, including the fact that land was made available for Hindu and Sikh refugees from West Punjab and the fact that the Muslim landlords left for Pakistan (Grewal 1990, 181). However, even in areas where demographic changes were minimal, new legislation imposed a ceiling of 30 acres of land per owner (India, Government of Punjab 1953, sec. 2, para. 3). The creation of the 30-acre limit and enhancements of tenants' rights through a series of new laws strengthened poor peasants (Uppal 1969). Nevertheless, the provincial demand for land was minimal because of the more equitable distribution of land during the colonial period, and landed farmers maintained control of the provincial bureaucracy and legislature, which effectively scotched further land redistribution and maintained their dominance (B. Singh 2005, 165). Thus, the urban bourgeoisie and landed farmers began to dominate the politics of East Punjab via an alliance between the Sikh religious party Akali Dal and the Congress Party (Arora 1956; Puri 1983).

As a related aside, scholars note that by the 1950s the landed farmers in western Punjab (then part of Pakistan) yielded even greater power: their predominance in the postcolonial Pakistani army facilitated not just their stifling of land redistribution but also efforts to undertake democratic politics that would favor other provinces, especially by the more populous and anti-landlord peasantry of East Bengal (Sayeed 1959).

With regard to landlords, the division of Bengal radically changed the social structure of eastern India. The predominantly Hindu landlords lost their lands in East Bengal, which became part of Pakistan, and passed the East Bengal State Acquisition and Tenancy Act of 1950 to acquire and redistribute land controlled by the primarily Hindu *zamindars* (Ahmed and Timmons 1971). As a result, their participation in the politics of West Bengal, which remained in India, was severely curtailed: the landlords could not prevent land reform in West Bengal carried out under the West Bengal Estates Acquisition Act of 1953 and the West Bengal Land Reforms Act of 1955. However, both in Pakistani East Bengal (R. Mukherjee 1972) and Indian West Bengal (Ray and Ray 1975), the *jotedars* (landed peasants-cum-rural bourgeoisie) gained from land reforms. Such changes in the agrarian sector were complemented by the indigenous urban bourgeoisie's displacing of their foreign competitors from Calcutta, a process that began in the 1930s and 1940s (Goswami 1989).

For three decades (until 1977) the provincial Congress Party dominated West Bengal politics, backed by a coalition of urban bourgeoisie that included large industrialists based in Calcutta (P. Gupta 1982, 40–42) and *jotedars* (Bandyopadhyay 2006) who used their moneylending and business activities to dominate peasants and capture district-level political leadership

(A. Mukhopadhyay 1980, 75). The social coalition underlying the Congress Party was apparent even to contemporary foreign observers (Franda 1968).

Poor peasants and landless laborers in West Bengal also suffered from the capture of the redistribution process by the rural bourgeoisie. Here, even the substantive tenancy reforms introduced by the popularly elected Communist Party in 1977 maintained the private landownership structure while confirming only the peasants' rights to use such land (Rudra 1981). Although such reforms enhanced the socioeconomic status of poor peasants (Harriss 1993; Lieten 1996), they made their usage rights dependent on administrative fiat and continued support from the Communist Party (Herring 1989). Moreover, once it was entrenched in local governments, the Communist Party made fewer efforts to deliver fiscal grants and employment opportunities in government schemes (Bardhan and Mookerji 2006, 325).

Similar coalitions between the rural bourgeoisie who dominated district- and village-level politics (Sirsikar 1964) and urban bourgeoisie based in Bombay (Carras 1971) came to dominate the postcolonial politics of the Bombay Presidency and its successor provinces of Maharashtra and Gujrat, although there was no sociopolitical upheaval in those provinces (Kamat 1980).

Also land reforms in the northern region benefited the rural bourgeoisie—specifically, the class of rural bourgeoisie who were an admixture of landed peasants and moneylenders. Moreover, due to the weak industrial base in the province, the rural bourgeoisie alone began to dominate regional politics via provincial Congress Party organizations (Brass 1981). The landlords of the United Provinces lost their political dominance (Metcalf 1967) after land redistribution during the 1950s via the Uttar Pradesh Zamindari Abolition and Land Reforms Act of 1950, which was based on the recommendations of the pre-independence United Provinces Zamindari Abolition Committee appointed in 1946 (India, Government of Uttar Pradesh 1948). Similar to East Bengal, in the United Provinces the land reforms were facilitated by the migration of the large Muslim *taluqdars* and *zamindars* from the province into Pakistan after 1947 (Kudaisya 2006, 405) and by empowered landed peasants (Elder 1962). Similarly, in Bihar land reform was carried out through the Bihar Land Reforms Act of 1950, which empowered tenants who supported the provincial Congress Party (R. Roy 1968) with occupancy rights (Dhar 2000, 124–138).

In terms of excluding peasants from land redistribution, Uttar Pradesh, the successor province of the United Provinces, provides the paradigmatic example for northern India. There, land reforms dissolved the large landlords' holdings but left landed farmers unaffected and even protected them from peasants' demands. According to the United Provinces Zamindari Abolition Committee Reports of 1948, 98.51 percent of provincial landowners paid 250 rupees or less as annual land revenue to the government, and 1.49 percent of the landowners paid more than 250 rupees annually. The former segment owned 42.23 percent of the cultivable land, while the latter owned 57.77 percent (India, Government of United Provinces 1948, 1:441–443; Moore and Moore 1955, 13–25). However, by 1972, only 0.4 percent of the cultivable land had been distributed, most of it in sparsely populated areas, and approximately half of the redistributed land was unsuitable for cultivation. This meant that half the peasantry was landless or owned subsistence-level farms with 2.5 or fewer acres (Newell 1972, 224).

Although cooperative farming would have benefited the landless and poor peasants, the recommendations of the government committee on land reforms that a system be imposed akin to the Mexican *ejidal* system of cooperative farms attached to government monitoring and credit agencies—deemed the most suitable option after field research and comparative analyses were conducted with Israeli kibbutzim and Soviet kolkhoz farms—were not applied by the Congress Party state government (India, Government of Uttar Pradesh 1948, 1:311–336).

Given the existing dominance of the rural bourgeoisie due to the *ryotwari* system of land ownership, the rural bourgeoisie, who usually came from the middle castes, came to dominate the politics of the successor provinces of the Madras Presidency, as well. The postcolonial socioeconomic dominance by landed peasants and the rural bourgeoisie was evident: at the village level, in the state of Tamil Nadu carved out of the southern Madras Presidency (Mines 2005, 12–14); at the state level in Andhra Pradesh, created by amalgamating the princely state of Hyderabad and the northern Madras Presidency (Kohli 1988); and at the state level in Karnataka, created from the central areas of the Madras Presidency and the princely state of Mysore (Manor 1977). The dominant classes' support for the INC in the southern Indian states remained constant until the internal party split of 1969, which marginalized the local elites in Tamil Nadu (Forrester 1976) and Andhra Pradesh (Bernstorff 1973).

The Malabar area where the *ryotwari* system actually functioned like the *zamindari* system, however, saw political developments similar to those in northern and eastern India. As explicated in Chapter 2, this area witnessed the violent Moplah Rebellion that failed due to lack of elite support. Postcolonial land reforms in the state of Kerala, created from the amalgamation of parts of the princely states of Travancore and Cochin with the Malabar, also removed the large *janmi* landlords (Radhakrishnan 1989). Nevertheless, here, too, the rural bourgeoisie and urban professionals played a prominent role through both the provincial Congress Party and the Communist Party (B. Ahmed 1966, 395–396; Gough 1968–1969).

Nevertheless, peasants made the most significant advances in the state of Kerala. The long-standing tenant-landlord conflicts led to land reforms and social-welfare mechanisms that exceeded those in the rest of India (Dréze and Sen 1998; Radhakrishnan 1989). Other than Kerala, the southern region's overall inequality in landholdings remained comparable to what existed after land reforms in northern India (Sharma 1994, A14, table 2), yet again revealing that the greatest beneficiaries of regional land reform programs had not been landless or poor peasants but the landed farmer–based rural bourgeoisie (Sharma 1994, A15, table 3).

Thus, unlike for the domestic bourgeoisie, decolonization was a mixed blessing for the Indian peasantry. As attested above, peasants' influence on the shaping of postcolonial institutions was noticeable by its absence. One reason was perhaps that the civil conflict and collapse of British rule, which led to the partition of India, sidelined pressing issues of socioeconomic equity for the immediate requirements of restoring law and order. However, the key underlying factor was the influence of the urban and rural bourgeoisie on the ruling Congress Party. As a result, on the one hand, the postcolonial constitution ensured Indian peasants' political freedoms via free and fair elections based on universal adult suffrage, accompanied by civil liberties. On the other hand, peasants' poverty and inequality of wealth, based in inadequate postcolonial land reforms that benefited the rural bourgeoisie, maintained peasants' dependence on local elite-led parties and consequent political and economic marginalization.

Thus, in 1958, eight years after decolonization, 22 percent of rural households were landless, while 74.42 percent of rural households owned fewer than 5 acres of land and controlled only 16.77 percent of land, while the average landholding by the rural Indian household was 6.05 acres (Mahalanobis 1958, 49–50). These trends were exacerbated during the next two decades (National Sample Survey Office 1996, 22).

Conclusion

In summary, this chapter delineates two phases of political competition in late colonial India and how they affected the rebelling elite and peasant groups. The first phase, in which the colonial regime sought to compromise by broadening the franchise, led to electoral competition among the various political parties that arose to support or oppose the rebellions of the 1920s and early 1930s. The victory of the Congress Party, representing the rural bourgeoisie, propelled the landlords to use religion as a cross-class identity to retain popular support. However, this period also witnessed the increasing political influence of the indigenous urban bourgeoisie, who chose to align with the Congress Party and influence its economic policy. The second phase, whose catalyst was the British entry into World War II, witnessed the collapse of the fragile equilibrium, with new and old interests being channeled electorally under British control. British demands on Indian society for the war effort caused social splintering in Bengal and Punjab along religious lines and culminated in the massive political violence that led to the partition of British India. The study of the postcolonial economy reveals that, while peasants received political freedom, the rural and urban elites who supported the Congress Party acquired most of the economic benefits.

The findings presented here challenge explanations of the Indian partition as arising from pan-Indian religious antipathy between the two largest religious communities: Islam and Hinduism (Dhulipala 2016). They do so in two distinct ways: (1) by explicating the subnational class conflicts, going all the way back to the 1920s, that underlay the religious violence of the mid-1940s and (2) by revealing how religious identity and political competition were constructed and exploited by threatened regional elite classes, *not* national leaders, during the 1930s and 1940s. This dovetails with Ayesha Jalal's (1985) contention that the partition occurred due to decisions by national-level leaders that were contingent on provincial-level political competition, as well as Joya Chatterji's (1994) argument that such religious competition was the external expression of economic conflicts between peasants and landlords.

The findings on state formation in India partially support Maya Tudor's (2013) explanation that postcolonial democracy in India was the outcome of the Congress Party's high level of organization; articulation and implementation of substantive programs of socioeconomic reform, from land redistribution to the emancipation of untouchable castes; and broad representation of popular and elite interests across regional, ethnic, and linguistic divides. Tudor contrasts the Congress Party's achievements with those of the elitist and pro-British Muslim League, which lacked grassroots organization and social programs, forcing it to rely initially on religious identity to create the mobilization that led to the partition, prevented Pakistani democratic institutions from channeling social tensions, and ultimately caused recurrent military coups and Pakistan's territorial disintegration in 1971.

However, this chapter also challenges Tudor's (2013) theses by showing that broad elite consensus in postcolonial India was as much a matter of conscious ideology and policy as it was an inadvertent outcome of strategic interactions among elites in the 1930s, which led to the division of India and the consequent decimation of landlords' political and economic power. Specifically, the partition caused the exit of Punjabi landed farmers and significant segments of northern Indian landlords from the United Provinces to Pakistan and resulted in most Bengali landlords' losing their land. This implies that the Congress Party and the bourgeoisie it represented were the last class standing. Consequently, the elite alliance that undergirded the Congress Party did not serve the interests of the vast majority of Indians. Even today, large numbers of peasants remain desperately poor and lack social rights, such as access to health care (Mudur 2005; PricewaterhouseCoopers 2007) and primary education (Desai and Kulkarni 2008; Jeffery, Jeffery, and Jeffery 2005). This provides further evidence that, despite successfully rebelling, Indian peasants were unable to control the destiny of their national regime.

6

International Capital and State Formation

British Mediation and the Creation of Zimbabwe

The analysis of Zimbabwe's transition to majority rule from settler colonialism, presented in this chapter, shows how British investors, represented by the British government, influenced the conflict and subsequent peace agreement between the Black rebels and the White settler regime. British investments in Nigerian Petroleum and South African precious metals and diamonds, which as fixed assets were prone to takeover by their home governments, initially increased the duration of the conflict and subsequently shaped the terms of its resolution. In contrast, the guerrillas and the settlers' dependence on foreign sponsors made them vulnerable to pressures arising from their sponsors' unwillingness to provide continued support. Thus, continued conflict and the peace agreement ultimately sidelined the economic and political interests of the primary stakeholders in the conflict, with the Black African guerrillas ostensibly representing the rural poor and the Rhodesian government representing the White settler–controlled domestic businesses and commercial agriculture.

The first part of the study focuses on the Rhodesian Whites' motives for declaring unilateral independence from Britain in 1965, their continued belligerence against both Britain and intensifying Black opposition through the mid-1970s, and their desire for a negotiated transition to Black majority rule after 1978. In line with the broader theory, the analysis discovers two distinct causes for the origins, sustenance, and weakening of the Rhodesian regime: (1) the White settlers' desire to retain their wealth and (2) the costs of doing so. Specifically, as the incumbent elites, the Rhodesian Whites separated from

Britain to retain political power based on the control of agricultural land and minerals. However, their capacity to continue for fifteen years was contingent on British unwillingness to use force against or enforce sanctions on Rhodesia, as well as rapidly building domestic industries and outright smuggling. Finally, the regime's decline was caused by the increasing economic and human cost of fighting the guerrillas through the 1970s. These causes forced the Whites first to attempt an Internal Settlement to introduce Black majority rule in 1978, and later to agree to the British-mediated Lancaster House negotiations of 1979.

The second part of the study analyzes the trajectory of Black political opposition. The investigation supports the broader argument that allied elites' interests come to dominate peasant rebellions. As explained in Chapter 2, the rebellion was popular among poor, rural Blacks because of its core cause of wresting control of agricultural land from the White settlers, while the rebellion's proximate cause was the shared religion between the rural poor and the elites who led the guerrilla movement. However, the examination of the rebellion's dynamics and leadership in this study demonstrates how repression forced opposition leaders into exile, and these leaders' consequent reliance on Black African governments made the guerrillas susceptible to pressure from their sponsors. In turn, the foreign supporters' preferences were shaped by their own interests, including the costs of continued conflict. Thus, whereas peasant support was required for the rebellion's success, the peasants' interests were relegated to the background during the Lancaster House negotiations of 1979.

The following study evaluates British actions, from failed mediation in the mid-1960s to the mid-1970s, which nearly delivered independence and diplomatic recognition under White minority rule, to the successful mediation of the Lancaster House negotiations of 1979 and supervision of the 1980 elections, which facilitated the transition to Black majority rule. The analysis, including evidence from the immediate post-transition period, reveals that rather than by a normative commitment to decolonization and democratization, British actions were shaped by economic ties, initially with apartheid South Africa and subsequently with independent African countries—specifically, Nigeria. From the mid-1960s to the mid-1970s, economic reliance on South Africa prevented Britain from enforcing sanctions against the White Rhodesians. From the mid-1970s, however, Britain's trade ties increased with Nigeria, which supported the Black rebels, while the economic strength and international standing of South Africa, the White settler regime's primary backer, declined considerably. As a result, between 1978 and 1980, Britain first sought international recognition for the Internal Settlement–based regime and then shifted support to the Lancaster House negotiations and supervised the 1980 elections. Whereas the negotiations undermined land redistribution, Britain used its supervisory role during the elections to secretly attempt to create a coalition between selected Black and White parties while refusing to stop violence and intimidation by the Zimbabwe African National Union (ZANU). Thus, while Black leaders of the rebellion achieved political power and the Whites retained economic power, the masses became marginalized both economically and politically through abrogated land redistribution and violent repression of Black ethnic minorities.

From Belligerent Prosperity to Reluctant Agreement: White Rhodesia's Path to Internal Settlement

The British colony of (Southern) Rhodesia became self-governing under property-based suffrage—implied White minority rule—in 1923. Unlike in the dominions of Canada, Australia, and New Zealand, Britain maintained reserved powers in Rhodesia on issues of foreign affairs, protecting African rights and lands, constitutional amendments, and revenue from railways and mining. However, the White settler–dominated governments of Rhodesia racially segregated control of land via a series of laws and policies, most prominent among which were the Land Apportionment Act of 1930, the Land Husbandry Act of 1958, and Land Tenure Act of 1962. This system of racialized control over the most fertile agricultural land made the prosperity of Whites contingent on their continued political domination, which in turn pushed the Black majority to rebel (Arrighi 1966; R. Palmer 1977; Riddell [1980] 2013; Rifkind 1968).

Although Britain never granted Rhodesia full dominion status, it continued to buttress the White minority implicitly through the 1950s. The final attempt at institutionalizing a semi-dominion status that granted a large degree of self-governance was the Central African Federation formed in 1953, which merged Northern Rhodesia (now Zambia) with Southern Rhodesia and Nyasaland (now Malawi). However, rising African nationalism in Northern Rhodesia and Nyasaland and Southern Rhodesians' unwillingness to make political concessions led to the dissolution of the federation in 1963, an outcome predicted by the so-called Monckton Commission Report (*Report of the Advisory Commission* 1960). Subsequently, Zambia and Malawi achieved independence under Black majority rule (Horowitz 1970).

As the Central African Federation collapsed, the White settlers of Southern Rhodesia, led by the Rhodesian Front (RF), which was dominated by White farmers, began a series of negotiations with Britain centered on the settlers' determination to retain power and Britain's insistence on granting independence and diplomatic recognition only under Black majority rule.

After British Prime Minister Harold Wilson refused to intervene militarily because of military incapacity and misperceived domestic sympathy for the White minority (Watts 2002), the settlers executed a Unilateral Declaration of Independence (UDI) in 1965 under an RF government headed by Prime Minister Ian Smith.

Initially, the UDI regime remained unaffected by the sanctions Britain imposed in 1965, which were reaffirmed by the United Nations in 1968. Although no country officially recognized the UDI regime, France, West Germany, Switzerland, and Japan partially circumvented the sanctions (J. Wood 2012). South Africa's apartheid regime supplied goods, loans, and (along with Portugal via its colony of Mozambique) petroleum (Good 1973, 126–144). Due to massive economic ties, the rupturing of which could destabilize the British economy itself, Britain refused to countenance either sanctions or a military confrontation with South Africa (Henshaw 1996; Shadow Cabinet: Circulated Paper 1978; Smock 1969).

The United States undermined its own and United Nations sanctions via the Byrd Amendment of 1971, which permitted importation of Rhodesian chrome, arguing that sanctions were both illegal and ineffective. This stance was justified by identifying chrome as critical to American industry and Rhodesia as a "reliable, non-Communist supply of chrome for national defense" (Yates 1972). Ironically, the Soviet Union, then America's largest supplier of chrome, was reportedly buying chrome from Rhodesia at steep discounts to sell it to American companies (L. White 2015, 141–145). Most egregiously, both Labour Party and Conservative Party governments in Britain did not enforce the sanctions on the British oil companies Shell and British Petroleum, which were surreptitiously supplying oil to Rhodesia (Nossiter 1978).

As a result, White Rhodesians combined import-substitution industrialization policies with infrastructure built during the federation period to foster rapid economic growth (Stoneman 1980). Rapid development also profited White agriculturalists. Beef producers, backed by government loans and subsidies, used South African front companies that provided false papers of origin to continue, and even increase, exports to the international market, including West African countries via Gabon, and to Britain itself (Nhamo 2002). Although the production of tobacco, the primary Rhodesian export to Britain, declined significantly due to sanctions, the state-owned Tobacco Corporation, founded in 1966, created a monopsony that shielded farmers from the sanctions' worst effects. This parastatal arrangement rendered them dependent on the government and, in effect, undermined a significant source of White political opposition (Rowe 2001, 63–95).

Through the 1960s until 1972, Britain's pressure relied on a series of conferences, which are further explicated in the penultimate section of the chapter. These conferences led to the agreement in 1971 to grant independence and diplomatic recognition under minority rule if the Black population was in agreement. At this high point of the UDI regime, the Pearce Commission from Britain toured Rhodesia in early 1972 to investigate Black African public opinion about the White settler regime. However, in the atmosphere of lessened repression before and during the British tour, a peaceful African movement arose to protest minority rule. The movement was headed by the United African National Council (UANC), led by the Methodist Bishop Abel Muzorewa, and backed by the banned guerrilla organizations ZANU and the Zimbabwe African People's Union (ZAPU) (L. White 2015, 214, 220). From protests at the Salisbury Airport that greeted the British team (*British Movietone* 1972) to councils in remote villages that they consulted (L. White 2015, 220), the answer to Rhodesian independence under minority rule was a resounding no.

However, the key development of 1972 was the escalation of the Black African insurgency. This escalation was due to Portugal's inability to control the Tete province of Mozambique against the Black African insurgents of the Mozambican Liberation Front (FRELIMO), who in turn permitted the Zimbabwe African National Liberation Army (ZANLA), the military wing of ZANU, to operate freely in Tete (Weitzer 1990, 83). The collective punitive measures undertaken by the Rhodesian Security Forces (RSF)—which included the shutting down of shops, clinics, schools, churches, businesses, and mills in affected areas—also reduced the regime's legitimacy (Moorcraft and McLaughlin 1982, 38). However, the most destructive policy was the creation of the 236 protected villages, to which 400,000 rural Blacks were relocated both to protect them from guerrillas and prevent them from supporting guerrillas (Ottaway 1978). Far from their farmland and cattle, and overcrowded and therefore prone to outbreaks of disease, these villages came to epitomize Rhodesian repression of Black Africans and loss of popular legitimacy (Cilliers 1985, 79–103; Ranger 1985, 266–268).

The insurgency further intensified after Portugal's Carnation Revolution of 1974 and subsequent rapid withdrawal from Mozambique, which simultaneously opened 764 miles of border to guerrilla incursions. Because the revolutionary government of Mozambique enforced international sanctions, this regime change also made the Rhodesian economy entirely dependent on South Africa (Mtisi, Nyakudya, and Barnes 2009, 144–145). Accompanying the deteriorating security situation was an economic downturn caused by the Arab oil embargo that crippled the Rhodesians' capacity to carry out the conflict (A. Wilkinson 1973, [1980] 2013). Indeed, the war's outcome seemed increasingly uncertain, as guerrilla attacks on White civilians increased and the Rhodesians lost more territory to rebel control (*The Economist* 1977; A. Wilkinson [1980] 2013, 114).

Even at this stage, the Rhodesians were willing to commit to majority rule only in principle. Under pressure from South Africa's President John Vorster, who threatened to cut off financial and military support (I. Smith 1997, 207–209), the Rhodesians restarted negotiations in 1975 with representatives of ZANU and ZAPU ("South African Government Cabinet Minutes on Rhodesia" [1976] 2013). However, these initial negotiations failed because the Rhodesians refused to accept Black majority rule (Nkomo 1984, 156–157). External mediation by the United States in September 1976 also failed (United Press International 1976), as did that of Britain, to broker a peace agreement in October of that year in Geneva (U.S. Department of State 1976b). Nevertheless, at South Africa's urging, the Rhodesians accepted the core principle of Black majority rule during the Geneva Conference (Graham 2005). Consequently, the British agreed to restart mediation with American backing to begin the transition away from White minority rule (United States 1977a).

However, the military call-ups intensified and economic uncertainties of conflict further worsened, such that White skilled professionals began emigrating from the country in increasing numbers—7,072 in 1976, 10,908 in 1977, and up to 13,709 in 1978 (Mlambo 2005, 165). It was at this juncture in 1978, facing unbearable costs of war and a severe economic downturn that South Africa threatened to exacerbate, and having ceded to Black majority rule in principle, that the Rhodesian regime moved toward an Internal Settlement with moderate Black African leaders. The Rhodesians primarily negotiated with two Black leaders from Shona-dominated parties: Bishop Abel Muzorewa, from the UANC, and the Methodist pastor Ndabaningi Sithole, from a moderate wing of ZANU. Despite these negotiations, the attack on the main oil depot in the capital Salisbury (now Harare) on December 11, 1978, by guerrillas, who set a fire that lasted six days and destroyed enormous amounts of scarcely available petroleum, demonstrated the rising costs of continued conflict to the White population (Cilliers 1985, 49).

The settlement led to a general election in 1979 for one hundred parliamentary seats, with twenty-eight reserved for Whites. Twenty seats were retained for White voters and White candidates and seventy-two seats were opened for Blacks voting on a Common Roll. A further eight seats for Whites were to be nominated by White members of Parliament and elected by all members of Parliament. The guaranteed independence of the military, police, civil service, and judiciary from political interference also implied that Whites retained control over these key areas (C. Murphy 1979; Mutunhu 1978, 5). These safeguards could be removed only by a parliamentary supermajority of seventy-eight votes, which gave the White members a blocking veto (Mutunhu 1978, 5).

From the Common Roll, the two major winners were from the majority Shona ethnic group: Bishop Muzorewa's UANC won fifty-one seats, and Sithole's ZANU won twelve. The pro-Rhodesian Ndebele United National Federal Party, led by Kayisa Ndiweni, won nine seats. The RF, led by Ian Smith, won all twenty-eight seats from the White Roll. After the election, a government of Blacks and Whites emerged led by Prime Minister Muzorewa. Twelve cabinet positions were held by Blacks; five were given to the Whites, including the Ministries of Agriculture, Finance, Justice, and Transportation; and the three most important positions dealing with the insurgency were delivered to Blacks, including the Ministry of Defense (headed by Muzorewa himself) and the Ministry of Law and Order (Burns 1979).

The settlement failed to take root because of continued guerrilla activities by ZANU (led by Robert Mugabe) and ZAPU (led by Joshua Nkomo), which had been excluded from the elections, as well as lack of international recognition and defections by important White and Black leaders (Mtisi, Nyakudya, and Barnes 2009, 163). Two British observers, Lord Boyd (Alan Lennox-Boyd) and Lord (Pratap) Chitnis, arrived in Rhodesia to independently monitor and evaluate the elections held in March 1979. Based on polling arrangements and the numbers of people who voted—approximately 62 percent of the eligible population, according to Rhodesian records—Lord Boyd deemed it a qualified success, while Lord Chitnis argued it was a failure because Black voters were unaware of the constitutional aspects and were coerced into voting (Delap 1979).

British officials also acknowledged that enclaves of power remained with the Whites. In his memoir, Robin Renwick, who then headed the Rhodesia Department of the Foreign and Commonwealth Office (FCO), recalls informing the newly installed Conservative Party Prime Minister Margaret Thatcher that "the Zimbabwe-Rhodesia constitution was unlike any other on the basis of which we [Britain] had granted independence, as the real power remained in the hands of the Rhodesian military commanders" (Renwick 2013). Official records show that Thatcher agreed with Renwick that such an imbalance "must be remedied before the country could be brought to independence" (U.S. Department of State 1979).

Nevertheless, British leaders and their American counterparts agreed that a significant and substantive political change had occurred, and recognizing the new regime became a distinct possibility. The Conservative Party implicitly accepted the conclusions of Lord Boyd's report. Furthermore, Thatcher sought to recognize the new regime in a first step toward international recognition and implicitly to drop sanctions (United Kingdom 1979h).

Conservative congressmen and senators in the United States also pressured President Jimmy Carter to recognize the Internal Settlement regime. A Senate resolution calling for the lifting of sanctions against Rhodesia was defeated in a 48–42 vote (Tamarkin 1990, 238). The subsequent Case-Javits Amendment, approved by a 59–36 vote in the Senate, called for the removal of sanctions if the president recognized good-faith efforts—not substantive changes—by the Rhodesian government to transition to Black majority rule and the successful conducting of free and fair elections (Tamarkin 1990, 239).

The High Cost of International Support: Why Black African Leaders Softened on Land Redistribution

Even before the Black African insurgency escalated due to the use of spirit mediums, as explicated in Chapter 2, the Rhodesian regime began imprisoning, exiling, or killing Black African guerrillas from ZANLA and the Zimbabwe People's Revolutionary Army (ZIPRA), the military wings of ZANU and ZAPU, respectively. As described in Chapter 2, the strategy of repression fragmented the rebels by fostering disunity among leaders and between leadership and members. But, as explained below, it also made ZANLA and ZIPRA reliant on Black African states for funding and safe havens, which led to the foreign sponsors' interests outweighing those of the guerrillas' domestic peasant base. Due to the rising costs of the conflict, Black African states began encouraging ZANU and ZAPU to unite and adopt the same platform, which favored access to state institutions over land redistribution. Consequently, the core grievance underlying the Chimurenga Rebellion—that is, racialized control over agricultural land—was given up by the guerrilla leaders to achieve political power.

Angola, Botswana, Mozambique, Tanzania, and Zambia came to be known collectively as the front-line states during the period. Nigeria also became deeply involved in supporting the guerrillas. The reliance on foreign backing affected the rebellion in three ways: (1) the front-line states attempted to unite and strengthen the capacity of the guerrillas; (2) the front-line states made ZANU and ZAPU vulnerable to their own interests; and (3) the front-line states simultaneously increased ZANU's and ZAPU's leverage with Britain and the United States. The reasons that underlay ZANU's and ZAPU's willingness to compromise can be explained via the front-line states' influence over these organizations and the high costs to Zambia and Mozambique of continued conflict.

The influence of the front-line states on ZANU and ZAPU is best seen in their three major attempts to unite the groups to increase the guerrillas' capacity to fight the Rhodesian regime. In 1972, they supported a breakaway faction of ZAPU, led by James Chikerema and George Nyandoro, in its efforts to form the Front for the Liberation of Zimbabwe (FROLIZI) (Moorcraft and McLaughlin 1982, 87). Nevertheless, FROLIZI failed to create unity and became ineffective after drawing away not just funding from ZANU and ZAPU but also recruits from exiled Zimbabweans in Zambia, the same pool that ZANU and ZAPU used for their soldiers (Kirk 1975, 6–7). In December 1974, President Kenneth Kaunda of Zambia, President Julius Nyerere of Tanzania, and President Seretse Khama of Botswana, along with Samora Machel, who was expected to become the president of Mozambique, forced ZAPU and ZANU to merge into Bishop Muzorewa's UANC (U.S. Central Intelligence Agency 1976, 3).

The 1975 negotiations occurred in the dramatic setting of a railway carriage on the Victoria Falls Bridge connecting Zambia and Rhodesia. However, the ZANU leaders fell out with one another. ZAPU's Nkomo snatched the leadership of the UANC from Muzorewa to continue negotiations with Prime Minister Smith, with backing from President Kaunda (U.S. Central Intelligence Agency 1976, 3). After this fiasco, young guerrillas from ZANLA and ZIPRA, disappointed by squabbles among senior leaders within and between ZANU and ZAPU, successfully approached the front-line states to acquire funding for a unified military wing called the Zimbabwe People's Army (ZIPA). They conducted several raids in Rhodesia and appeared uninvited at the Geneva Conference in 1976 but ultimately fragmented in 1977 (Moorcraft and McLaughlin 1982, 41–42, 87–88).

Meanwhile, the costs of continued conflict began to rise for these countries, especially Zambia and Mozambique. The most prominent attack in Zambia occurred a week before the first Black majority–based elections following the Internal Settlement, when Rhodesia attempted to capture or assassinate Joshua Nkomo in Lusaka, destroying Nkomo's house and killing at least ten people, including his guards (Ottaway 1979). The most economically harmful of such raids was conducted after the Internal Settlement had already been reached, in November 1979, when Rhodesian forces destroyed bridges and roads connecting Zambia to Malawi and Mozambique, "forcing Zambia into total dependence for its foreign trade needs on the southern railway route" through Rhodesia (*New York Times* 1979b). Other such raids included one in February 1979, in retaliation for ZIPRA's shooting down of an Air Rhodesia passenger airliner with a shoulder-fired missile supplied by the Soviet Union and killing of the survivors (*New York Times* 1979a).

The Rhodesians attacked Mozambique more frequently and with greater intensity because of the ZANLA bases located in the country. The most infamous of these raids was Operation Eland, which targeted the rebel and refugee camp in the Mozambican town of Nyadzonya in August 1976, killing 1,300 people, including hundreds of guerrillas and a few members of the Mozambican forces (Emerson 2014, 41). Even the day before Ian Smith announced the acceptance of Black majority rule, Operation Dingo, carried out by the RSF against the ZANLA base camp near the Mozambican towns of Chimoio and Tembue, led to 1,200 casualties among the guerrillas (*New York Times* 1977). Moreover, the Rhodesians attempted to destroy all communications and transportation infrastructure, especially in Mozambique, including roads, railway lines, and bridges (Emerson 2014, 30–31). The Rhodesians also sponsored the rebel Mozambican National Resistance (RENAMO), which used tribal allegiances to rebel against the Marxist Mozambican government led by FRELIMO (Emerson 2014, 33–35; M. Hall 1990, 39–40).

The RSF's raids on Zambian and Mozambican infrastructure, which badly affected their economies, made Zambia and Mozambique single-mindedly pursue the transfer of power in Rhodesia as their core objective. Press conferences and interviews with Zimbabwean leaders as early as 1976 reveal this transformation. By comparison, economic issues that underlay the ongoing insurgency became open to negotiations and compromise. As Mugabe and Nkomo arrived at the Geneva Conference in 1976, organized by Britain after a peace initiative by U.S. Secretary of State Henry Kissinger failed, Nkomo announced that he intended to "work out a constitution that . . . remove[d] the causes" of the conflict, while Mugabe said the "theme of the conference must be the transference of power and the achievement of independence" (*AP Television* 1976). When asked after two days of negotiations whether farmers (by implication, White farmers) would be allowed to own land under the new system, Mugabe replied, "For a beginning they can. . . . [I]t is preferable that the land belongs to the people as such[;] that's traditional and also is in accord with our socialist ideals" (Snow 1976). Thus, he suggested that ZANU could compromise on the critical issue of landownership.

President Machel of Mozambique urged Mugabe to join the Lancaster House negotiations of 1979, indicating that refusal to do so would lead Mozambique and the other front-line states to recognize the Internal Settlement–based regime (L. White 2015, 256–257). During the subsequent negotiations, which would lead to a ceasefire and the first democratic elections, British Prime Minister Thatcher communicated to President Machel that agricultural land could not be expropriated; instead, it would have to be acquired by the Black majority regime through adequate compensation that Britain and other countries could fund (United Kingdom 1979j). In a letter to Thatcher in early 1980, Machel stated that he did not seek to influence the political and economic aspects of the settlement and simply expressed his opposition to "any racist policy whatsoever" (United Kingdom 1980i).

Foreign Investments and Zimbabwe's Transition: Unprincipled Mediation and Unfaithful Supporters

On December 2, 1966, the first Anglo-Rhodesian conference after the UDI occurred aboard the British navy's light cruiser *HMS Tiger*. The British delegation, led by Prime Minister Harold Wilson, proposed six principles on which a future settlement could be based. First, unimpeded progress to majority rule, already enshrined in the 1961 Constitution, would have to be maintained and guaranteed by the Rhodesian regime. Second, the settlement would need to include guarantees against retrogressive amendments to the constitution. Third, immediate improvement in the political status of the African population was a requirement. Fourth, progress would need to be made toward ending racial discrimination. Fifth, the British government would have to be satisfied that any basis proposed for independence was acceptable to the people of Rhodesia as a whole, implying the Black majority. Sixth, it would be necessary to ensure that, regardless of race, there was no oppression of majority by minority or of minority by majority. Furthermore, to achieve this set of goals, the British proposed certain interim implementation procedures: an end to the rebellion and UDI by the White minority government, the installation of a British-appointed governor to preside over an administration representing the population, security forces responsible to the governor, the liberation of political detainees, and the restoration of peaceful and democratic political activity (Good 1973, 175–176).

However, during the conference itself, Prime Minister Wilson stated that he was willing "to countenance independence before majority rule"; he supported Ian Smith's continuing as prime minister of an interim Rhodesian government and the stripping of any "power [by the British] to override the powers of the interim government in defense and law and order matters" (Good 1973, 195–196). The Rhodesians rejected the proposals, despite the assurances from Britain. Subsequent negotiations on *HMS Fearless* in 1968, in which the British agreed to postpone majority rule for ten or fifteen years, also failed (Rowe 2001, 12).

In 1971, a British Conservative Party government led by Prime Minister Edward Heath, pressured by the right-wing Monday Club members of Parliament, who used Rhodesian funding to create and sustain the Anglo-Rhodesian Society to support White minority rule (Pitchford 2011, 152; Seyd

1972, 464–487), attempted yet again to negotiate a solution. The resulting tour of Rhodesia by the Pearce Commission, as discussed earlier, revealed Black opposition to the transfer of power to the White minority government. The only positive revelation to both Britain (BBC 1972) and leaders of the front-line states (Nyerere 1972) was that future negotiations would have to include Black African political representatives.

After the escalation of the conflict through the 1970s, which imposed unbearable costs on both the Rhodesians and the front-line states, the Rhodesians agreed to negotiate with the Black African leaders then united under the UANC. However, both the conference on August 26, 1975, and subsequent secret negotiations with Joshua Nkomo proved inconclusive on the central issue of Black majority rule.

Consequently, fearing that infighting among Black groups, Rhodesian intransigence, and British impotence would create a scenario akin to the scenario in neighboring Angola, which was witnessing Cuban and Soviet intervention, Kissinger attempted to shape a solution (Gleijeses 2002, 390). Acting in tandem with South African Prime Minister John Vorster, Kissinger invited Ian Smith to a conference in Pretoria. Facing South African threats to withdraw financial and military support, which was key to Rhodesia's survival, Smith conceded to Black majority rule within two years (United Press International 1976). The front-line states initially appeared amenable to the proposed solution (*Chicago Tribune* 1976), although Nkomo and Bishop Muzorewa expressed reservations about the two-year transition period and the "imposed" nature of the agreement formulated in Pretoria without Black participation (Associated Press 1976).

Based on this agreement, a constitutional conference was organized in Geneva in December 1976 under the chairmanship of Britain (Tamarkin 1990, 143–144). Right at the start of the conference, the participating Rhodesian Whites felt that Britain had implicitly sided with the Black African groups by not recognizing Smith and his team as the Rhodesian government delegation (United States 1976). More important, the African representatives of ZAPU, ZANU, and the UANC, by then ostensibly united as the Patriotic Front, failed to reach consensus among themselves (U.S. Department of State 1976d). They also could not agree with the Smith team regarding the new constitution, opposing especially the two-year transition period and demanding a more rapid transfer of power (U.S. Department of State 1976b, 1976c). Despite the failure of the talks, it became apparent to the conference participants that the core hurdle of Black majority rule had been conceded by Smith. He was negotiating to extend the time period and conditions for the transfer of power—specifically, regarding the timing of the cessation of hostilities (Graham 2005, 54–55).

Upon the failure of the Geneva Conference, the British outlined four preconditions for agreeing to mediate any future negotiations: (1) that future negotiations have support from the front-line states—particularly, Angola, Botswana, Mozambique, Tanzania, and Zambia; (2) that the "new conditions exist," possibly implying a military scenario favoring the African guerrillas; and (3) that the Smith government agree to the outcomes. Most important, the British stated that, as "Mugabe and his group" of ZANU rebels would settle "for nothing less than their maximum conditions," a future conference could not "proceed unless Nkomo join[ed] Muzorewa and Sithole in renewed deliberations. In short, a Nkomo-Mugabe split may have been a precondition of a new conference" (U.S. Department of State 1976c). In 1977, an Anglo-American proposal clearly outlined the conditions under which Rhodesia would receive independence and official recognition from Britain, as well as the process—involving British assumption of the interim administration—that would precede the elected government's takeover of power (United States 1977a).

The following year, to avoid these preconditions and given the rising costs of continued conflict, the Rhodesian government reached an "Internal Settlement" with the moderate Black African leaders Bishop Muzorewa and Ndabaningi Sithole. The settlement led to elections in April 1979, after which Bishop Muzorewa attempted to gain recognition for the rechristened Zimbabwe-Rhodesia from the United States and Britain, meeting with President Jimmy Carter (U.S. Department of State 1979) and Prime Minister Thatcher ("Press Office: Bulletin," 1979) in quick succession. Bishop Muzorewa hoped that diplomatic recognition would lead to the lifting of economic sanctions and political marginalization of the guerrillas. Although the United States initially denied recognition to the new regime, U.S. officials indicated that this could change if recognition was granted by Britain (*ITN Source* 1979). Given the Case-Javits Amendment earlier that year, the U.S. stance strengthened Britain's position as the arbiter of the new regime's destiny.

Thatcher's stance on the Internal Settlement was, in turn, shaped by her balancing of Britain's relationship with Black African states, especially those in the Commonwealth that supported the guerrillas, and South Africa, Rhodesia's primary military and economic sponsor. On the one hand, Thatcher acknowledged to U.S. Secretary of State Owen Vance that Rhodesia was part of a broader southern African problem (implying White minority rule) that encompassed South Africa, Namibia, and Mozambique. Thus, it was imperative to acquire international acceptance from the regime, particularly from Black African leaders such as Nyerere (Tanzania), Kaunda (Zambia), and Machel (Mozambique) (United Kingdom 1979g).

On the other hand, Thatcher considered any actions against South Africa as impinging on vital British interests, although she declared that no British political leader supported apartheid. This contradiction merited a handwritten marginal remark from President Carter himself: "I hope they are not giving support to Smith" (United States 1977b). Indeed, Thatcher's sentiments on Rhodesia, and on South Africa by extension, had economic rationales that enjoyed bipartisan support in Britain. South Africa supplied valuable and scarce commodities, such as platinum, chromium, gold, and diamonds, as well as uranium from Namibia. Even the prior Labour Party government led by Prime Minister James Callaghan refused to impose economic sanctions on South Africa to pressure it to support the Anglo-American peace proposals of 1977 (U.S. Department of State 1977a). Callaghan subsequently opposed President Carter's efforts to impose sanctions on petroleum supplies to South Africa (U.S. Department of State 1977b).

Also, the right wing of Thatcher's Conservative Party, led by the Monday Club, continued to support the White minority. Julian Amery, a club member and member of Parliament, met with Thatcher in July 1979 to make the case that Britain's economic reliance on South African natural resources made it imperative for her to recognize the Internal Settlement, lest the country fall to communist forces like neighboring Angola and Mozambique (United Kingdom 1979n). However, as Amery himself acknowledged in the course of the same conversation, there would also be negative repercussions of such a decision on Britain's economic ties with Nigeria (United Kingdom 1979n). In reality, aside from Nigerian petroleum supplies on which Britain relied, British companies controlled and imported agricultural products and natural resources from Black African countries, including coffee from Kenya, cocoa from Ghana, and cobalt and copper from Zambia.

In light of these competing economic interests, the Foreign and Commonwealth Office (FCO) presented a study of what the international economic repercussions from African and Asian countries would be if Britain granted diplomatic recognition to the Internal Settlement regime. Specifically, a study by the FCO in May 1979 analyzing Britain's economic interlinkages with Rhodesia and Black African countries noted a shift in the relative economic power of South Africa and Nigeria (United Kingdom 1979a). Regarding Nigeria, it noted that "visible exports worth [£]1,114.4 million net, invisible receipts worth [£]108.8 million, and direct investment with a bulk value of [£]508 million would be at stake." If the British government recognized the Internal Settlement, it argued, Nigeria would nationalize British Petroleum's stake in the country's petroleum extraction and supply industry. It contrasted these losses with the minor gains from accepting the Internal Settlement, noting that, "by comparison, British exports to Rhodesia in 1965 at 1978 prices totaled [£]123.4 million" and estimating the book value of British assets in Rhodesia in 1974 at £113.6 million (United Kingdom 1979b).

Other evaluations also revealed a changing international economic balance: the waning of South African economic strength and influence in the continent, accompanied by the rise of Nigeria. According to William Bowdler, who was then the U.S. ambassador to South Africa, South Africa's economy was slowing down, and the country was faced with balance-of-payments problems, growing vulnerability to international sanctions, increasingly violent domestic political unrest among non-Whites, and political-military uncertainties in Namibia and Rhodesia (U.S. Department of State 1976a). The change in the relative power of South Africa and Nigeria was most apparent in Nigerian economic policy. Specifically, when Nigeria did nationalize British Petroleum, Nigeria's president, General Olusegun Obasanjo, told Australia's Prime Minister Malcolm Fraser that the expropriation had occurred because Britain was supplying oil to South Africa, which was also being boycotted by Black African countries because of its apartheid system (United Kingdom 1979k).

Despite these shifts in the regional balance of power, Britain also feared the costs of absorbing the projected 150,000 White refugees from Rhodesia into Britain, an exodus South Africa's prime minister indicated was entirely possible (United Kingdom 1980l). The claim was supported by the commander of the RSF, General Peter Walls (United Kingdom 1980k). However, British support for the White settlers—and, by implication, the Internal Settlement—were publicly justified by Prime Minister Thatcher in the interests of Zimbabweans: the flight of the White populace would ruin Zimbabwe economically, she argued, akin to the earlier experiences of decolonization in Congo, Angola, and Mozambique (United Kingdom 1980l).

Thatcher was aware that the Internal Settlement allowed Whites to retain control over the security forces and bureaucracy of Zimbabwe-Rhodesia (U.S. Department of State 1979). British officials secretly noted that several conditions for a free and fair election remained unmet. The Internal Settlement's "election was held under conditions of martial law and with ZANU and ZAPU banned," for example, and the Constitution, "approved by a referendum of Whites only," contained "a number of clauses" that left "serious doubt as [to] whether real power" would be "exercised by representatives of the Black majority" (United Kingdom 1979e). However, Thatcher wrote a response in the document's margin: "Tell me another country in Africa which has one person one vote for 4 different Political Parties?" Moreover, she compared the integration of the RSF with Black "terrorists" (her term) to the proposition that the British Army accept the Irish Republican Army and argued that the capacity of any new government ultimately relied on its ability to maintain internal security, which the (White-controlled) RSF was capable of doing (United States 1977b).

Thatcher attempted to convince European and African leaders of the Internal Settlement's validity and popular legitimacy within Rhodesia using three rationales. First, the nature of the Internal Settlement Constitution was within the purview of the country's sovereign rights. Second, the government was elected in free and fair elections. And third, elections were based on universal adult suffrage. She argued with French President Valéry Giscard d'Estaing that the Conservative Party's election observers (implying Lord Boyd) had evaluated the elections as "free and fair," and the nature of the Rhodesian Constitution was an internal matter, to be decided by its people (United Kingdom 1979d).

In August 1979, right before the Commonwealth Heads of Government meeting (CHOGM) in Lusaka, Zambia, British Foreign Secretary Peter Carrington attempted to do the same with Kenya's President Daniel arap Moi, by claiming that Ian Smith was "relegated to a subordinate and inactive position" and that "it was impossible to ignore a turn-out of nearly 65 percent" of voters for the election (United Kingdom 1979o). President Moi sympathetically responded that the constitutional protections based on race "created the possibilities of attacks on the communities who were given entrenched rights under it," implying the Whites. Instead, he called for the "protection of property and rights of individuals," clarifying that it "was essential to generate confidence; elections could not be held in an atmosphere of hate." He stipulated that the guerrilla leaders—ZANU's Mugabe and ZAPU's Nkomo—had to be encouraged to return and participate in an election (United Kingdom 1979o). Carrington could push back on the elections only by casting aspersions at the level of popular support enjoyed by the guerrillas, arguing that "Nkomo and Mugabe might not necessarily have won much support" if they had been allowed to run in the Internal Settlement elections (United Kingdom 1979o).

Most important, Thatcher and Carrington tried to convince President Nyerere of Tanzania, a prominent supporter of the guerrillas, before the CHOGM meeting. During the conversation, Nyerere revealed what the front-line states had agreed to the previous evening. "They did not believe that a situation had been reached in Rhodesia where there was a government that should be recognized and sanctions lifted," he said, adding that "it was not a matter of whether there had been free and fair elections: it was the constitution that was the main problem" (United Kingdom 1979l). Later, he explicitly mentioned that neither reserving parliamentary seats for the Whites—something that existed in Tanzania's post-independence constitution—nor the requirement for a strong, independent administration was a problem. Rather, the problem was the power for the White minority entrenched therein (United Kingdom 1979l).

In essence, the front-line states were opposed in principle to a negotiated transition that maintained safeguards for the White minority. This position became apparent when Nyerere subsequently proposed the front-line states' preferred solution: a modified democratic constitution acceptable to the Commonwealth countries, implying the Black African and Asian countries that were the overwhelming majority of the organization's members; fresh elections based on this constitution; and the monitoring of these elections to ensure they remained free and fair, to the satisfaction of the Commonwealth. If these conditions were met, Nyerere promised, the front-line states were willing to stop supporting the guerrilla forces of ZANU and ZAPU, which by then had united as the Patriotic Front (PF) (United Kingdom 1979l).

Nyerere's assertions were reaffirmed at the CHOGM. Thatcher herself outlined the key developments: the CHOGM recognized Britain as the sole principal intermediary; member states committed to stop supporting the guerrillas; member states sought the end of sanctions; member states would not recognize the guerrillas as the sole representatives of Rhodesia; and member states would accept the electoral verdict, whatever the outcome (United Kingdom 1979c). The British agreed to the CHOGM's proposal in part because they calculated that South Africa's failure to prevent Cuban and Soviet military intervention in Angola—and a desire to prevent further losses of men and materiel—would make Prime Minister P. W. Botha accept the electoral outcome after the British-mediated settlement (United Kingdom 1980e).

The subsequent Lancaster House Agreement brokered by the British between the belligerent groups stipulated elections under British supervision. To protect White interests, the agreement provided twenty parliamentary seats for the White Roll, a reduction of eight from the Internal Settlement. The agreement also protected White farmers, who still occupied two-fifths of all agricultural land, by introducing the "willing buyer, willing seller" principle, permitting government acquisition of land only via purchasing at market prices (R. Palmer 1990). To make the land-purchase scheme credible, Britain promised to deliver £500 million, and the United States indicated a contribution of $200 million, although Britain ultimately paid only £20 million, and the United States did not pay anything (Lebert 2006, 44–46). These terms were ensured by a ten-year moratorium on all constitutional amendments.

Under the purview of Christopher Soames, as the British governor, Zimbabwe-Rhodesia reverted to being the British colony of Southern Rhodesia in December 1979. This began the period of campaigning and elections that would lead to the formation of the new government in 1980. Four major Black parties ran separately: ZANU-PF, led by Robert Mugabe; ZAPU, led by Joshua Nkomo; the UANC, under Abel Muzorewa; and ZANU (Ndongo), led by Ndabaningi Sithole. The former two parties represented the guerrillas, and the latter two parties had participated in the Internal Settlement. The RF and a few other splinter parties contested seats reserved for the Whites.

At this point, it is important to note that the RSF came to represent Rhodesian Whites during the transfer of power. This was based on an informal—the minutes state, "under the counter"—arrangement reached between Prime Minister Thatcher and General Peter Walls during the Lancaster House negotiations, wherein General Walls would have formal and informal direct access to Governor Lord Soames "just as the Chiefs of Staff had direct access to her" to maintain law and order as the only "disciplined force in the country" (United Kingdom 1979m, 2–3). Thatcher sent a message to Lord Soames a few days later to confirm in writing that she wanted General Walls to have direct access without having to go through others (United Kingdom 1979i).

More revealing, during her conversation with Walls, Thatcher also mentioned that members of her family lived in Zimbabwe-Rhodesia, "in the front line of the defence of the Western way of life," thus indicating her personal and ideological commitment to an amicable transition (United Kingdom 1979m, 5). Using such terms also implied that she viewed the RSF as representing the White minority because Britain's justification for refusing to use force against the UDI regime in 1965 centered on the possibility of mutiny if British troops were asked to fire on "kith and kin." In addition, the Rhodesian White settlers' justification for continuing minority rule was defending the country against communism. Nevertheless, despite expressing a mélange of institutional, ethnic, and ideological solidarity, Thatcher avoided granting General Walls permission to conduct cross-border raids against guerrillas, suggesting instead that such a decision would fall under the purview of Lord Soames (United Kingdom 1979m, 4–5).

As electioneering began, a series of reports by ZAPU and the UANC accusing the ZANU-PF of intimidating the former parties' election workers elicited British warning about taking actions, which were conveyed to leaders of African and Western countries (United Kingdom 1980h). Yet, instead of increasing policing or penalizing ZAPU, Lord Soames and the team of British officials who were overseeing the elections and subsequent transfer of power leveraged the violence to create a secret preelectoral coalition between Nkomo's Ndebele-supported ZAPU, Muzorewa's Shona-backed UANC, and the Whites of the RF. Soames secretly posited that "Nkomo's position was key" to gaining international recognition for the new country; deescalating the conflict; and stopping other African countries, especially Zambia and Botswana, from supporting the guerrillas (United Kingdom 1980m).

Governor Soames's actions followed a British plan that preceded the Lancaster House negotiations: to create a postindependence government that would simultaneously represent the Ndebele, the Shona, and the Whites but exclude the Shona-backed ZANU-PF (United Kingdom 1979g). Britain's favored outcomes for the election, from most to least preferred, were later expressed in communications among General Walls of the RSF, Prime Minister Thatcher, and Foreign Secretary Carrington. First, if the ZANU-PF won fewer than forty of the eighty seats from the Common Roll, implying less than a majority of the Black African seats, Britain preferred a coalition among ZAPU, the UANC, and the RF, with some elements of the ZANU-PF. If the ZANU-PF received more than forty seats, Mugabe would be given a "leading role in the government," but in alliance with White members of Parliament, to form a national government. But if the ZANU-PF had an absolute majority of more than fifty seats, and Mugabe could not be denied a prominent role, then the British would impose a national government, implying an all-party coalition (United Kingdom 1980f).

The South Africans, represented by Foreign Minister Pik Botha, also preferred such coalitions. Botha asked the British to secretly broker an alliance between Muzorewa and Nkomo to deter or crush the ZANU-PF guerrillas militarily (United Kingdom 1980c). The next week, he suggested that Lord Soames "tighten the screws" on the ZANU-PF and strengthen Muzorewa's UANC by another 10–15 percent to create a broad-based coalition (United Kingdom 1980d).

After the ZANU-PF won fifty-seven of the eighty Common Roll seats, thereby acquiring an absolute majority in the one-hundred-seat Parliament, Britain persuaded Walls—who challenged the election's validity because of electoral violence perpetrated by the ZANU–PF—that restarting the conflict was futile (United Kingdom 1980k). Britain also asked the South Africans to accept the ZANU-PF's victory in exchange for British acceptance of the apartheid status quo in South Africa. Specifically, the British disavowed any efforts to push for "one man, one vote" (implying Black majority rule) in South Africa, and stated that Britain "recognized that [White South Africans] had built an economy and civilization that they did not wish destroyed" (United Kingdom 1980b).

The precedent Britain set by ignoring preelectoral violence perpetrated by the ZANU-PF and its wholehearted acceptance of Robert Mugabe as prime minister, in exchange for economic guarantees for the Whites, continued to shape Zimbabwean politics after the 1980 election. Soon after the transition, Zimbabwe faced another, albeit smaller, civil war between the Shona-dominated ZANU-PF and the Ndebele-supported ZAPU. The brutal Gukurahundi repression of the rebellion by the Fifth Brigade, which was primarily trained by North Korea, revealed Mugabe's authoritarian tendencies and the political system's inability to check them.

Yet British efforts ignored Black opposition in Zimbabwe. Prime Minister Thatcher mentioned that "Nkomo sought to come to the United Kingdom, [and] it was to be hoped that some way could be found of refusing to admit him" (United Kingdom 1983a, 4). A week later, when he was informed that Nkomo had entered Britain, Foreign Secretary Francis Pym suggested that Britain continue to support Mugabe "to pre-empt the risk that he might seek support from Communist governments, and . . . prevent Nkomo from staying in Britain for more than four weeks" (United Kingdom 1983a).

Instead, Britain focused on protecting the White settlers' interests, as exemplified by its efforts to obtain the release of White officers of the Zimbabwean Air Force who had been arrested and tried for destroying nine airplanes and damaging four others, including some that had recently been supplied by Britain, at the Thornhill Air Base in the city of Gweru in May 1983 (Cowell 1983). However, during a private meeting at the British High Commissioner's residence in New Delhi, on the sidelines of the CHOGM in November 1983, Mugabe responded to Thatcher's inquiry about three officers who had been re-detained after being acquitted by the court in a way that paradoxically revealed the primary British interests in Rhodesia. Mugabe asked why positive achievements of the ZANU-PF government had been ignored by Britain, then remarked that the "majority of the white community were content. They still had their privileges, except the privilege of ruling. They had a far higher standard of living and occupied prominent posts. Firms had not been nationalized and had even been encouraged to expand" (United Kingdom 1983c).

Britain also continued to balance its ties with South Africa and Black African countries. In 1980, as the civil war in Namibia between Black guerrillas and the South African–controlled White minority regime began to escalate, the British sought to veto any economic sanctions on South Africa. However, Britain wanted to do so jointly with France and the United States because "a solitary British veto could be very damaging" to Britain's "overall interests in Black Africa, including . . . extensive commercial ones" (United Kingdom 1980a). Subsequently, at the CHOGM in 1985, while reiterating Britain's opposition to apartheid, Thatcher strongly opposed a group of Commonwealth leaders on the issue of imposing sanctions on South Africa, including not only premiers of the Black African states but also Prime Minister Brian Mulroney of Canada, Prime Minister Robert Hawke of Australia, and Prime Minister Rajiv Gandhi of India (United Kingdom 1985).

Conclusion

This study of the transfer of power from White minority–ruled Rhodesia to Black majority–based Zimbabwe highlights how British companies' investments in Africa influenced its decision making during the Lancaster House negotiations of 1979 and the elections of 1980. Shifts in the relative economic power of South Africa and Nigeria in the 1970s—the former backing the White settlers, and the latter supporting the Black guerrillas—influenced Britain's decision to mediate and impose Black majority rule. However, Britain's attempt to balance its still formidable investments in South Africa with those in Nigeria led to its undermining of democratization in two seemingly contradictory ways. By helping the Whites and, by extension, South Africa, Britain conspired to create coalitions to stop Mugabe's ZANU-PF from taking power, and to placate the Black guerrillas and their foreign sponsors, Britain refused to take action against electoral violence committed by the ZANU-PF.

The background to the internationalization of the Rhodesian conflict through economic ties that spanned Africa, Europe, America, and Asia is presented in the first two sections of the chapter on the trajectories of the White settler–backed Rhodesian regime and the Black guerrillas who fought against it, respectively. The Rhodesian regime was backed via covert ties with European countries such as France and Germany, as well as the communist Soviet Union. The Black opposition, faced with the banning of political parties and frequent detention of its leaders, fled to various African countries, which allowed them to fight an increasingly successful guerrilla war. Despite the benefits that both the Whites and the Blacks accrued from such connections, these links made them vulnerable to pressure from their foreign sponsors: Rhodesia, from South Africa; and the guerrillas, from various Black African states. Accounting for such dependence, British mediation in 1978–1980 became centered on placating the foreign sponsors, at the cost of the belligerent domestic groups.

The findings presented here challenge two popular explanations for Britain's behavior during the negotiations and the subsequent general elections. First, they discredit the idea that Britain's positions were shaped by its commitment to decolonizing and democratizing Zimbabwe (Watts 2006, 146; N. White 2014). Second, they also do not support the claim by Lord Soames, the last British governor of Southern Rhodesia, that Britain's actions were shaped by its expectation and acceptance of the election's predicted outcome—that is, the outright victory of Robert Mugabe (Soames 1980).

Instead, the collected evidence demonstrates that the economic costs of deteriorating relations with the Black African states—particularly Nigeria because of Britain's increasing dependence on supplies of Nigerian petroleum—combined with the expected cost of absorbing fleeing Whites influenced Britain's decisions regarding Rhodesia in 1978–1980. Communications among British officials also reveal that Britain did not equate Black majority rule with democratization, either in terms of arranging secret coalitions to stop the ZANU-PF or publicly declining to stop the ZANU-PF from using violence against its Black competitors, including ZAPU and the UANC. Furthermore, Britain did not accept the outcome of the elections as a given. In fact, uncertainty regarding the electoral outcome allowed Britain to consider different coalitions of Black and White parties.

Therefore, the influence of international capital on British mediation and the consequent peace agreement, which transformed White-dominated Rhodesia into Black majority–ruled Zimbabwe, hews to the general explanation presented in this book. The effect of British companies' investments in fixed assets—exemplified by Nigerian petroleum and South African precious metals and diamonds—affected the longevity and resolution of the conflict because British companies could not easily divest their assets, which, being fixed, were also prone to government takeover in these countries. On the one hand, Britain could not stop Black African countries from sponsoring the guerrillas and apartheid South Africa from backing the White settler regime. On the other hand, shifts in the relative power of South Africa and Nigeria led to British mediation and the conflict's conclusion, but on terms that undermined both democratization and land redistribution.

Conclusion

A New Research Agenda for Politics in Agrarian Societies

Why do peasant rebellions create state institutions dominated by elites who marginalize peasants? The studies of three countries, and of regions within each, presented in the book, center on two queries. First, how and why do rebellions occur? And second, how and why are new states formed? Prior research has explored the origins of rebellions separately (Moore 1966; Scott 2009; Skocpol 1979; E. Wood 2003), from the processes of popular mobilizations (McCarthy and Zald [2001] 2006; Tarrow 1998; Tilly 1995; Weinstein 2006) to the causes and processes of state institution formation (Acemoglu and Robinson 2006; Bates 2001; Tsebelis 1991, 2002). The model and findings presented here bridge such explanations to present a holistic theory of how the origins of rebellions affect the process of state formation, using Mancur Olson's ([1965] 1971) insight on barriers to collective action and John McCarthy and Mayer Zald's ([2001] 2006) insight that groups need resources to overcome such barriers. In addition, the book argues that peasant rebellions in large agrarian societies require elite allies to provide resources, and allied elites subsequently use their greater cohesion and resources to control peasants and bargain among themselves to select new state institutions.

The posited theory is confirmed using studies of peaceful and violent rural rebellions and state formation in Mexico from 1910 to the mid-1930s, India from the 1910s to 1950, and Zimbabwe from the mid-1960s to 1980. Chapters 1–3 address the first inquiry, explicating the causes of elite participation in peasant rebellions in various regions of Mexico, India, and Zimbabwe and their outcomes. Addressing the second inquiry, Chapters 4–6 explicate the processes and outcomes of elite bargains, followed by brief presentations of the resulting new institutions' effects on different social classes.

The narratives regarding peasant rebellions and state formation presented in the book's subnational- and national-level studies reveal that peasant rebellions carry within them the seeds of their own disappointment. Grievances alone are insufficient to propel such rebellions because barriers exist that prevent peasants from acting collectively. Leaving their fields untended during the sowing or harvesting season, risking death and the loss of whatever little they own from the retaliation of incumbent elites and state forces, and the costs of rebelling in terms of provisions and materiel are too onerous a burden for peasant rebels to bear, especially if the accrued benefits of lowered land rents and political freedoms and free education could be gained without taking these risks and bearing the costs. These barriers therefore make local elite allies critical determinants of rural rebellions. Shopkeepers and small-town barkeepers; lawyers; educated landed farmers and grain merchants; large bankers; and urban industrialists, as well as established landlords and hardy ranchers, can become the providers of leadership, party organizations, guns, and money that lower the tangible and intangible costs of participating in rebellions.

Yet although these allied elites help overcome barriers to collective action by delivering tangible and intangible resources, they subsequently use these same resources, and their own smaller population size and resultant cohesion, to co-opt and remarginalize peasants. Political parties and agrarian leagues controlled by such elites begin to articulate popular grievances and by doing so reshape them to suit elite grievances and vision of future institutions. When autonomous peasant groups cannot be co-opted, elites crush them through violent and peaceful means. The leaders of the popular organizations then bargain with one another to select state institutions that will deliver wealth and power to them and create representative institutions that entrench them as spokespeople and negotiators for peasants' interests. Under the guise of redistribution, economic policies increase the ruling party's control of cooperative farms or inordinately benefit the newly empowered rural elites. Industrialization policies profit the urban bourgeoisie by protecting them from foreign competition, at the cost of workers and peasants. When foreign investors predominate, economic policies curtail redistribution of wealth and impede domestic industrialization.

The theory backed by these studies addresses the dilemma that revolutionary outcomes remain insecure until they are institutionalized (Acemoglu and Robinson 2006, 24–27). In the vein of Carles Boix (2003, 35–37), this book shows that redistributive outcomes are institutionalized because bargains between newly empowered elites determine which new national-level state institutions are chosen. As explicated by George Tsebelis (1991), such bargains are multifaceted because they encompass several social cleavages, and multileveled because they involve elites' bargaining with one another and simultaneously negotiating with peasants to preserve the coalitions that empowered them in the first place. Possible gridlocks are resolved when the rising costs of internecine conflict threaten to outweigh existing and future economic and political benefits, compelling elites to seek and institutionalize compromise solutions (Bates 2001; Tilly 1985). The institutions created from elite compromises therefore do not increase peasants' liberty and prosperity but maintain incumbent elites' wealth and power (Bates 1981). The elites' specific demands from the state vary depending on what is locally suitable to maintain their popular support (Boone 2003).

Ideologies—whether communist, theocratic, or libertarian—cannot inoculate peasants from marginalization because the problem lies not with the underlying grievances and goals of particular rebellions, fought as they are with the highest ideals of community and freedom against fearful odds. The problem lies instead with the demographic characteristics of social classes and the process of rebellion in agrarian societies: the large population size and poverty of peasants (to which authors attribute their revolutionary potential), in fact, cripples them, and elites' small population size and greater resources (the reason for their ostensible vulnerability to revolutions) actually facilitates their co-option of peasants and strategic selection of state institutions.

These insights therefore challenge structural theories of revolutions by accounting for the processes of rebellions and state formation. Hitherto, such theories have moved directly from the origins of rebellions in conflicts among social classes, unleashed by the process of socioeconomic modernization, to the new institutional arrangements (Luebbert 1991; Moore 1966; Rueschemeyer, Stephens, and Stephens 1992). These theories thus conflate cause with outcome by ignoring the intermediary effects of the process of mobilization (Kalyvas 1996, 11). Rather, as demonstrated by the studies of intended and unintended effects of peasant rebellions and state formation presented here, peasants' battles against repression cannot deliver emancipation.

The next section elucidates the two major takeaway points from this book in terms of its contributions to the general understanding of the causes of peasant rebellions and their subsequent effects on state formation. Specifically, dissenting elite classes play a critical role in such rebellions, and new state institutions arise from bargains among these elites. The third section presents and justifies three possible weaknesses in the development of the theory, design of the research, and selection of the case studies—in particular, regarding the distinct role of conflict in encouraging state formation, how the research design addresses the "degrees of freedom" problem, and why the Ndebele rebellion in Zimbabwe and the postcolonial formation of the Pakistani state were not selected for study. Finally, the diagnostic and prescriptive policy ramifications of the findings are presented. First, neither democratization nor socialist ideologies are capable of removing elites and emphasizing pro-peasant policies because of the dynamics of rebellion and state formation in agrarian societies. Second, scholars and policy makers would be better served by investigating the rise of dominant parties that characterized the postrevolutionary regimes in Mexico, India, and Zimbabwe.

What Are the Major Contributions of This Book?

This book makes two major contributions to the study of political development in agrarian societies. With regard to peasant rebellions, the comparative studies demonstrate the critical role elites play in agrarian rebellions because they provide both tangible and intangible resources that help the more numerous and poorer peasant rebels overcome barriers to collective action. Second, the book connects peasant rebellions to state formation by showing that postrevolutionary states are formed via bargains among the elites who previously allied with peasant rebels because the elites' greater resources and cohesion allow them to capture peasants' interests. Thus, liberatory state formation is impossible because revolutions in agrarian societies perpetuate elite domination.

The study of peasant rebellions presented in the case studies of various regions in Mexico, India, and Zimbabwe reveal the critical role of elite classes in determining the success of agrarian rebellions. Elites provide not only financial support and materiel, as they did in all three societies, but also intangible benefits such as knowledge of the surrounding environment (e.g., the spirit mediums in Zimbabwe), leadership skills (e.g., the revolutionaries in Mexico), and organizations that can sustain challenges over time (e.g., the Congress Party and its regional counterparts). The tradeoff for elite participation, which is also highlighted by the analyses of subnational rebellions, is peasants' ceding control to elites. Thus, elite class participation in peasant rebellions translates into elite influence over peasants and, ultimately, the next stage of state formation.

These studies draw on Boix's (2003) insights that social groups' incentives are contingent on the specificity of assets they control. Thus, the preferences of landlords, members of the bourgeoisie, and peasants vary based on their control of land, capital and specialized skills, or labor. Moreover, the studies nuance the characteristics of classes based on a region's culture, institutions, and history. Thus, the elite class in colonial India's Punjab could appear as landed farmers in the Canal Colonies made up of former servicemen, yet their beneficial relationship with the colonial army and their contentious relationship with city-based merchants and moneylenders made them behave like landlords, *not* peasants. In Zimbabwe, the Black middle classes extended from domestic help in cities, service employees, and small-business owners who lived in or interacted with cities. To the tiny minority of White Rhodesians, the Black middle class may have appeared poor, almost at par with the vast Black peasantry, but their initial leadership allowed the rebellion to survive repression and exile from 1965 until its slow return in 1972 and ultimate triumph in 1979. The homesteading ranchers in western-central Mexico owned land, but their preferences were more similar to those of bankers in Mexico City than to those of southeastern landlords living in haciendas and employing hundreds of indigenous peasants. As implied by these examples, combining the historicist approach highlighting local particularities with a positivist one focusing on discovering generalizable truths offers an empirically grounded general theory of rebellions and state formation.

By presenting a theory that revolves around the rise and fulfilment of subnational elite classes, I argue against the possibility of liberatory state formation in agrarian societies. Prior theories of revolutions, extending from those focusing on coalitions among social classes (Acemoglu and Robinson 2006; Boix 2003; Moore 1966; Paige 1975; Rueschemeyer, Stephens, and Stephens 1992) to those focusing on sclerotic (Huntington 1968) or collapsing (Skocpol 1979) state institutions, consider revolutions national-level phenomena in which mass mobilizations are undertaken, societies metamorphose, and new institutions are constructed at the national level. These theories, therefore, do not account for the diversity of causes, leaders, and, most important, social classes that lead and dominate sub-national rebellions, which jointly constitute national-level revolutions. Indeed, the subnational turn in historiography, pioneered by the subaltern studies approach, has long noticed this myopia and addressed it by investigating the local blind spots of national-level studies (Ludden 2002). However, such bottom-up approaches are inadequate in explaining national-level state formation, focused as they are on uncovering and understanding local-level phenomena, especially regarding marginalized groups previously displaced in favor of national leaders.

This problem is best elucidated by the regionalist approach to the Mexican Revolution pioneered by Thomas Benjamin and Mark Wasserman (1990), which deconstructs the revolution's unified narrative by examining the distinct causes and outcomes of provincial rebellions during the revolutionary period. Perhaps because its primary aim is deconstructing the national-level narrative, such scholarship cannot explain the formation of the postrevolutionary state under the Partido Revolucionario Institucional (PRI) in 1929 that lasted until 2000. In other words, Benjamin and Wasserman's focus on revolutionaries ignores the revolution. Yet national-level political-economic explanations led by Stephen Haber, Armando Razo, and Noel Maurer (2003), who reveal the interdependence of political-military caudillos and business interests that underlay Mexico's economic development and political stability, also do not adequately account for the origins of the caudillos who shaped the postrevolutionary state. In other words, their revolution lacks revolutionaries.

In contrast, the explanatory narratives presented in this book show that state formation can occur in a centripetal manner, wherein local dynamics shape new state institutions. The characteristics of new states' formation therefore arise from strategic interactions among actors empowered by local rebellions, as well as the class interests that they represent. As a result, Barrington Moore (1966) and Maya Tudor's (2013) argument, that a pan-Indian class coalition organized by the Congress Party led by Mahatma Gandhi undergirded the postcolonial Indian state, is shown to be the result of loosely connected regional rebel coalitions with distinct demands.

Some of these rebel coalitions, such as the one in the eastern province of Bengal, not only fell outside the ambit of a broader Gandhian coalition but also actively opposed it because Bengali landlords and dependent bourgeoisie were the most prominent members of the provincial Congress Party (J. Chatterji 2002). In the northwestern province of Punjab, landed farmers' dependence on colonial military recruitment policies, and consequent official protection from encroaching market forces represented by urban merchants and moneylenders who patronized the Congress Party, created provincial political dynamics that rejected the Congress Party in favor of the Unionist Party, which subsequently fractured into the Akali Dal, representing Sikhs and the Muslim League (Yong 2005). Interactions among these regional coalitions, and their inability to agree on redistributive policies and political representation, ultimately caused the Partition and the formation of the postcolonial Indian state.

Responding to Possible Weaknesses: Concept, Research Design, and Case Selection

Scholars make choices about theoretical focuses, appropriate research designs, and suitable cases to focus on certain aspects of the subject of inquiry. As all theories and relevant findings act as lenses, they consequently provide an imperfect evaluation of the totality of the studied topic. Therefore, this section presents and justifies four possible drawbacks with this study—one each in terms of theory development and research design, and two in terms of case selection. In particular regarding the theoretical focuses, the book does not theorize and test the relationship between conflict and state making. Second, this section explains why the comparative research design does not fall prey to problems of degrees of freedom as a result of too many study variables' chasing too few observations in the regional- and national-level studies. Finally, it explains why the broader study does not account for a smaller regional rebellion in Zimbabwe's Ndebele-dominated areas and explicate the process of postcolonial state formation in Pakistan and Bangladesh, which were carved out of British India.

In all three countries, the rising costs of conflict forced elites to seek the compromise solutions that became the bases of state formation. In Mexico, the warlords fought until the repeated failures of at least three coalitions in the 1920s to capture national power resulted in economic instability and significant loss of life. The apparent stalemate forced the warlords, backed by their elite-class supporters, to negotiate to form a new party that effectively froze the status quo and started state formation. In India during the mid-1940s, the stalemated politics between the Congress Party and the Muslim League, which centered on religion and were backed by distinct class coalitions, caused waves of massive violence. Unable to guarantee the lives and property of each other's supporters as British authority weakened, the parties sought partition and, therefore, the formation of the postcolonial Indian state. In Zimbabwe, the effect of conflict was most apparent because the stalemated conflict forced the indigenous insurgents, led by Mugabe's Zimbabwe African National Union (ZANU), and the White settlers, represented by the Rhodesian state, to negotiate and compromise. The Lancaster House negotiations became the linchpin around which the Zimbabwean state formed in the 1980s; thus, accounting for the conflict supports the hypothesis that elite classes negotiate to choose self-serving institutions. Because conflict is factored in as a cost for non-negotiation, increases in conflict intensity made compromises more attractive to competing elite groups.

Although conflict is regarded as imposing costs that elites seek to avoid, the critical role of conflict in state formation remains somewhat underexplored in the narrative presented above. At first glance, the explanation of state formation appears to support Robert Bates's (2001) contention that economic prosperity is contingent on incumbent elites' capacity to terminate domestic conflict and foster economic growth, both of which are achieved by state institutions that deter aggression from domestic competitors and reassure private investors. This insight, in turn, is developed from Charles Tilly's

(1985) historicist notion of state making as an elite strategy to resolve similar problems. Moreover, because all three of the societies studied here continue to suffer from poverty and various degrees of political repression, accounting for the process of conflict could reveal that the interaction of peasants' poverty with elite classes' control of resources, both of which are needed to carry out rebellions, precludes the establishment of "open-access" state institutions that maximize economic benefits and political representation for individual citizens and instead establishes "natural states" dominated by elite classes who collaborate to retain power to extract rent from state institutions (North, Wallis, and Weingast 2009).

The comparative research design is vulnerable to criticisms regarding degrees of freedom because the number of studied variables, in the analyses of both the subnational rebellions and subsequent state formation, exceeds the number of regions and countries selected for comparison. It could therefore be argued that the number of observed variations in the cases is insufficient to test the posited variables. This is an important critique of case studies, in the vein of statistical research that reports "only one measure on any pertinent variable" by aggregating "variables together into single indices to get fewer independent variables" (George and Bennett 2004, 28). However, the goal of this book is to show how similar problems and structures emerge despite the many differences for which a true statistical test would struggle to account. In particular, the goal is to demonstrate how different types of rebellions and regimes can be explained using the same causal mechanism—that is, via coalitions between peasants and elites—followed by elite bargains. By doing so, my historical comparative approach successfully yields new insights and potential theories that can be further tested.

In terms of selected cases, the analysis of rebellions and state formation does not cover those in areas dominated by the Ndebele group in the southwestern Matabeleland districts of Rhodesia. The Ndebele, who make up almost 20 percent of the country's population, were represented by the Zimbabwe African People's Union and its military wing, the Zimbabwe People's Revolutionary Army (ZIPRA). The central reason for not analyzing the rebellion in Matabeleland led by ZIPRA was its strategy to construct a conventional army while maintaining a low-intensity agrarian rebellion. Specifically, ZIPRA avoided violent agrarian rebellion similar to that mounted by the Shona rebels (as discussed in Chapter 2), despite similar grievances against White Rhodesians regarding economic and political marginalization, because the Ndebele also feared postcolonial domination by the Shonas, who made up nearly 80 percent of the population (Cilliers 1985, 37). Furthermore, although ZIPRA survived the initial transition to Black majority rule, the Shona-dominated ZANU, led by Robert Mugabe, sidelined it politically and ruthlessly crushed its military capacity in a civil war during the 1980s (P. Jackson 2011).

Finally, this book does not address the trajectory of postcolonial Pakistani politics, which culminated in territorial fragmentation in the face of a secessionist peasant rebellion in East Bengal. The trajectory of Pakistan from 1947 through its disintegration in 1971 attests to the importance of the expression of political and economic grievances as ethnolinguistic conflicts when representative institutions are unable to channel such modes of opposition peacefully. Thus, Pakistan's history mirrors the crisis that led to partition itself and reaffirms that the religious cleavages that led to the creation of Pakistan as a nation-state separate from India merely reflected deeper socioeconomic cleavages.

At independence, Pakistan became dominated by two elite classes from West Pakistan: émigré landlords and allied middle classes from northern India who had founded and led the Muslim League, and Punjabi landlords who depended on military service and were originally from the Unionist Party. However, the majority of Pakistan's population lived in the province of East Bengal in East Pakistan, which also provided the most foreign-exchange earnings through jute exports and whose politics were dominated by the anti-landlord *jotedars* originally from the Krishak Praja Party (KPP). Furthermore, due to British recruitment policies, Bengalis were nearly nonexistent in the armed forces.

Although the temporary subsuming of the Unionist Party and the KPP within the Muslim League forced the creation of Pakistan in 1947, as discussed in Chapter 5, the stark differences between the class makeup of the elites and their representation in the armed services resulted in a postcolonial scenario in which representative democracy favoring the East Bengali majority implied the loss of West Pakistani elites' power over state institutions. The Muslim League lacked organizational presence and ameliorative programs in the vein of the state-led development policies or the anti-caste reform movements introduced by the Congress Party (Tudor 2013). Thus, after ratifying a constitution in 1956, the country was unable to channel political competition within democratic institutions and faced military coups.

The first military dictator, General Ayub Khan, attempted to incorporate the younger generation of West Pakistani elites under the leadership of Zulfiqar Ali Bhutto, the American-educated scion of a major landed family in the West Pakistani province of Sindh. Such attempts to create broad legitimacy for the regime, however, did not extend to East Pakistan. Consequently, the most populous wing of Pakistan, which provided most of its foreign-exchange earnings, neither shared power in democratic governance nor was represented in the military. Furthermore, the government attempted to impose Urdu, the language of the Muslim elite émigrés from northern India who composed less than 6 percent of the entire Pakistani population, on Bengalis as the national language. Subsequent East Bengali demands for autonomy, West Pakistani military and then civilian elites' unwillingness to relinquish power to the popularly elected Awami League from East Pakistan, and, ultimately, civil war and Indian intervention caused the secession of East Pakistan as the new country of Bangladesh (Cohen 2004, 73–75)—thus ironically reaffirming that the cleavages around which the anticolonial movement and postcolonial Indian state formed were socioeconomic, *not* religious.

Policy Ramifications and Avenues for Future Research

Scholarship on revolutions and rebellions implicitly assumes that these processes liberate peasants at least by creating economic well-being or providing political representation, if not both. The first part of this section explains to policy makers why this book's findings challenge such expectations. Neither of these expected outcomes was achieved in the three countries I studied. Instead, peasants were remarginalized, with the source of exploitation and repression shifting from one elite class to another. Liberal democratic and communist ideologies are no curatives to the dilemma presented by the interaction of class interests and collective-action barriers in agrarian societies. Rather, this section concludes by urging scholars to study the phenomenon of dominant parties that appear as a result of elite bargains to control the state, for their form and functions could reveal the mind and sinews of domination by elite classes.

Scholars in the past two decades have provided intellectual credence to policies forwarded by various state agencies and nongovernmental organizations in the United States and Western Europe to support peaceful and violent rebellions in developing societies that aim to establish liberal democratic institutions. Some have argued that democratization secures and maintains human rights (Bueno de Mesquita et al. 2005; Cingranelli and Filippov 2010; Davenport and Armstrong 2004); others have argued that it fosters equitable economic development (Acemoglu et al. 2015; Gerring et al. 2005). However, as this book's studies of postcolonial India and Zimbabwe demonstrate, democratic institutions formed through peasant rebellions provide neither adequate representation nor equitable development because they are designed to reflect elites' priorities rather than local peasants' realities.

Indeed, liberal democratic institutions' guarantees of free popular participation and fair contestation for power have failed to remove entrenched elites. Instead, elites persist with popular support in countries such as the Philippines and Liberia. In the Philippines, political leaders belong to regional landowning families (McCoy 2009), including former President Corazon Aquino, the leader of the anti-Marcos democratic movement, as well as her son Benigno Aquino III, who served as president until 2016. In Liberia, after more than a century of one-party rule and two decades of civil war, the creole landed and business elites continue to influence politics, though to a lesser extent and in cooperation with segments of the indigenous elites, through democratically elected parties and leaders such as President Ellen Johnson Sirleaf (Gerdes 2013, 199–200).

For the same reasons, ironically, peasant rebellions fail to establish socialist governing institutions, which also end up repressing peasants economically and politically. In the 1970s and 1980s, the Soviet Union and China patronized numerous revolutionary movements in Asia and Africa in the hope of establishing communist political-economic institutions. Yet revolutionary elites' modernization strategies in countries such as Ethiopia and Mozambique denied political freedoms to peasants and failed to deliver equitable economic development. In Ethiopia, the Derg government brutally repressed the population, created famine conditions, prevented relief, and killed thousands (Young 1997). The collectivization and modernization policies of the Marxist-Leninist Frente de Libertação de Moçambique (FRELIMO) politically repressed and economically impoverished peasants, eventually creating popular support for the Resistência Nacional Moçambicana (RENAMO) insurgency originally started by the South African apartheid regime and the White Rhodesians (Bowen 2000).

The ultimate failure of peasant rebellions should therefore give pause to sympathetic commentaries about the ongoing Maoist rebellions in India, particularly with regard to the nature of grievances, the involved classes, and the actual carrying out of these rebellions. In terms of constituent classes, Jonathan Kennedy and Sunil Purushotham (2012) argue that the long-term popular support for such rebellions comes from previously autonomous tribal populations whose grievances arise from the capture of labor and natural resources by local merchants and moneylenders supported by state institutions. They consider the elite supporters present in most such rebellions as marginal over the long term. The studies presented in this book, however, dovetail with John Harriss's (2011) central insight, based on gleaning a broad array of secondary research on the topic, that the goals of the Maoist leadership and peasant supporters are mutually incompatible. Harriss argues that, whereas economic and political grievances propel rebellions and peasants' trust supporting elites' capacity to genuinely represent them, the elite-driven strategy of using violence to attain the ultimate goal of capturing the state increases repression and undermines peasants' pragmatic goals of equitable development and political voice.

In terms of understanding institution formation in such societies, the most promising approach is to investigate the role of the dominant parties that came to control politics in Mexico, India, and Zimbabwe. Future research should test whether ruling elites create dominant parties to resolve the problem of policy instability that arises from broad elite coalitions. As Kenneth Arrow's (1951) seminal work explains, universal coalitions hinder the creation of specific policies because higher numbers of elites are required to form minimum winning coalitions.

Incumbent elites have two methods of creating stable policies: by empowering groups or individuals (such as legislative committees or career bureaucrats) to set agendas or force particular outcomes that can lead to increased policy stability (McKelvey 1979; Shepsle and Weingast 1981) or by selecting groups or individuals (such as a group of oligarchs or a president) who can act as veto players to dictate and override elites' preferences (Tsebelis 2002). These solutions can be institutionalized in dominant parties. With regard to membership, such parties represent incumbent elite classes, whether they are bourgeois or landowning; further, they include bureaucrats and are headed by presidents or prime ministers, thereby enabling them to "consign elite conflicts to intra-party disputes, supply strong incentives for elite coordination, and generate mechanisms for sanctioning defectors" (Smyth, Lowry, and Wilkening 2007).

Thus, dominant parties are not created by would-be dictators seeking to commit to power sharing with other political leaders and elite classes (Magaloni 2008; Reuter and Remington 2009). Rather, as is shown by the case studies presented here, dominant parties create dictators and authoritarian institutions to sustain elite-class agreements after extended conflicts are ended. Consequently, it is important for students of revolutions to remember that these conflicts were based on the aspirations and blood of the peasants, which such dominant parties ignored, co-opted, and repressed. These parties, as intermediary political organizations, then became not the bearers of popular interests but their cenotaphs, symbolizing the rebellions as their source of legitimacy, but burying the aspirations of the vast majority of poor peasants who started them.

References

Abimbola, Adesoji. 2010. "The Boko Haram Uprising and Islamic Revivalism in Nigeria." *Africa Spectrum* 45.2:95–108.

Acemoglu, Daron, Suresh Naidu, Pascual Restrepo, and James A. Robinson. 2015. "Democracy Does Cause Growth." Unpublished paper. http://economics.mit.edu/files/11227. Accessed April 20, 2016.

Acemoglu, Daron, and James A. Robinson. 2006. *The Economic Origins of Dictatorship and Democracy.* New York: Cambridge University Press.

———. 2008. "Persistence of Power, Elites, and Institutions." *American Economic Review* 98.1:267–293.

Aceves, Maria T. F. 2009. "José Guadalupe Zuno Hernández and the Revolutionary Process in Jalisco." In *State Governors in the Mexican Revolution, 1910–1952: Portraits in Conflict, Courage, and Corruption*, ed. Jürgen Buchenau and William H. Beezley, 95–108. Lanham, MD: Rowman and Littlefield.

Acharya, Poromesh. 1986. "Development of Modern Language Text-Books and the Social Context in 19th Century Bengal." *Economic and Political Weekly* 21.17:745–751.

———. 1989. "Education and Communal Politics in Bengal." *Economic and Political Weekly* 24.30:81–90.

Agiboba, Daniel E. 2013. "Why Boko Haram Exists: The Relative Deprivation Perspective." *African Conflict and Peacebuilding Review* 3.1:144–157.

Aguilar, Gustavo A. 2001. *Banca y desarrollo regional en Sinaloa: 1910–1994.* Mexico City: Alianza.

Aguilera Peña, Mario. 2014. *Guerrilla y población civil: Trayectoria de las FARC, 1949–2013.* Bogotá: Centro Nacional de Memoria Histórica and Instituto de Estudios Políticos, Universidad Nacional de Colombia.

Ahmad, Abul Mansur. 1970. *Amar Dakha Rajnitir Pachash Bachar.* Dhaka, Bangladesh: Naoroj Kitabistan.

Ahmed, Bashiruddin. 1966. "Communist and Congress Prospects in Kerala." *Asian Survey* 6.7:389–399.

Ahmed, Iftikhar, and John Timmons. 1971. "Current Land Reforms in East Pakistan." *Land Economics* 47.1:55–64.

Ahmed, Sufia. 1974. *Muslim Community in Bengal: 1884–1912.* Dhaka, Bangladesh: Oxford University Press.

Alao, Abiodun, John Mackinlay, and 'Funmi Olonisakin. 1999. *Peacekeeper, Politicians, and Warlords: The Liberian Peace Process.* New York: United Nations University Press.

Alavi, Hamza. 1988. "Pakistan and Islam: Ethnicity and Ideology." In *State and Ideology in the Middle East and Pakistan*, ed. Fred Halliday and Hamza Alavi, 64–111. New York: Monthly Review.

Alavi, Seema. 2011. "Fugitive Mullahs and Outlawed Fanatics: Indian Muslims in Nineteenth Century Trans-Asiatic Imperial Rivalries." *Modern Asian Studies* 45.6:1337–1382.

Ali, Imran. 1987. "Malign Growth? Agricultural Colonization and the Roots of Backwardness in the Punjab." *Past and Present* 114 (February): 110–132.

———. 1988. *The Punjab under Imperialism: 1885–1947.* Princeton, NJ: Princeton University Press.

Almada, Francisco R. 1964–1965. *La Revolución en el Estado de Chihuahua*, vol. 1. Chihuahua: Patronato del Instituto de Estudios Históricos de la Revolución Mexicana.

Altamirano, Graziella. 2000. "Confiscaciones revolucionarias en Durango." *Secuencia* 46:121–162.

Ambedkar, Bhimrao R. 1946. *Pakistan or the Partition of India*, 3d ed. Bombay: Thacker.

Anderson, Rodney D. 1974. "Mexican Workers and the Politics of Revolution, 1906–1911." *Hispanic American Historical Review* 54.1:94–113.

Ankerson, Dudley. 1984. *Agrarian Warlord: Saturnino Cedillo and the Mexican Revolution in San Luis Potosí.* Dekalb: Northern Illinois University Press.

Ansell, Ben W., and David J. Samuels. 2014. *Inequality and Democratization: An Elite Competition Approach.* New York: Cambridge University Press.

Appleby, R. Scott. 2000. *The Ambivalence of the Sacred: Religion, Violence, and Reconciliation.* Lanham, MD: Rowman and Littlefield.

———. 2003. "Retrieving the Missing Dimension of Statecraft: Religious Faith in the Service of Peacebuilding." In *Faith-Based Diplomacy: Trumping Realpolitik*, ed. Douglas Johnstons, 231–258. Oxford: Oxford University Press.

AP Television. 1976. "Switzerland and Rhodesia Conference: SYND 24 1976 Nkomo and Mugabe Arrive to Geneva for Rhodesia Conference and Deliver Statements," October 24. http://www.aparchive.com/metadata/youtube/c4313311df11f6abec1c1de571299d50.

Archivo General Agrario, Mexico City. n.d. Guadalupe Victoria, 23/170.

———. n.d. Ignacio, 23/692.

———. n.d. Pasaje, 23/75.

———. n.d. Peñón Blanco, 25/726.

Arnold, David. 1977. *The Congress in Tamilnad: Nationalist Politics in South India, 1919–1937.* London: Curzon.

Arnold, Ralph. 1921. "The Oil Situation: Production in United States and Mexico in Its Relation to Recent Drastic Cut in Price of Crude Oil Discussed at Petroleum and Gas Session on Feb. 16." *Mining and Metallurgy* 2.171:20–22.

Arora, Satish K. 1956. "The Reorganization of the Indian States." *Far Eastern Survey* 25.2:27–30.

Arrighi, Giovanni. 1966. "The Political Economy of Rhodesia," *New Left Review* 1.39:35–65.

Arrow, Kenneth. 1951. *Social Choice and Individual Values*. New York: Wiley.

Associated Press. 1914. News report 15/1464, Mexico City, September 7. Doc. 6 of 6, Manuscritos de Venustiano Carranza, Centro de Estudios de Historia de Mexico, Mexico City.

———. 1976. "Blacks Reject Kissinger Plan for Rhodesia," October 5.

Baden-Powell, Baden H. 1892a. *The Land-Systems of British India, Book 3: The System of Village or Mahál Settlements*. Oxford: Clarendon.

———. 1892b. *The Land-Systems of British India, Book 4: The Raiyatwari and Allied Systems*. Oxford: Clarendon.

Bagchi, Amiya K. 1972. *Private Investment in India, 1900–1939*. Cambridge: Cambridge University Press.

Bailey, David C. 1974. *Viva Cristo Rey! The Cristero Rebellion and the Church-State Conflict in Mexico*. Austin: University of Texas Press.

Baker, Christopher J. 1976. *The Politics of Southern India, 1920–1937*. Cambridge: Cambridge University Press.

———. 1984. *An Indian Rural Economy, 1880–1995: The Tamilnad Countryside*. New Delhi: Oxford University Press.

Bamford, P. C. 1925. *Histories of the Non-Cooperation and Khilafat Movements*. Delhi: Government of India Press.

Bandyopadhyay, Sekhar. 1990. "Community Formation and Communal Conflict: Namasudra-Muslim Riot in Jessore-Khulna." *Economic and Political Weekly* 25.46:2563–2568.

———. 1994. "From Alienation to Integration: Changes in the Politics of Caste in Bengal, 1937–1947." *Indian Economic Social History Review* 31.3:349–391.

———. 1998. "Changing Borders, Shifting Loyalties: Religion, Caste and the Partition of Bengal in 1947." Working Paper No. 2. Wellington, New Zealand: Asian Studies Institute, Victoria University of Wellington.

———. 2006. "Freedom and Its Enemies: Politics of Transition in West Bengal, 1947–1949." *Journal of South Asian Studies* 29.1:43–68.

Banerjee, Abhijit, and Lakshmi Iyer. 2005. "History, Institutions, and Economic Performance: The Legacy of Colonial Land Tenure Systems in India." *American Economic Review* 95.4:1190–1213.

Banerjee, Sukanya. 2010. *Becoming Imperial Citizens: Indians in the Late-Victorian Empire*. Durham, NC: Duke University Press.

Bardhan, Pranab, and Dilip Mookerjee. 2006. "Pro-poor Targeting and Accountability of Local Governments in West Bengal." *Journal of Development Economics* 79:303–327.

Barnett, Marguerite R. 1976. *The Politics of Cultural Nationalism in South India*. Princeton, NJ: Princeton University Press.

Barrier, N. Gerald. 1967a. "The Arya Samaj and Congress Politics in the Punjab, 1894–1908." *Journal of Asian Studies* 26.3:363–379.

———. 1967b. "The Punjab Disturbances of 1907: The Response of the British Government in India to Agrarian Unrest." *Modern Asian Studies* 1.4:353–383.

Basedau, Matthias, and Johannes Vüllers. 2010. "Religion and Armed Conflict in Sub-Saharan Africa, 1990 to 2008—Results from a New Database." Paper presented at the SGIR 7th Pan-European International Relations. Stockholm, September 9–11.

Bates, Robert, 1981. *Markets and States in Tropical Africa*. Berkeley: University of California Press.

———. 2001. *Prosperity and Violence*. New York: W. W. Norton.

———. 2009. *Prosperity and Violence*, 2d ed. New York: W. W. Norton.

Batista, Juan, and Teodoro Martinez. 1916. Letter 66/7332, January. Manuscritos de Venustiano Carranza, Centro de Estudios de Historia de México, Mexico City.
Bayly, Christopher A. 1970. "The Development of Political Organization in the Allahabad Locality, 1880–1925." PhD diss., Oxford University.
———. 2001. *Origins of Nationality in South Asia: Patriotism and Ethical Government in the Making of Modern India*. New York: Oxford University Press.
Bayly, Christopher, and Timothy Harper. 2005. *Forgotten Armies: The Fall of British Asia, 1941–1945*. Cambridge, MA: Harvard University Press.
Bayly, Susan. 1999. *Caste, Society and Politics in India: From the Eighteenth Century to the Modern Age*. New York: Cambridge University Press.
BBC News. 1977. "Smith Keeps Power in Rhodesia." August 31.
Beaglehole, T. H. 1977. "From Rulers to Servants: The I.C.S. and the British Demission of Power in India." *Modern Asian Studies* 11.2:237–255.
Beals, Carleton, 1932. *Porfirio Diaz: Dictador de México*. Philadelphia: J. R. Lippincott.
Beames, John. (1867) 1961. *Memoirs of a Bengal Civilian*. London: Chatto and Windus.
Behal, Rana P. 1985. "Forms of Labour Protest in Assam Valley Tea Plantations, 1900–1930." *Economic and Political Weekly* 20.4:19–26.
Behuria, Ashok K. 2010. "The Islamist Impulse Haunting Pakistan." *Strategic Analysis* 35.1:12–16.
Bell, F. O. 1948. "Parliamentary Election in Indian Provinces." *Parliamentary Affairs* 1.2:20–29.
Benford, Robert D., and David A. Snow. 2000. "Framing Processes and Social Movements: An Overview and Assessment." *Annual Review of Sociology* 26:611–639.
Benjamin, Thomas. 1980. "Revolución interrumpida—Chiapas y el interinato presidencial—1911." *Historia Mexicana* 30.1:79–98.
———. 1983. "Una historia poco gloriosa: Informe de Rafael Cal y Mayor al General Emiliano Zapata, 1917." *Historia Mexicana* 32.4:597–620.
———. (1989) 1996. A Rich Land, a Poor People: Politics and Society in Modern Chiapas. Albuquerque: University of New Mexico Press.
———. 2004. "¡Primero viva Chiapas! La revolución mexicana y las rebeliones locales." In *Los rumbos de otra historia*, 3d ed., ed. Juan Pedro Viqueria and Mario Humberto Ruiz, 175–193. Mexico City: Universidad Nacional Autónoma de México.
Benjamin, Thomas, and Mark Wasserman, eds. 1990. *Provinces of the Rebellion: Essays on Regional Mexican History 1910–1929*. Albuquerque: University of New Mexico Press.
Bernstorff, Dagmar. 1973. "Eclipse of 'Reddy Raj'? The Attempted Restructuring of the Congress Party Leadership in Andhra Pradesh." *Asian Survey* 13.1:959–979.
Besserer, Federico, Jose Diaz, and Raul Santana. 1980. "Formación y consolidación del sindicalismo minero en Cananea." *Revista Mexicana de Sociología* 42.4:1321–1353.
Beverly, Henry. 1874. "The Census of Bengal." *Journal of the Statistical Society of London* 37.1:69–113.
Bhagat, R. B. 2001. "Census and the Construction of Communalism in India." *Economic and Political Weekly* 36.46/47:4352–4356.
Bhagwati, Jagdish. 1985. "Indian Economic Policy and Performance: A Framework for a Progressive Society." In *Essays in Development Economics, Volume 1: Wealth and Poverty*, ed. Jagdish Bhagwati, 32–58. Cambridge, MA: MIT Press.
Bhattacharya, Jnanabrata. 1978. "An Examination of Leadership Entry in Bengal Peasant Revolts, 1937–1947." *Journal of Asian Studies* 37.4:611–635.

———. 1987. "Language, Class and Community in Bengal." *Comparative Studies of South Asia, Africa and the Middle East* 7.1–2:56–63.

Bhebe, Ngwabi. 1989. "The Nationalist Struggle, 1957–1962." In *Turmoil and Tenacity*, ed. Canaan Banana, 50–115. Harare, Zimbabwe: College Press.

———. 1999. *The ZAPU and ZANU Guerrilla Warfare and the Evangelical Lutheran Church in Zimbabwe*. Harare, Zimbabwe: Mambo.

Billings, Dwight B. 1990. "Religion as Opposition: A Gramscian Analysis." *American Journal of Sociology* 96.1:1–31.

Birla, Ghanshyam D. 1955. "Letter to Sir Tej Bahadur Sapru. London, October 31, 1931." In *In the Shadow of the Mahatma: A Personal Memoir*, ed. Ghanshyam D. Birla, 38–40. Calcutta: Orient Longmans.

"Birla Encourages Mill Laborers to Strike: Rural Participation in Delhi Agitation." 1986. F.24/Cong/42-D.1, August 17, 1942. In *Quit India Movement Secret Documents*, vol. 2, ed. P. N. Chopra, 134–135. New Delhi: Interprint.

Bisbee Daily Review. 1906. "Junta Admits Interest in Revolt," June 10, 16.

Biswas, A. K. 1995. "Paradox of Anti-Partition Agitation and Swadeshi Movement in Bengal (1905)." *Social Scientist* 23.4/6:38–57.

Bluntschli, Johann K. 1892. *Theory of the State*, 2d ed. Oxford: Clarendon.

Bohara, Alok K., and Neil J. Mitchell. 2006. "Opportunity, Democracy, and the Exchange of Political Violence: A Subnational Analysis of Conflict in Nepal." *Journal of Conflict Resolution* 50.1:108–128.

Boix, Carles. 2003. *Democracy and Redistribution*. New York: Cambridge University Press.

Bolt, William. 1771. *Considerations on Indian Affairs: Particularly Respecting the Present State of Bengal and Its Dependencies*, 2d ed. London: J. Almon.

Boone, Catherine. 2003. *Political Topographies of the African States: Territorial Authority and Institutional Choice*. New York: Cambridge University Press.

Bortz, Jeffrey. 2003. "Authority Re-seated: Control Struggles in the Textile Industry during the Mexican Revolution." *Labor History* 44.2:171–188.

Bose, Sugata. 1986. *Agrarian Bengal*. Cambridge: Cambridge University Press.

Bourdillon, Michael F. C. 1976. *The Shona Peoples: An Ethnography of the Contemporary Shona, with Special Reference to their Religion*. Salisbury (Harare), Zimbabwe: Mambo.

Bowen, Merle L. 2000. *The State against the Peasantry: Rural Struggles in Colonial and Postcolonial Mozambique*. Charlottesville: University of Virginia Press.

Brading, David A. 1975. *Estructura de la producción agrícola en el Bajío, 1700 a 1850*. Mexico City: Siglo Vientiuno.

Bradley, Ben. 1937. "The Indian Election." *Labour Monthly*, no. 4 (April): 237–239.

Brass, Paul R. 1970. "Muslim Separatism in United Provinces: Social Context and Political Strategy before Partition." *Economic and Political Weekly* 5.3–5:167–186.

———. 1981. "Congress, the Lok Dal, and the Middle-Peasant Castes: An Analysis of the 1977 and 1980 Parliamentary Elections in Uttar Pradesh." *Pacific Affairs* 54.1:5–41.

———. 1997. *Theft of an Idol*. Princeton, NJ: Princeton University Press.

Bratton, Michael. 2007. "Formal versus Informal Institutions in Africa." *Journal of Democracy* 18.3:96–110.

Bratton, Michael, and Nicholas Van de Walle. 1997. *Democratic Experiments in Africa: Regime Transitions in Comparative Perspective*. Cambridge: Cambridge University Press.

Brennan, Lance, 1972. "Political Change in Rohilkhand, 1932–1952." PhD diss., University of Sussex.

———. 1984. "The Illusion of Security: The Background to Muslim Separatism in the United Provinces." *Modern Asian Studies* 18.2:237–272.

Brewer, James C. 1963. "To Richard Nolte." Letter, November 25. Institute of Current World Affairs, Washington, DC. http://www.icwa.org/wp-content/uploads/2015/11/JCB-27.pdf.

Brewster, Keith. 2005. "*Caciquismo* in the Sierra Norte de Puebla: The Case of Gabriel Barrios Cabrera." In *Caciquismo in Twentieth-Century Mexico*, ed. Alan Knight and Wil Pansters, 113–130. London: Institute for the Study of Americas.

Brickhill, Jeremy. 1995. "Daring to Storm the Heavens: The Military Strategy of ZAPU, 1976–1979." In *Soldiers in Zimbabwe's Liberation War*, ed. Ngwabi Bhebe and Terence Ranger, 48–72. London: James Currey.

Brimmer, Andrew F. 1955. "The Setting of Entrepreneurship in India." *Quarterly Journal of Economics* 69.4:553–576.

British Broadcasting Corporation (BBC). 1972. "British Foreign Secretary Comments on Pearce Commission Findings in Rhodesia," Alec D. Home, to BBC reporter, 6393/72, Can 10705, May 23. BBC, London.

British Movietone. 1972. "Pearce Commission in Rhodesia," January 17. http://www.aparchive.com/metadata/youtube/b60ef5c4f09c4ae8939d8886162f6de5.

Brittain, James J. 2010. *Revolutionary Social Change in Colombia: The Origin and Direction of the FARC-EP*. New York: Pluto.

Broomfield, John H. 1968. *Elite Conflict in a Plural Society: Twentieth Century Bengal*. Berkeley: University of California Press.

Brown, Jonathan C. 1993. *Oil and Revolution in Mexico*. Berkeley: University of California Press.

Brown, Judith M. 1972. *Gandhi's Rise to Power: Indian Politics, 1915–1922*. Cambridge: Cambridge University Press.

Bruce, Robert. 1983. "Economic Change and Agrarian Organization in 'Dry' South India 1890–1940: A Reinterpretation." *Modern Asian Studies* 17.1:59–78.

Buchanan (Hamilton), Francis. 1833. *A Geographical, Statistical, and Historical Description of the District, or Zila, of Dinajpur, in the Province, or Soubah, of Bengal*. Calcutta: Baptist Mission Press.

Buchenau, Jürgen, and William H. Beezley, eds. 2009. *Governors in the Mexican Revolution*. Lanham, MD: Rowman and Littlefield.

Bueno de Mesquita, Bruce, George W. Downs, Alastair Smith, and Feryal M. Cherif. 2005. "Thinking inside the Box: A Closer Look at Democracy and Human Rights." *International Studies Quarterly* 49.3:439–457.

Burns, John F. 1979. "Muzorewa Names a Cabinet, Reserving Key Roles for Himself and Smith." *New York Times*, June 31. http://www.nytimes.com/1979/05/31/archives/muzorewa-names-a-cabinet-reserving-key-roles-for-himself-and-smith.html.

Burrows, Frederick J. 1980a. "To Field Marshall Viscount Wavell," March 19, 1947. In *The Transfer of Power: 1942–47*, vol. 9, ed. Nicholas Mansergh, 985–986. London: His Majesty's Stationery Office.

———. 1980b. "To Rear-Admiral Viscount Mountbatten of Burma," April 11, 1947. In *The Transfer of Power: 1942–47*, vol. 10, ed. Nicholas Mansergh, 203. London: His Majesty's Stationery Office.

Butler, Matthew. 1999. "The 'Liberal' Cristero: Ladislao Molina and the Cristero Rebellion in Michoacán, 1927–1929." *Journal of Latin American Studies* 31.3:645–671.

———. 2004. "The Church in 'Red Mexico': Michoacán Catholics and the Mexican Revolution, 1920–1929." *Journal of Ecclesiastical History* 55.3:520–541.

———. 2006. "Revolution and the Ritual Year: Religious Conflict and Innovation in Cristero Mexico." *Journal of Latin American Studies* 38.3:465–490.

Butler, S. Harcourt. 1906. *Oudh Policy: The Policy of Sympathy*. Allahabad, India: Pioneer.

Buve, Raymond T. J. 1988. "'Neither Carranza nor Zapata!': The Rise and Fall of a Peasant Movement That Tried to Challenge Both, Tlaxcala, 1910–19." In *Riot, Rebellion, and Revolution: Rural Social Conflict in Mexico*, 2d ed., ed. Friedrich Katz, 338–375. Princeton, NJ: Princeton University Press.

Byers, Bruce A., Robert N. Cunliffe, and Andrew T. Hudak. 2001. "Linking the Conservation of Culture and Nature: A Case Study of Sacred Forests in Zimbabwe." *Human Ecology* 29.2:187–218.

Cahill, Kevin J. 1998. "The U.S. Bank Panic of 1907 and the Mexican Depression of 1908–1909." *Historian* 60.4:795–811.

Calles, Plutarco E. (1928) 2002. "Mexico Must Become a Nation of Institutions and Laws." In *Mexico Reader: History, Culture, Politics*, ed. Gilbert M. Joseph and Timothy J. Henderson, 421–425. Durham, NC: Duke University Press.

Camin, Hector A. 1977. *La frontera nómada: Sonora y la Revolución Mexicana*. Mexico City: Siglo Veintiuno.

Capetillo, Alonso. 1925. *La rebelión sin cabeza: Génesis y desarrollo del Movimiento Delahuertista*. Mexico City: Botas.

Cárdenas, Enrique. 1994. *La hacienda pública y la política económica 1929–1958*. Mexico City: Colegio de México.

Cárdenas, Olga. 2000. "Amelia Robles y la revolución zapatista en el Estado de Guerrero." In *Estudios sobre el zapatismo*, ed. Laura Espejel López, 303–320. Mexico City: Instituto Nacional de Antropología e Historia.

Cardero, María E. 1977. "Evolución financiera de México: 1920–1932." *Revista Mexicana de Sociologia* 39.4:1335–1362.

Carr, Barry, 1973. "Las peculiaridades del norte mexicano, 1880–1927: Ensayo de interpretación." *Historia Mexicana* 22.3:320–346.

Carranza, Venustiano. 1916. "To Cabrera L." Letter 74/8097, April 16. Manuscritos de Venustiano Carranza, Centro de Estudios de Historia de México, Mexico City.

———. n.d.(a). Doc. 12/13693. Manuscritos de Venustiano Carranza, Centro de Estudios de Historia de México, Mexico City.

———. n.d.(b). "To Unknown. Subject: Ley Agraria Complementaria del Estado de Yucatán, Bases Generales." Letter 150/17068. Manuscritos de Venustiano Carranza, Centro de Estudios de Historia de Mexico, Mexico City.

Carras, Mary C. 1971. "Congress Factionalism at the State and District Level in Maharashtra: Some Theories." *Economic and Political Weekly* 6.3/5:325–340.

Carriedo, Roberto. 2005. "The Man Who Tamed Mexico's Tiger: General Joaquin Amaro and the Professionalization of Mexico's Revolutionary Army." PhD diss., University of New Mexico, Albuquerque.

Casahonda Castillo, José. 1963. *50 años de revolución en Chiapas*. Tuxtla Gutiérrez: Instituto de Ciencias y Artes de Chiapas.

Castellano, Isaac M. 2015. *Civil War Interventions and Their Benefits: Unequal Return*. Lanham, MD: Lexington.

Castro, Pedro. 2002. "Antonio Díaz Soto y Gama, agrarista." *Investigación y Análisis Sociopolítico y Psicosocial*, no. 2:257–282.

Catanach, I. J. 1970. *Rural Credit in Western India: Rural Credit and the Co-operative Movement in the Bombay Presidency, 1875–1930*. Berkeley: University of California Press.

Cell, John Whitson. 1992. *Hailey: A Study in British Imperialism, 1872–1969*. New York: Cambridge University Press.

Centeno, Miguel A. 1994. *Democracy within Reason: Technocratic Revolution in Mexico*. University Park: Pennsylvania State University.

Cerutti, Mario. 2000. *Propietarios, empresarios y empresa en el norte de México*. Mexico City: Siglo Veintiuno.

Cervantes, Luis G. 1916. "To Venustiano Carranza, March 1, Letter 69/7531." In *Manuscritos de Venustiano Carranza*. Mexico City: Centro de Estudios de Historia de México.

Chakrabarty, Bidyut. 1985. "Peasants and the Bengal Congress, 1928–1938." *South Asia Research* 5.1:29–47.

———. 1989. "The Communal Award of 1932 and its Implications in Bengal." *Modern Asian Studies* 23.2:493–523.

———. 1990. *Subhas Chandra Bose and Middle Class Radicalism: A Study in Indian Nationalism, 1928–1940*. London: I. B. Tauris.

———. 2004. The *Partition of Bengal and Assam, 1932–1947: Contour of Freedom*. London: Routledge Curzon, 2004.

Chance, John K. 1978. *Race and Class in Colonial Oaxaca*. Stanford, CA: Stanford University Press.

Chand, Tara. 1983. *History of the Freedom Movement in India*, vol. 3. New Delhi: Publications Division, Ministry of Information and Broadcasting.

Chassen, Francie R. 2005. "Los precursos de la revolución en Oaxaca." In *La revolución en Oaxaca, 1910–1930*, ed. Víctor Raúl Martínez Vázquez, 25–73. Oaxaca, Mexico: Instituto Estatal de Educación Pública de Oaxaca.

Chassen-López, Francie R. 2004. *From Liberal to Revolutionary Oaxaca: The View from the South, Mexico 1867–1911*. University Park: Pennsylvania State University Press.

Chatterjee, Partha. 1975. "Bengal: Rise and Growth of a Nationality." *Social Scientist* 4.1:67–82.

———. 1982. "Agrarian Structure in Pre-partition Bengal." In *Perspective in Social Sciences*, vol. 2, 113–225. Calcutta, Oxford University Press.

———. 1986. "The Colonial State and Peasant Resistance in Bengal, 1920–1947." *Past and Present* 110 (February): 169–204.

Chatterji, Basudev. 1992. *Trade, Tariffs, and Empire: Lancashire and British Policy in India, 1919–1939*. Delhi: Oxford University Press.

Chatterji, Joya. 1994. *Bengal Divided: Hindu Communalism and Partition, 1932–1947*. Cambridge: Cambridge University Press.

———. 2002. *Bengal Divided: Hindu Communalism and Partition, 1932–1947*, 2d ed. Cambridge: Cambridge University Press.

Chaudhuri, Buddhadeb. (1983) 2005. "Agrarian Relations: Eastern India." In *The Cambridge Economic History of India*, vol. 2, ed. Dharma Kumar and Meghnad Desai, 86–176. Cambridge: Cambridge University Press.

Chaudhuri, Kirti N. (1983) 2005. "Foreign Trade and Balance of Payments (1757–1947)." In *The Cambridge Economic History of India*, vol. 2, ed. Dharma Kumar and Meghnad Desai, 804–877. Cambridge: Cambridge University Press.

Chávez, Alicia H. 1984. "Militares y negocios en la Revolución Mexicana." *Historia Mexicana* 34.2:181–212.

Chevalier, Francois. 1960. "Un factor decisivo de la revolución agraria en México: El levantamiento de Zapata (1911–1919)." *Cuadernos Americanos* 113.6:165–187.
Chibber, Vivek. 2003. *Locked in Place: State Building and Late Industrialization in India*. Princeton, NJ: Princeton University Press.
Chicago Tribune. 1976. "Hint Rhodesia Ready to OK Kissinger Plan." September 23.
Chichicastepec, Municipio Mixitlán. n.d. 267.1/1277. Archivo General Agrario, Mexico City, box 19, folder 1.
Chimhanda, Christopher C. 2003. "ZAPU and the Liberation Struggle in Zimbabwe." Master's thesis, University of Cape Town.
Chiriyankandath, James. 2001. "Democracy under the Raj: Elections and Separate Representation in British India." In *Democracy in India*, ed. Niraja G. Jayal, 53–81. Delhi: Oxford University Press.
Chongo, Clarence. 2015. "Decolonizing Southern Africa: A History of Zambia's Role in Zimbabwe's Liberation Struggle, 1964–1979." Master's thesis, University of Pretoria.
Cilliers, Jakkie K. 1985. *Counter-insurgency in Rhodesia*. London: Croom Helm, 1985.
Cingranelli, David, and Mikhail Filippov. 2010. "Electoral Rules and Incentives to Protect Human Rights." *Journal of Politics* 72.1:243–257.
Clarke, D. G. 1980. "Zimbabwe's International Economic Position and Aspects of Sanctions Removal." *Journal of Commonwealth and Comparative Politics* 18.1:28–54.
Coatsworth, John. 1978. "Obstacles to Economic Growth in Nineteenth-Century Mexico." *American Historical Review* 83.1:80–100.
Cockcroft, James D. 1967. "El maestro de primaria en la Revolución Mexicana." *Historia Mexicana* 16.4:565–587.
Cohen, Stephen P. 2004. *The Idea of Pakistan*. Washington, DC: Brookings Institution Press.
Cohn, Bernard S. 1969. "Structural Change in Indian Rural Society." In *Land Control and Social Structure in Indian History*, ed. Eric R. Frykenberg, 53–122. Madison: University of Wisconsin Press.
Collett, Nigel. 2005. *The Butcher of Amritsar: Colonel Reginal Dyer*. London: Hambledon Continuum.
Collier, Paul. 2000. "Doing Well out of War: An Economic Perspective." In *Greed and Grievance: Economic Agendas in Civil Wars*, ed. Mats Berdal and David Malone, 91–112. London: Lynne Rienner.
Collier, Paul, and Anke Hoeffler. 2000. "Greed and Grievance in Civil War." *Policy Working Paper, 2135*. Washington, DC: World Bank.
Collier, Ruth B., and David Collier. 1991. *Shaping the Political Arena: Critical Junctures, the Labor Movement, and Regime Dynamics in Latin America*. Princeton: Princeton University Press.
Contreras, Marcelino, and Eduviges Duran. 1916. Letter 65/7203, January 11. Manuscritos de Venustiano Carranza, Centro de Estudios de Historia de México, Mexico City.
Cooper, Adrienne. 1988. *Sharecropping and Sharecroppers' Struggles in Bengal, 1930–1950*. Calcutta: K. P. Bagchi.
Copland, Ian. 2002. "The Master and the Maharajas: The Sikh Princes and the East Punjab Massacres of 1947." *Modern Asian Studies* 36.3:657–704.
Cowell, Alan. 1983. "Zimbabwe Tries 6 Officers as Saboteurs." *New York Times*, May 24. http://www.nytimes.com/1983/05/24/world/zimbabwe-tries-6-officers-as-saboteurs.html.
Cozzi, Graziella A. 2010. *De las buenas familias de Durango: Parentesco, fortuna y poder, 1880–1920*. Mexico City: Instituto de Investigaciones Dr. José María Luis Mora.

Craik, Sir Henry (governor of Punjab). 1939. "The Viceroy of India, Lord Linlithgow." Letter R/3/1/61, September 13. India Office Records, London, January–December 1939.

Crane, Robert I. 1951. "The Indian National Congress and the Indian Agrarian Problem, 1919–1939." PhD diss., Yale University, New Haven, CT.

Crawley, William F. 1971. "Kisan Sabhas and Agrarian Revolt in the United Provinces 1920 to 1921." *Modern Asian Studies* 5.2:95–109.

Dale, Stephen F. 1977. "The Islamic Frontier in Southwest India: The Shahid as a Cultural Ideal among the Mappilas of Malabar." *Modern Asian Studies* 11.1:41–55.

Das, Arvind N. 1983. *Agrarian Unrest and Socio-economic Changes in Bihar, 1900–1980.* Delhi: Manohar.

Das, Suranjan. 1990. "Communal Violence in Twentieth Century Bengal: An Analytical Framework." *Social Scientist* 18.6/7:21–37.

Davenport, Christian, and David A. Armstrong. 2004. "Democracy and the Violation of Human Rights: A Statistical Analysis from 1976 to 1996." *American Journal of Political Science* 48.3:538–554.

De, Amalendu. 1977. "Bengali Intelligentsia's Attitudes to the Permanent Settlement." *Social Scientist* 5.8:18–40.

———. 1995. "The Social Thoughts and Consciousness of the Bengali Muslims in the Colonial Period." *Social Scientist* 23.4/6:16–37.

De Bonfil, Alicia O. S. 1966. *Aspectos del conflicto religioso de 1926 a 1929: Sus antecedentes y consecuencias.* Mexico City: Instituto Nacional de Antropología e Historia.

De Juan, Alexander. 2008. "A Pact with the Devil? Elite Alliances as Bases of Violent Religions Conflicts." *Studies in Conflict and Terrorism* 31.12:1120–1135.

De Juan, Alexander, and Johannes Vüllers. 2010. "Religious Peace Activism—the Rational Element of Religious Elites' Decision-Making Processes." Working Paper no. 130, April. German Institute for Global and Area Studies, Hamburg.

De Koning, Ruben. 2012. "The Big Men Commanding Conflict Resources in Africa: the DRC Case." In *African Conflicts and Informal Power: Big Men and Networks*, ed. Mats Utas, 224–247. London: Zed Books.

Del Angel, Gustavo A., and Carlos Marichal. 2003. "Poder y crisis: Historiografía reciente del crédito y la banca en México, siglos XIX y XX." *Historia Mexicana* 52.3:677–724.

De la Peña Marshall, Ricardo 2005. "Historia de la ganadería en Tabasco, de la conquista al Garridismo." In *Anuario de historia de la Universidad Juárez Autónoma de Tabasco*, vol. 1, 27–58. Villahermosa, Mexico: División Académica de Ciencias Sociales y Humanidades, Programa Integral de Fortalecimiento Institucional, Cuerpo Académico de Historia, Cultura y Vida Cotidiana, Secretaria de Educación Pública.

Delap, Mick. 1979. "The April 1979 Elections in Zimbabwe-Rhodesia." *African Affairs* 78.313:431–438.

De la Pedraja, René. 2006. *Wars of Latin America, 1899–1941.* Jefferson, NC: McFarland.

del Cid Gómez, Juan M. 2010. "A Financial Profile of the Terrorism of Al-Qaeda and Its Affiliates." *Perspectives on Terrorism* 4.4:3–27.

Desai, Sonalde, and Veena Kulkarni. 2008. "Changing Educational Inequalities in India in the Context of Affirmative Action." *Demography* 45.2:245–270.

Deshpande, Prachi. 2004. "Caste as Maratha: Social Categories, Colonial Policy and Identity in Early Twentieth-Century Maharashtra." *Indian Economic and Social History Review* 41.1:7–32.

DeVotta, Neil. 2000. "Control Democracy, Institutional Decay, and the Quest for Eelam: Explaining Ethnic Conflict in Sri Lanka." *Pacific Affairs* 73.1:55–76.

Dewey, Clive J. 1972. "The Official Mind and the Problem of Agrarian Indebtedness in India, 1870–1910." PhD diss., Cambridge University.

———. 1993. *Anglo-Indian Attitudes: The Mind of the Indian Civil Service*. London: Hambledon.

Dhar, Hiranmay. 2000. "Institutional Constraints to Land Reforms in Bihar." In *Land Reforms in India, Volume 5: An Unfinished Agenda*, ed. B. K. Sinha and Pushpendra, 124–138. Delhi: Sage.

Dhulipala, Venkat. 2016. *Creating a New Medina: State Power, Islam, and the Quest for Pakistan in Late Colonial North India*. New York: Cambridge University Press.

Díaz Soto y Gama, Antonio. 1959. *La cuestión agraria en México*. Mexico City: Universidad Nacional Autónoma de México.

Dietrich, Christopher. 2013. "The Sustenance of Salisbury in the era of Decolonization: The Portuguese Politics of Neutrality and the Rhodesian Oil Embargo, 1965–1967," *International History Review* 35.2:235–255.

Douglass, North C. 1991. "Institutions." *Journal of Economic Perspectives* 5.1:97–112.

Dréze, Jean, and Amartya Sen. 1988. *India, Economic Development and Social Opportunity*. Oxford: Clarendon.

Dulles, John W. F. 1961. *Yesterday in México: A Chronicle of the Revolution, 1919–1936*. Austin: University of Texas Press.

Duyvesteyn, Isabelle. 2005. *Clausewitz and African War: Politics and Strategy in Liberia and Somalia*. London: Frank Cass/ Routledge, Cass Military Studies Series.

The Economist. 1977. "A Siding Near the Road's End," December 3, 85–86.

Edelman, Marc. 2005. "Bringing the Moral Economy back in . . . to the Study of 21st-Century Transnational Peasant Movements." *American Anthropologist* 107.3:331–345.

Eisinger, Peter K. 1973. "The Condition of Protest Behavior in American Cities." *American Political Science Review* 67.1:11–28.

Elder, Joseph W. 1962. "Land Consolidation in an Indian Village: A Case Study of the Consolidation of Holdings Act in Uttar Pradesh." *Economic Development and Cultural Change* 11.1:16–40.

Ellis, Stephen, and Gerrie ter Haar. 2004. *Worlds of Power: Religious Thought and Political Practice in Africa*. New York: Oxford University Press.

———. 2007. "Religion and Politics: Taking African Epistemologies Seriously." *Journal of Modern African Studies* 45.3:385–401.

Emerson, Stephen A. 2014. *The Battle for Mozambique: The Frelimo-Renamo Struggle, 1977–1992*. Solihull, UK: Helion.

Erdman, Howard L. 1967. *The Swatantra Party and Indian Conservatism*. Cambridge: Cambridge University Press.

Estado de Coahuila, Comisión de Gobernación y Justicia. 1912. *Periódico Oficial*, April 3, file 1. Saltillo, Mexico: Archivo Poder Legislativo de Coahuila.

Estado de México. n.d. Santa Maria Jajalpa, Municipio Tenando del Valle, 23/10981. Archivo General Agrario, Mexico City.

Everingham, Mark. 1996. *Revolution and the Multiclass Coalition in Nicaragua*. Pittsburgh: University of Pittsburgh Press.

Fábregas, Andrés. 1979. "Los Altos de Jalisco: Caracteristicas generales." In *El Movimiento Cristero: Sociedad y conflicto en los Altos de Jalisco*, ed. José Díaz Estrella and Román Rodríguez Cruz, 11–92. Mexico City: Nueva Imagen.

Fair, Christine C. 2005. "Diaspora Involvement in Insurgencies: Insights from the Khalistan and Tamil Eelam Movements." *Nationalism and Ethnic Politics* 11.1:125–156.

Falcón, Romana. 1986. *La semilla en el surco: Adalaberto Tejeda y el radicalismo en Veracruz, 1883–1960*. Mexico City: Colegio de México.

———. 1988. "Esplendor y ocaso de los caciques militares: San Luis Potosí en la revolución mexicana." *Mexican Studies/Estudios Mexicanos* 4.2:265–293.

———. 1998. "Introduccíon: Cuautitlán y don Porfirio." In *Don Porfirio presidente . . . , nunca omnipotente: Hallazgos, reflexiones y debates, 1876–1911*, ed. Romana Falcón and Raymond Buve, 13–38. Mexico City: Universidad Iberoamericana, Departamento de Historia.

———. 2004. "Carisma y tradición: Consideraciones en torno a los liderazgos campesinos en la revolución mexicana: El caso de San Luis Potosí." In *Riot, Rebellion, and Revolution: Rural Social Conflict in Mexico*, 2d ed., ed. Friedrich Katz, 89–112. Princeton, NJ: Princeton University Press.

Fay, Albert H. 1911. *The Mining Industry during 1901*, vol. 19. New York: McGraw-Hill.

Fearon, James D. 2004. "Why Do Some Civil Wars Last So Much Longer than Others?" *Journal of Peace Research* 4.3:275–301.

Fearon, James D., and David D. Laitin. 2000. Violence and the Social Construction of Ethnic Identity. *International Organization* 54.4:845–877.

Federal Reserve Bulletin. 1929. "Foreign Exchange Rates, 1922–1928: Yearly Averages." January 1929. https://fraser.stlouisfed.org/files/docs/publications/FRB/pages/1925-1929/28191_1925-1929.pdf.

Ferguson, William. 2006. *Global Shadows: Africa in the Neoliberal World Order*. Durham, NC: Duke University Press.

Figueroa, Francisco. 1965. "To Francisco Madero [November 11, 1911]." In *Documentos históricos de la revolución mexicana: Revolución y régimen maderista*, vol. 2, ed. Isidro Fabela, 264–266. Mexico City: Jus.

Figueroa, Julio R. 2002. *Siglo XX: Muerte y resurrección de la iglesia católica en Chiapas*. Chiapas, Mexico: Programa de Investigaciones Multidisciplinarias, Universidad Nacional Autónoma de México.

Findley, Michael G. 2013. "Bargaining and the Interdependent Stages of Civil War Resolution." *Journal of Conflict Resolution* 57.5:905–932.

Floud, Francis. 1941. *Report of the Land Revenue Commission, Bengal, 1938–1940*, vol. 1. Calcutta: Superintendent of Government Printing, Bengal.

Flower, Ken. 1987. *Serving Secretly: An Intelligence Chief on Record: Rhodesia into Zimbabwe, 1964–1981*. London: John Murray.

Fondo Genovevo de la O. n.d. Box 122, folder 2, p. 17, box 124, folder 2, pp. 36–37. Archivo General de la Nación, Mexico City.

Forrester, Duncan. 1976. "Factions and Filmstars: Tamil Nadu Politics since 1971." *Asian Survey* 16.3:283–296.

Fox, Richard G. 1985. *Lions of the Punjab: Culture in the Making*. Berkeley: University of California Press.

Francis, W. 1908. *Imperial Gazetteer of India, Provincial Series: Madras*, vol. 2. Calcutta: Superintendent of Government Printing.

Franda, Marcus. 1968. "West Bengal." In *State Politics in India*, ed. Myron Weiner, 247–320. Princeton, NJ: Princeton University Press.

Franklin, Henry. 1963. *Unholy Wedlock: The Failure of the Central African Federation*. London: G. Allen and Unwin.

Fry, Peter. 1976. *Spirits of Protest: Spirit: Mediums and the Articulation of Consensus amongst the Zezuru of Southern Rhodesia*. Cambridge: Cambridge University Press.

Fukazawa, H. (1983) 2005. "The Land and the People: Western India." In *The Cambridge Economic History of India*, vol. 2, ed. Dharma Kumar and Meghnad Desai, 177–206. Cambridge: Cambridge University Press.

Gait, E. A. 1902. *Report on the Census of India, 1901, Volume 6: The Lower Provinces of Bengal and their Feudatories*, pt. 1. Calcutta: Bengal Secretariat Press.

Gait, E. A., B. C. Allen, and H. F. Howard. 1909. *Imperial Gazetteer of India, Provincial Series: Eastern Bengal and Assam*. Calcutta: Superintendent of Government Printing.

Gallagher, John. 1973. "Congress in Decline: Bengal, 1930 to 1939." *Modern Asian Studies* 7.3:589–645.

Gamboa, Federico, Tuxtla Gutiérrez, Chiapas. 1912. Letter to Francisco I. Madero, Mexico City, January 10. Francisco Madero Collection, Archivo General de la Nación, Mexico City, box 14, folder 324.1, p. 010466.

Garcia, Jonathan, and Richard G. Parker. 2011. "Resource Mobilization for Health Advocacy: Afro-Brazilian Religious Organizations and HIV Prevention and Control." *Social Science and Medicine* 72.12:1930–1938.

García de León, Antonio. 1994. *Resistencia y utopía: Memorial de agravios y crónica de revueltas y profecías acaecidas en la provincia de Chiapas durante los últimos quinientos años de su historia*, 2d ed. Mexico City: Era.

Garner, Paul. 1985. "Federalism and Caudillismo in the Mexican Revolution: The Genesis of the Oaxaca Sovereignty Movement (1915–1920)." *Journal of Latin American Studies* 17.1:111–113.

———. 1990. "Oaxaca: The Rise and Fall of State Sovereignty." In *Provinces of the Revolution: Essays on Regional Mexican History, 1910–1929*, ed. Thomas Benjamin and Mark Wasserman, 163–184. Albuquerque: University of New Mexico Press.

Garrido, Luis J. 1986. *El partido de la revolución institucionalizada*. Mexico City: Siglo Veintiuno.

Gent, Stephen E. 2011. "Relative Rebel Strength and Power Sharing in Intrastate Conflicts." *International Interactions* 37.2:215–228.

George, Alexander L., and Andrew Bennett. 2004. *Case Studies and Theory Development in the Social Sciences*. Cambridge, MA: Belfer Center for Science and International Affairs and MIT Press.

Gerdes, Felix. 2013. *Civil War and State Formation: The Political Economy of War and Peace in Liberia*. Frankfurt: Campus.

Gerring, John, Philip Bond, William T. Barndt, and Carola Moreno. 2005. "Democracy and Economic Growth: A Historical Perspective." *World Politics* 57.3:323–364.

Ghosh, Shyamali. 1974. "Fazlul Haq and Muslim Politics in Pre-Partition Bengal." *International Studies* 13.3:441–464.

Gilmartin, David. 1998. "A Magnificent Gift: Muslim Nationalism and the Election Process in Colonial Punjab." *Comparative Studies in Society and History* 40.3:415–436.

Ginzberg, Eitan. 2000. "Formación de la infraestructura política para una reforma agraria radical: Adalberto Tejeda y Cuestión Municipal en Veracruz, 1928–1932." *Historia Mexicana* 49.4:673–727.

Gleijeses, Piero. 2002. *Conflicting Missions: Havana, Washington, and Africa*. Chapel Hill: University of North Carolina Press.

———. 2013. *Visions of Freedom: Havana, Washington, Pretoria, and the Struggle for Southern Africa, 1976–1991*. Chapel Hill: University of North Carolina Press.

Godwin, Peter, and Ian Hancock. 1993. *"Rhodesians Never Die": The Impact of War and Political Change on White Rhodesia, c. 1970–1980.* London: Pan Macmillan.

Gómez-Galvarriato, Aurora, and Gabriella Recio. 2007. "The Indispensable Service of Banks: Commercial Transactions, Industry, and Banking in Revolutionary Mexico." *Enterprise and Society* 8.1:68–115.

González, Valentín L. 1980. *Los compañeros de Zapata.* Mexico City: Ediciones de Gobierno del Estado Libre y Soberano de Morelos.

Good, Robert C. 1973. *U.D.I.: The International Politics of the Rhodesian Rebellion.* London: Faber and Faber.

Goswami, Omkar. 1987. "Changes in Industrial Control in Eastern India 1930–1950: An Exploratory Essay." In *Myth and Reality: The Struggle for Freedom in India, 1945–1947,* ed. Amit K. Gupta, 172–196. New Delhi: Manohar.

———. 1989. "Sahibs, Babus, and Banias: Changes in Industrial Control in Eastern India, 1918–1950." *Journal of Asian Studies* 48.2:289–309.

Gough, Kathleen. 1968–1969. "Peasant Resistance and Revolt in South India." *Pacific Affairs* 41.4:526–544.

———. 1981. *Rural Society in Southeast India.* Cambridge: Cambridge University Press.

Gould, Harold, 1984. "Politics of Agrarian Unrest in UP: Who Co-Opted Whom?" *Economic and Political Weekly* 19.49:2084–2088.

Graham, John. 2005. "Britain and Rhodesia: Route to Settlement," ed. Michael Kandia and Sue Onslow. Seminar held at the Institute of Contemporary British History, Cold War Studies Centre, London School of Economics, National Archives of the United Kingdom, Richmond, UK, July 5. https://www.kcl.ac.uk/sspp/departments/icbh/witness/PDFfiles/Rhodesia2.pdf.

Greene, Kenneth. 2007. *Why Dominant Parties Lose: Mexico's Democratization in Comparative Perspective.* New York: Cambridge University Press.

Greenhill, Kelly M., and Major Solomon. 2006. "The Perils of Profiling: Civil War Spoilers and the Collapse of Intrastate Peace Accords." *International Security* 31.3:7–40.

Greenough, Paul. 1982. *Prosperity and Misery in Modern Bengal.* New York: Oxford University Press.

Grewal, J. S. 1990. *The New Cambridge History of India: The Sikhs of the Punjab.* Cambridge: Cambridge University Press.

Griffiths, Percival. 1967. *The History of the Indian Tea Industry.* London: W. Clowes and Sons.

Gupta, Bishnupriya. 1997. "Collusion in the Indian Tea Industry in the Great Depression: An Analysis of Panel Data." *Explorations in Economic History* 34.2:155–173.

Gupta, Prasanta S. 1982. "The Congress Party in West Bengal: A Study of Factionalism, 1947–1967." PhD diss., Calcutta University.

Haber, Stephen H. 1992. "Assessing the Obstacles to Industrialization: The Mexican Economy, 1830–1940." *Journal of Latin American Studies* 24.1:1–32.

Haber, Stephen, Armando Razo, and Noel Maurer. 2003. *The Politics of Property Rights: Political Instability, Credible Commitments, and Economic Growth in Mexico, 1876–1929.* New York: Cambridge University Press.

Haber, Stephen, and Laura E. P. Varela. 1993. "La industrialización de México: Historiografía y análisis." *Historia Mexicana* 42.3:649–688.

Hacchethu, Krishna, 2008–2009. "The Communist Party of Nepal (Maoist): Transformation from an Insurgency Group to a Competitive Political Party." *European Bulletin of Himalayan Research,* nos. 33–34:39–71.

Haldar, Gopal. 1986. *A Comparative Grammar of East Bengal Dialects*. Calcutta: Puthipatra.

Hall, Linda. 1995. *Oil, Banks, and Politics: The United States and Postrevolutionary Mexico, 1917–1924*. Austin: University of Texas Press.

Hall, Linda, and Don M. Carver. 1984. "Oil and the Mexican Revolution: The Southwestern Connection." *The Americas* 41.2:229–244.

Hall, Margaret. 1990. "The Mozambican National Resistance Movement (RENAMO): A Study in the Destruction of an African Country." *Africa* 60.1:39–68.

Hansen, Thomas B. 2001. *Wages of Violence: Naming and Identity in Postcolonial Bombay*. Princeton, NJ: Princeton University Press.

Hardgrave, Robert. 1977. "The Mappilla Rebellion, 1921: Peasant Revolt in Malabar." *Modern Asian Studies* 11.1:57–99.

Harriss, John. 1993. "What Is Happening in Rural West Bengal? Agrarian Reform, Growth and Distribution." *Economic and Political Weekly* 28.24:1237–1247.

———. 2011. "What Is Going On in India's 'Red Corridor'? Questions about India's Maoist Insurgency—Literature Review." *Pacific Affairs* 84.2:309–327.

Hart, John M. 1987. *Revolutionary Mexico: The Coming and Process of the Mexican Revolution*. Berkeley: University of California Press.

Hartzell, Caroline, Matthew Hoddie, and Donald Rothchild. 2001. "Stabilizing the Peace after Civil War: An Investigation of Some Key Variables." *International Organization* 55.1 (Winter): 183–208.

Hartzell, Caroline, and Matthew Hoddie. 2007. *Crafting Peace: Power Sharing Institutions and the Negotiated Settlement of Civil Wars*. University Park: Pennsylvania State University Press.

Hasan, Mushirul. 1980. "Communalism in the Provinces: A Case Study of Bengal and the Punjab, 1922–1926." *Economic and Political Weekly* 15.33:1395–1406.

Hasenclever, Andreas, and Volker Rittberger. 2003. "Does Religion Make a Difference? Theoretical Approaches to the Impact of Faith on Political Conflict." In *Religion in International Relations: The Return from Exile*, ed. Pavlos Hatzopolous and Fabio Petito, 107–146. New York: Palgrave Macmillan.

Hashmi, Taj-ul-Islam. 1988. "The Communalization of Class Struggle: East Bengal Peasantry, 1923–1929." *Indian Economic and Social History Review* 25:171–204.

———. 1992. *Pakistan as Peasant Utopia: The Communalization of Class Politics in Eastern Bengal, 1920–1947*. Boulder, CO: Westview.

Hastings, Adrian. 1997. *The Construction of Nationhood: Ethnicity, Religion, and Nationalism*. Cambridge: Cambridge University Press.

Hauser, Walter, 1961. "The Bihar Kisan Sabha, 1929–1949: A Study of an Indian Peasant Movement." PhD diss., University of Chicago.

Haynes, Douglas E. 2012. *Small Town Capitalism in Western India: Artisans, Merchants and the Making of the Informal Economy, 1870–1960*. New York: Cambridge University Press.

Helmke, Gretchen, and Steven Levitsky. 2004. "Informal Institutions and Comparative Politics: A Research Agenda." *Perspectives on Politics* 2.4:725–740.

Henshaw, Peter J. 1996. "Britain, South Africa and the Sterling Area: Gold Production, Capital Investment and Agricultural Markets, 1931–1961." *Historical Journal* 39.1:197–223.

Herrera, María del Carmen C. 1996. *Empresarios y políticos: Entre la restauración y la revolución*. Mexico City: Instituto Nacional de Estudios de la Revolución Mexicana.

Herrera Cruz, Miriam. 2011. "El movimiento de soberanía en la Mixteca de Oaxaca (1915–1920): Una muestra de la diversidad regional." Paper presented at the Segundo Congreso Nacional de Estudios Regionales y la Multidisciplinariedad en la Historia, Tlaxcala, Mexico, September 28–30.

Herring, Ronald J. 1989. "Dilemmas of Agrarian Communism: Peasant Differentiation, Sectoral and Village Politics." *Third World Quarterly* 11.1:89–115.

Hindus of Bengal. 1936. "To Secretary of State for India, Lord Zetland." Letter C/80, June 4. Hindu Mahasabha Papers, Nehru Memorial Museum Library, New Delhi.

Hitchcock, R. H. 1925. *A History of the Malabar Rebellion, 1921.* Madras, India: Government Press.

Hodder-Williams, Richard. 1980. "Political Scenarios and Their Economic Implications." *Journal of Commonwealth and Comparative Politics* 18.1:55–68.

Hoddie, Matthew, and Caroline A. Hartzell. 2003. "Civil War Settlements and the Implementation of Military Power-Sharing Arrangements." *Journal of Peace Research* 40.3 (May): 303–320.

———. 2005. "Signals of Reconciliation: Institutions-Building and the Resolution of Civil Wars." *International Studies Review* 7.1:21–40.

Hogden, W. Murray. 1981. "An Imperial Dilemma: The Reluctant Indianization of the Indian Political Service." *Modern Asian Studies* 15.4:751–769.

Horowitz, Dan. 1970. "Attitudes of British Conservatives towards Decolonization in Africa." *African Affairs* 69.274:9–26.

Horvath, Gyula. 1997. "La Apertura Política en México." In *Estudios sobre transiciones democr*áticas en América Latina, ed. Adam Anderle and José Girón, 23–28. Oviedo, Spain: Universidad de Oviedo.

Hostetter, Luis, American Consul at Hermosillo, Mexico. 1913a. To Secretary of State. Telegram, March 6. Records of the Department of State Relating to Internal Affairs of Mexico, 1910–1939. General Records of the U.S. Department of State, file no. 812.00/6522, Record Group (RG) 59, U.S. National Archives and Records Administration (hereafter, NARA).

———. 1913b. To Secretary of State. Letter, March 17. Records of the Department of State Relating to Internal Affairs of Mexico, 1910-1939. General Records of the U.S. Department of State. File No. 812.00/6855, RG 59, NARA.

———. 1913c. To Secretary of State. Letter, March 18. Records of the Department of State Relating to Internal Affairs of Mexico, 1910-1939. General Records of the Department of State. File No. 812.00/6784, RG 59, NARA.

Hubert, Cochet. 1988. "Gandería y aparcería en la Sierra de Coalcomán." In *Paisajes agrarios de Michoacán*, ed. Hubert Cochet, Eric Léonard, and Jean Damien de Surgy, 217–225. Zamora, Mexico: Colegio de Michoacán.

Huerta, Gumersino, and Antonio Macario. 1916. Letter 65/7196, January 10. Manuscritos de Venustiano Carranza, Centro de Estudios de Historia de Mexico, Mexico City.

Human Rights Watch. 2006. "Funding the 'Final War': LTTE Intimidation and Extortion in the Tamil Diaspora." *Human Rights Watch Report* 18.1. Accessed April 4, 2016. https://www.hrw.org/reports/2006/ltte0306/ltte0306webwcover.pdf.

Hunter, William H. 1920a. *Disorders Inquiry Committee, 1919–1920: Report.* Calcutta: Superintendent of Government Printing.

———. 1920b. *Evidence Taken before the Disorders Inquiry Committee*, vol. 4. London: His Majesty's Stationery Office.

Hunter, William W. 1876. *The Indian Musalmans.* London: Trubner.

———. 1877. *A Statistical Account of Bengal, Volume 5: Districts of Dacca, Bakarganj, Faridpur, and Maimansinh*. London: Trubner.

Huntington, Samuel P. 1968. *Political Order in Changing Societies*. New Haven, CT: Yale University Press.

Huque, Azizul. 1931. *A Plea for Separate Electorates in Bengal*. Calcutta: n.p.

Hurd, John M. (1983) 2005. "Railways." In *The Cambridge Economic History of India*, vol. 2, ed. Dharma Kumar and Meghnad Desai, 737–761. Cambridge: Cambridge University Press.

Imaz, Cecilia. 1981. "La izquierda y la reforma política en México: Situación actual y perspectivas de la democracia." *Revista Mexicana de Sociolgía* 43.3:1103–1120.

India, Government of Punjab. 1953. *The Punjab Security of Land Tenures Act, 1953*. Chandigarh, India: Printing and Stationery Department.

India, Government of United Provinces. 1948. *Report of the United Provinces Zamindari Abolition Committee*, vol. 1. Allahabad: Superintendent of Government Printing and Stationery.

India, Government of Uttar Pradesh. 1948. *Report of the United Provinces Zamindari Abolition Committee*, 2 vols. Allahabad: Superintendent of Printing and Stationery.

India, Ministry of Law and Company Affairs. 1979. *Report of the High-Powered Expert Committee on Companies and Monopolies and Restrictive Trade Practices Act*. New Delhi: Government of India Press.

Investors India Year Book. 1914. Calcutta: Place, Siddons, and Gough.

Iqbal, Iftekhar. 2009. "Return of the Bhadralok: Ecology and Agrarian Relations in Eastern Bengal, c. 1905–1947." *Modern Asian Studies* 43.6:1325–1353.

Irish, Bell R. 2009. "The Amritsar Massacre: The Origins of the British Approach of Minimal Force on Public Order Operations." Master's thesis, School of Advanced Military Studies United States Army Command and General Staff College, Fort Leavenworth, KS.

Irschick, Eugene. 1969. *Political and Social Conflict in Southern India: The non-Brahmin movement and Tamil Separatism, 1916–1929*. Berkeley: University of California Press.

Islam, Mufakharul M. 1978. *Bengal Agriculture, 1920–1940: A Quantitative Study*. Cambridge: Cambridge University Press.

Ispahani, Mirza A. H. 1976. *Quaid-i-Azam Jinnah as I Knew Him*. Karachi: Elite.

ITN Source. 1979. "USA: Muzorewa Meets with Vance and Carter," July 12, BGY511110206. http://www.itnsource.com/shotlist//RTV/1979/07/12/BGY511110206/?s=*.

Itzcoatl, Antonio Pascual, and Antonio Mixcoatl. 1915. Letter 28/2981, February 20 (Esteban Coatl Avila, escritor). Manuscritos de Venustiano Carranza, Centro de Estudios de Historia de México, Mexico City.

Jackson, Paul. 2011. "The Civil War Roots of Military Domination in Zimbabwe: The Integration Process Following the Rhodesian War and the Road to ZANLA Dominance." *Civil Wars* 13.4:371–395.

Jackson, Robert H. 1990. *Quasi-States: Sovereignty, International Relations and the Third World*. Cambridge: Cambridge University Press.

Jacobs, Ian. 1982. *La revolución mexicana en Guerrero: Una revuelta de los rancheros*. Austin: University of Texas.

Jalal, Ayesha. 1985. *The Sole Spokesman: Jinnah, the Muslim League and the Demand for Pakistan*. Cambridge: Cambridge University Press.

Jalal, Ayesha, and Anil Seal. 1981. "Alternative to Partition: Muslim Politics between the Wars." *Modern Asian Studies* 15.3:415–454.

Jannuzi, F. Tomasson. 1974. *Agrarian Crisis in India: The Case of Bihar*. Delhi: Sangam.

Javid, Hassan. 2012. "Class, Power, and Patronage: The Landed Elite and Politics in Pakistani Punjab." PhD diss., London School of Economics.

Jeffery, Roger, Patricia Jeffrey, and Craig Jeffrey. 2005. "Social Inequalities and the Privatization of Secondary Schooling in North India." In *Education Regimes in Contemporary India*, ed. Radhika Chopra and Patricia Jeffery, 41–61. New Delhi: Sage.

Johnston, Hank, and Jozef Figa. 1988. "The Church and Political Opposition: Comparative Perspectives on Mobilization against Authoritarian Regimes." *Journal for the Scientific Study of Religion* 27.1:32–47.

Joseph, Gilbert M. 1980. "*Caciquismo* and the Revolution: Carrillo Puerto in Yucatan." In *Caudillo and Peasant in the Mexican Revolution*, ed. David Brading, 193–221. Cambridge: Cambridge University Press.

———. 1982. *Revolution from Without: Yucatán, Mexico and the United States, 1880–1924*. New York: Cambridge University Press.

Joseph, Gilbert M., and Jürgen Buchenau. 2013. *Mexico's Once and Future Revolutions: Social Upheaval and the Challenge of Rule since the Late Nineteenth Century*. Durham, NC: Duke University Press.

Joseph, Gilbert M., and Allen Wells. 1982. "Corporate Control of a Monocrop Economy: International Harvester and Yucatán's Henequen Industry during the Porfiriato." *Latin American Research Review* 17.1:69–99.

———. 1990. "Yucatán: Elite Politics and Rural Insurgency." In *Provinces of the Rebellion: Essays on Regional Mexican History 1910–1929*, ed. Thomas Benjamin and Mark Wasserman, 93–131. Albuquerque: University of New Mexico Press.

Kabir, Humayun. 1943. *Muslim Politics: 1906–1942*. Calcutta: Gupta, Rahman and Gupta.

Kaihko, Ilmari. 2012. "Big Man Bargaining in African Conflicts." In *African Conflicts and Informal Power: Big Men and Networks*, ed. Mats Utas, 181–204. London: Zed Books.

Kalyvas, Stathis N. 1996. *The Rise of Christian Democracy in Europe*. Ithaca, NY: Cornell University Press.

———. 2003. "The Ontology of 'Political Violence': Action and Identity in Civil Wars." *Perspectives on Politics* 1.3:475–494.

Kamat, A. R. 1980. "Politico-Economic Developments in Maharashtra: A Review of the Post-Independence Period." *Economic and Political Weekly* 15.40:1669–1678.

Kaminsky, Graciela L., and Carmen M. Reinhart. 1999. "The Twin Crises: The Causes of Banking and Balance-of-Payments Problems." *American Economic Review* 89.3:473–500.

Katz, Friedrich. 1974. "Labor Conditions on Haciendas in Porfirian Mexico: Some Trends and Tendencies." *Hispanic American Historical Review* 54.1:1–47.

———. 1976. "Agrarian Changes in Northern Mexico in the Period of Villista Rule, 1913–1915." In *Contemporary Mexico: Papers of the IV International Congress of Mexican History*, ed. James Wilkie, Michael Meyer, and Edna Monzon de Wilkie, 259–273. Los Angeles: University of California, Los Angeles, Latin American Center.

———. 1998. *The Life and Times of Pancho Villa*. Stanford, CA: Stanford University Press.

Kay, George. 1970. *Rhodesia: A Human Geography*. London: University of London Press.

Keddie, Nikki R. 1998. "The New Religious Politics. Where, When, and Why Do Fundamentalists Appear." *Comparative Studies in Society and History* 40.4:696–723.

Keen, David. 2012. *Useful Enemies: When Waging Wars Is More Important than Winning Them*. New Haven, CT: Yale University Press.

Kennedy, Jonathan, and Sunil Purushotham. 2012. "Beyond Naxalbari: A Comparative Analysis of Maoist Insurgency and Counterinsurgency in Independent India." *Comparative Studies in Society and History* 54.4:832–862.

Kenny, Michael. 2004. *The Politics of Identity: Liberal Political Theory and the Dilemmas of "Difference."* Cambridge: Polity.

Khosla, Gopal D. 1989. *Stern Reckoning: Survey of Events Leading Up to and Following the Partition of India*. Delhi: Oxford University Press.

King, Mary E. 2015. *Gandhian Nonviolent Struggle and Untouchability in Southern India: The 1924–25 Vykom Satyagraha and Mechanisms of Change*. Delhi: Oxford University Press.

"Kiran Shankar Roy Is Reported to Have Accepted Rs. Two Lakh from CWC to Organize Disturbances." 1986. F.28/Cong/42-A-J. September 26, 1942. In *Quit India Movement Secret Documents*, vol. 2, ed. P. N. Chopra. New Delhi: Imprint.

Kirk, Tony. 1975. "Politics and Violence in Rhodesia." *African Affairs* 74.294:3–38.

Kirschner, Shanna. 2010. "Knowing Your Enemy: Information and Commitment Problems in Civil Wars." *Journal of Conflict Resolution* 54.5:745–770.

Kirshner, Alan M. 1976. *Tomás Garrido Canabal y el Movimiento de los Camisas Rojas*. Mexico City: Secretaría de Educación Pública, Dirección General de Divulgación.

Knight, Alan. 1986. *The Mexican Revolution: Counterrevolution and Reconstruction*, vol. 2. Lincoln: University of Nebraska Press.

———. 1997. "Habitus and Homicide: Political Culture in Revolutionary Mexico." In *Citizens of the Pyramid: Essays on Mexican Political Culture*, ed. Wil G. Pansters, 107–129. Lafayette, IN: Purdue University Press.

———. 2005. "*Caciquismo* in Twentieth-Century Mexico." In *Caciquismo in Twentieth-Century Mexico*," ed. Alan Knight and Wil Pansters, 1–51. London: Institute for the Study of Americas and University of London.

Kochanek, Stanley A. 1971. "The Federation of Indian Chambers of Commerce and Industry and Indian Politics." *Asian Survey* 11.9:866–885.

———. 1974. *Business and Politics in India*. Berkeley: University of California Press.

Kohli, Atul. 1988. "The NTR Phenomenon in Andhra Pradesh: Political Change in a South Indian State." *Asian Survey* 28.10:991–1017.

Kriger, Norma. 1988. "The Zimbabwe War of Liberation: Struggles within the Struggle." *Journal of Southern African Studies* 14.2:304–322.

Krishan, Gopal. 2004. "Demography of the Punjab (1849–1947)." *Journal of Punjab Studies* 11.1:77–89.

Krishan, Shri. 2005. *Political Mobilization and Identity in Western India*. New Delhi: Sage.

Krishnamurty, J. (1983) 2005. "The Occupational Structure." In *The Cambridge Economic History of India*, vol. 2, ed. Dharma Kumar and Meghnad Desai, 533–552. Cambridge: Cambridge University Press.

Krishnan, V. V. Kunhi. 1993. *Tenancy Legislation in Malabar, 1880–1970*. New Delhi: Northern Book Centre.

Kudaisya, Gyanesh. 2006. *Region, Nation, "Heartland": Uttar Pradesh in India's Body Politic*. New Delhi: Sage.

Kuhnen, Frithjof. 1982. *Man and Land: An Introduction into the Problems of Agrarian Structure and Agrarian Reform*. Saarbrucken, Germany: Breitenbach.

Kumar, Dharma. 1975. "Landownership and Inequality in Madras Presidency: 1853–54 to 1946–47." *Indian Economic and Social History Review* 12.3:229–261.

———. (1983) 2005. "South India: Agrarian Relations." In *The Cambridge Economic History of India*, vol. 2, ed. Dharma Kumar and Meghnad Desai, 207–241. Cambridge: Cambridge University Press.

Kumar, Kapil, 1994. *Peasants in Revolt: Tenants, Landlords, Congress and the Raj in Oudh 1886–1992*. Delhi: Manohar Publishers.

Kydd, Andrew. 2003. "Which Side Are You On? Bias, Credibility, and Mediation." *American Journal of Political Science* 47.4:597–611.

LaFrance, David G. 2007. *Revolution in Mexico's Heartland: Politics, War, and State Building in Puebla, 1913–1920*. Lanham, MD: Rowman and Littlefield.

Lahiri, Pradip K. 1991. *Bengali Muslim Thought, 1818–1947: Its Liberal and Rational Trends*. Calcutta: K. P. Bagchi.

Lan, David. 1985. *Guns and Rain: Guerrillas and Spirit Mediums in Zimbabwe*. Berkeley: University of California Press.

———. 1989. "Resistance to the Present by the Past: Mediums and Money in Zimbabwe." In *Money and Morality of Exchange*, ed. Jonathan Parry and Maurice Bloch, 191–208. Cambridge: Cambridge University Press.

Lansing, Robert. 1916. "To Venustiano Carranza." Letter 66/7305, January 26. Manuscritos de Venustiano Carranza, Centro de Estudios de Historia de México, Mexico City.

Latham, C. J. K. 1986. "Mwari and the Divine Heroes: Guardians of the Shona." Master's thesis, Rhodes University, Grahamstown, South Africa.

Lebert, Tom. 2006. "An Introduction to Land and Agrarian Reform in Zimbabwe." In *Promised Land: Competing Visions of Agrarian Reform*, ed. Peter Rosset, Raj Patel, and Michael Courville, 40–56. Oakland, CA: Food First.

Le Billion, Philippe. 2001. "The Political Ecology of War: Natural Resources and Armed Conflicts." *Political Geography* 20.5:561–584.

Lecomte-Tilouine, Marie. 2004. "Ethnic Demands within Maoism: Questions of Magar Territorial Autonomy, Nationalist, and Class." In *Himalayan People's War: Nepal's Maoist Rebellion*, ed. Michael Hutt, 112–135. Bloomington: Indiana University Press.

Leongómez, Eduardo P. 2005. "Actores armados, dinámicas y estrategias." In *Nuestra guerra sin nombre: Transformaciones del conflicto en Colombia*, ed. Francisco Gutiérrez, María Emma Wills, and Gonzalo Sánchez Gómez, 98–118. Bogotá: Instituto de Estudios Políticos Relaciones Internacionales, Universidad Nacional de Colombia, and Grupo Editorial Norma.

Lerner, Victoria. 1980. "Los fundamentos socioeconómicos del cacicazgo en el México postrevolucionario: El caso de Saturnino Cedillo." *Historica Mexicana* 29.3:375–446.

Levi-Faur, David. 2006. "A Question of Size? A Heuristics for Stepwise Comparative Research Design." In *Innovative Comparative Methods for Policy Analysis: Beyond the Quantitative-Qualitative Divide*, ed. Benoit Rihoux and Heiki Grimm, 43–66. New York: Springer.

Lewis, Stephen E. 2005. *The Ambivalent Revolution: Forging State and Nation in Chiapas, 1910–1945*. Albuquerque: University of New Mexico Press.

Lewy, Guenter. 1974. *Religion and Revolution*. New York: Oxford University Press.

Ley Agraria Complementaria del Estado de Yucatán. 1916. Doc. 150/17086, May. Manuscritos de Venustiano Carranza, Centro de Estudios de Historia de México, Mexico City.

Lichbach, Mark I. 1994. "What Makes Rational Peasants Revolutionary? Dilemma, Paradox, and Irony in Peasant Collective Action." *World Politics* 46.3:383–418.

Lieten, Georges K. 1982. "Strikers and Strike-Breakers: Bombay Textile Mills Strike, 1929." *Economic and Political Weekly* 17.14/16:697–704.

———. 1996. "Land Reforms at Center Stage: The Evidence of West Bengal." *Development and Change* 27.1:111–130.

Lieuwen, Edwin. 1968. *Mexican Militarism: The Political Rise and Fall of the Revolutionary Army, 1910–1940*. Albuquerque: University of New Mexico Press.

Lockwood, David. 2012. *The Indian Bourgeoisie: A Political History of the Indian Capitalist Class in the Early Twentieth Century*. London: I. B. Tauris.

Logan, William. (1887) 2004. *Malabar Manual*. New Delhi: Asian Educational Services.

Lohman, Charles M., and Robert I. MacPherson. 1983. *Rhodesia: Tactical Victory, Strategic Defeat*. Quantico, VA: Marine Corps Education and Development Command.

López Gutiérrez, Gustavo. (1932) 1939. *Chiapas y sus epopeyas libertarias*, 3 vols. Chiapas, Mexico: Tuxtla Gutiérrez.

Lozoya, Jorge A. 1970. *El ejercito mexicano, 1911–1965*. Mexico City: Colegio de México.

Ludden, David. 2002. "Introduction: A Brief History of Subalternity." In *Reading Subaltern Studies: Critical History, Contested Meaning and the Globalization of South Asia*, ed. David Ludden, 1–42. London: Anthem.

Luebbert, Gregory M. 1991. *Liberalism, Fascism or Social Democracy*. New York: Oxford University Press.

Mabry, Donald J. 1978. "Mexican Anticlerics, Bishops, Cristeros, and the Devout in the 1920s: A Scholarly Debate." *Journal of Church and State* 20.1:81–92.

Machado, Manuel A., Jr. 1972. "The United States and the De la Huerta Rebellion." *Southwestern Historical Quarterly* 75.3:303–324.

Machingura, Dzinashe, and Mozambican Information Agency. 1977. "The Zimbabwe People's Army: An Interview with Dzinashe Machingura." *Issue: A Journal of Opinion* 7.1:15–18.

Magaloni, Beatriz. 2008. "Credible Power-Sharing and the Longevity of Authoritarian Rule." *Comparative Political Studies* 41.4/5:715–741.

Mahalanobis, P. C. 1958. "The National Sample Survey: Eighth Round: July 1954–March 1955, Number 10. First Report on Land Holdings, Rural Sector." *Sankhya* 19.1–2:29–180.

Maldonado, Gustavo, Tuxtla Gutiérrez, Chiapas. 1912. Letter to Juan Sánchez Azcona, Mexico City, January 30. Francisco Madero Collection, Archivo General de la Nación, Mexico City, box 23, folder 594–2, pp. 017507–017509.

Mandair, Arvind-Pal. 2015. "Sikhs, Sovereignty and Modern Government." In *Religion as a Category of Governance and Sovereignty*, ed. Trevor Stack, Naomi R. Goldenberg, and Timothy Fitzgerald, 115–142. Leiden: E. J. Brill.

Manor, James. 1977. "Structural Changes in Karnataka Politics." *Economic and Political Weekly* 12.44:1865–1869.

Mansoob, Murshed, and Scott Gates. 2005. "Spatial Horizontal Inequality and the Maoist Insurgency in Nepal." *Review of Development Economics* 9.1:121–134.

Markovits, Claude. 1985. *Indian Business and Nationalist Politics, 1931–1939*. Cambridge: Cambridge University Press.

Marten, Kimberly. 2012. *Warlords: Strong-Arm Brokers in Weak States*. Ithaca, NY: Cornell University Press.

Martínez, Gabino, and Juan Ángel Chávez Ramírez. 1988. *Durango: Un volcán en erupción*. Mexico City: Fondo de Cultura Económica.

Martínez, Jesús M. 1982. *La Confederación Revolucionaria Michoacana del Trabajo*. Mexico City: Eddisa.

Marwell, Gerald, and Pamela Oliver. 1993. *The Critical Mass in Collective Action: A Micro-social Theory*. Cambridge: Cambridge University Press.

Marx, Karl. (1852) 1954. *Eighteenth Brumaire of Luis Napoleon*. Moscow: Progress.

Maxwell, D. J. 1993. "Local Politics and the War of Liberation in North-East Zimbabwe." *Journal of Southern African Studies* 19.3:359–386.

Mazarire, G. Chikozho. 2011. "Discipline and Punishment in ZANLA: 1964–1979." *Journal of Southern African Studies* 37.3:571–591.

Mazumder, Rajit K. 2003. *The Indian Army and the Making of Punjab*. Delhi: Permanent Black/Orient Longman.

McAdam, Doug. 1982. *Political Process and the Development of Black Insurgency*. Chicago: University of Chicago Press.

McAdam, Doug, Sidney Tarrow, and Charles Tilly. 2001. *Dynamics of Contention*. Cambridge: Cambridge University Press.

———. 2009. "Comparative Perspectives on Contentious Politics." In *Comparative Politics: Rationality, Culture and Structure*, ed. Mark I. Lichbach and Alan S. Zuckerman, 260–290. New York: Cambridge University Press.

McBride, George M. 1929. *The Land System in Mexico*. New York: American Geographical Society.

McCarthy, John D., and Mayer N. Zald. 2001. "The Enduring Vitality of the Resource Mobilization Theory of Social Movements." In *Handbook of Sociological Theory*, ed. Jonathan H. Turner, 533–65. New York: Springer.

McCoy, Alfred W., ed. 2009. *An Anarchy of Families: State and Family in the Philippines*. Madison: University of Wisconsin Press.

McKelvey, Richard D. 1979. "General Conditions for Global Intransitivities in Formal Voting Models." *Econometrica* 47.5:1085–1112.

McKenna, Thomas M. 1998. *Muslim Rulers and Rebels: Everyday Politics and Armed Separatism in the Southern Philippines*. Berkeley: University of California Press.

Mecham, J. Lloyd. 1942. "Federal Intervention in Mexico." In *Hispanic American Essays: A Memorial to James Alexander Robertson*, ed. Alva C. Wilgus, 256–280. Chapel Hill: University of North Carolina Press.

"Meeting between Cabinet Delegation, Wavell, Ismail, Chundrigar, Raufshah, and Khaliquzzaman, 8 April 1946." 1980. In *The Transfer of Power: 1942–47*, vol. 7, ed. Nicholas Mansergh, 166. London: His Majesty's Stationery Office.

Menkhaus, Ken. 2006. "Governance without Government in Somalia." *International Security* 31.3:74–106.

Menon, V. P. 1957. *The Transfer of Power in India*. Princeton, NJ: Princeton University Press.

Merchant, Luis A. 2002. *Colapso y reforma: La integración del sistema bancario en el México revolucionario, 1913–1932*. Mexico City: Miguel Ángel Porrúa–Universidad Autónoma de Zacatecas.

Meredith, Martin. 1980. *The Past Is Another Country: Rhodesia, U.D.I. to Zimbabwe*. London: Pan.

Metcalf, Thomas R. 1967. "Landlords without Land: The U.P. Zamindars Today." *Pacific Affairs* 40.1/2:5–18.

———. 1969. "Social Effects of British Land Policy in Oudh." In *Land Control and Social Structure in Indian History*, ed. Frykenberg, Eric R., 143–162. Madison: University of Wisconsin Press.

Meyer, David S. 2004. "Protest and Political Opportunities." *Annual Review of Sociology* 30:125–145.

Meyer, Eugenia. 1980. *La lucha obrera en Cananea, 1906*. Mexico City: Instituto Nacional de Antropología e Historia.

Meyer, Jean. 1971. "Los obreros en la Revolución Mexicana: Los 'Batallones Rojos.'" *Historia Mexicana* 21.1:1–37.

———. 1974. *Iglesia y el estado, Volumen 3: Los Cristeros*, trans. A. G. Del Camino. Mexico City: Siglo Veintiuno.

———. 1976. *The Cristero Rebellion: The Mexican People between Church and States, 1926–1929*, trans. Robert Southern. Cambridge: Cambridge University Press.

Meyer, Lorenzo, Rafael Segovia, and Alejandra Lajous. 1978. *Los inicios de la institucionalización, 1928–1934*. Mexico City: Colegio de México.

Middlebrook, Kevin J. 1981. "Political Change in Mexico." *Proceedings of the Academy of Political Science* 34.1:55–66.

Migdal, Joel S. 2001. *State in Society: Studying How States and Societies Transform and Constitute One Another*. New York: Cambridge University Press.

Mill, John S. 1859. "Return to an Order of the House of Commons, Dated 9 June, 1857, Showing under What Tenures, and Subject to What Land Tax, Lands Are Held under the Several Presidencies of India." In *Annals of British Legislation*, vol. 4, ed. Leone Levi, 239–245. London: Smith, Elder.

Miller, Barbara. 1984. "The Role of Women in the Mexican Cristero Rebellion: Las Señoras y las Religiosas." *The Americas* 40.3:303–323.

Millon, Robert P. 1969. *Zapata: The Ideology of a Peasant Revolutionary*. New York: International Publishers.

Mines, Diane P. 2005. *Fierce Gods: Inequality, Ritual, and the Politics of Dignity in a South Indian Village*. Bloomington: Indiana University Press.

"The Mining News." 1914. *Engineering and Mining Journal* 98.17:725–766.

Misra, Bankey B., ed. 1963. *Select Documents on Mahatma Gandhi's Movement in Champaran, 1917–1918*. Patna, India: Government of Bihar.

———. 1970. *The Administrative History of India, 1834–1947: General Administration*. Bombay: Oxford University Press.

Misra, Maria. 1999. *Business, Race and Politics in British India, c. 1850–1960*. Oxford: Oxford University Press.

Mittal, S. K., and Kapil Kumar. 1978. "Baba Ram Chandra and Peasant Upsurge in Oudh: 1920–21." *Social Scientist* 6.11:35–56.

Mittra, H. N. 1921. *Punjab Unrest Before and After*, 2d ed. Shibpur, India: N. N. Mitter, Annual Register Office.

Mkandawire, Thandike. 2002. "The Terrible Toll of Post-colonial 'Rebel-Movements' in Africa: Towards an Explanation of the Violence against the Peasantry." *Journal of Modern African Studies* 40.2:181–215.

Mlambo, Alois, 2005. "Prelude to the 1979 Lancaster House Constitutional Conference on Rhodesia: The Role of International Economic Sanctions Reconsidered." *Historia* 50.1:147–172.

Momen, Humaria. 1972. *Muslim Politics in Bengal: A Study of Krishak Praja Party and the Elections of 1937*. Dhaka, Bangladesh: Sunny House.

Montes de Oca, Bruno, and Miguel Rebolledo. n.d. "To Venustiano Carranza." Letter 150/17117. Manuscritos de Venustiano Carranza, Centro de Estudios de Historia de México, Mexico City.

Montiel, Cristina J., and Maria E. J. Macapagal. 2006. "Effects of Social Position on Societal Attributions of an Asymmetric Conflict." *Journal of Peace Research* 43.2:219–227.

Moon, Penderel. 1998. *Divide and Quit*, 2d ed. Delhi: Oxford University Press.

Moorcraft, Paul L., and Peter McLaughlin. 1982. *The Rhodesian War: A Military History*. Johannesburg: Sygma.

Moore, Barrington. 1966. *Social Origins of Dictatorship and Democracy: Lord and Peasant in the Making of the Modern World*. Boston: Beacon.

Moore, Frank J., and Constance A. Moore. 1955. *Land Tenure Legislation in Uttar Pradesh*. Berkeley: University of California.

Morris, Morris D. (1983) 2005. "The Growth of Large-Scale Industry to 1947." In *The Cambridge Economic History of India*, vol. 2, ed. Dharma Kumar and Meghnad Desai, 553–676. Cambridge: Cambridge University Press.

———. 1984. *The Origins of the Civil Rights Movement*. New York: Free Press.

Mothibe, Tefetso H. 1996. "Zimbabwe: African Working Class Nationalism, 1957–1963." *Zambezia* 23.2:157–180.

Moyo, Gorden. 2017. "The Entrapment of Joshua Nkomo with Global Imperial Snares." In *Joshua Mqabuko Nkomo of Zimbabwe: Politics, Power, and Memory*, ed. Sabelo Ndlovu-Gatsheni, 115–148. Cham, Switzerland: Palgrave Macmillan.

Mtisi, Joseph, Munyaradzi Nyakudya, and Teresa Barnes. 2009. "War in Rhodesia, 1965–1980." In *Becoming Zimbabwe: A History from the Pre-colonial Period to 2008*, ed. Brian Raftopolous and Aloi Mlambo, 141–166. Harare, Zimbabwe: Weaver.

Mudur, Ganapati. 2005. "India Launches National Rural Health Mission." *British Medical Journal* 330.7497:920.

Mukherjee, Janam. 2015. *Hungry Bengal: War, Famine and the End of Empire*. New York: Oxford University Press.

Mukherji, Saugata. 1986. "Agrarian Class Formation in Modern Bengal, 1931–1951." Economic and Political Weekly 21.4:11–27.

Mukhopadhyay, A. K. 1980. *The Panchayat Administration in West Bengal*. Calcutta: World Press.

Mukhopadhyay, Dipali. 2014. *Warlords, Strongman Governors, and the State in Afghanistan*. New York: Cambridge University Press.

Muldoon, Andrew. 2009. *Empire Politics and the Creation of the 1935 Government of India Act: Last Act of the Raj*. Farnham, UK: Ashgate.

Murphy, Carlyle. 1978. "Rhodesian Raid Hits Mozambique." *Washington Post*, July 31. https://www.washingtonpost.com/archive/politics/1978/07/31/rhodesian-raid-hits-mozambique/e1bf1f96-08aa-45c9-86cc-325ea9be1ef0/?utm_term=.1be014fec4fb.

———. 1979. "Rhodesia Installs Black Rule." *Washington Post*, June 30. https://www.washingtonpost.com/archive/politics/1979/05/30/rhodesia-installs-black-rule/094a837e-949b4411-aa4a-07bf955129ac/?utm_term=.3349724f848e.

Murphy, Philip. 2006. "An Intricate and Distasteful Subject: British Planning for the Use of Force against the European Settlers of Central Africa, 1952–1965." *English Historical Review* 121.492:746–777.

Murshid, Tazeen M. 1995. *The Sacred and the Secular: Bengali Muslim Discourses, 1871–1977*. Calcutta: Oxford University Press.

Mutanda, Darlington. 2017. *The Rhodesian Air Force in Zimbabwe's War of Liberation, 1966–1980*. Jefferson, NC: McFarland.

Mutunhu, Tendai. 1978. "The Internal Settlement in Zimbabwe: A Sell-Out or an Advancement to African Majority Rule." *The Black Scholar: Journal of Black Studies and Research* 10.1:2–10.

Nacif, Benito. 2002. "Understanding Party Discipline in the Chamber of Deputies: The Centralized Party Model." In *Legislative Politics in Latin America*, ed. Scott Morgenstern and Benito Nacif, 254–284. Cambridge: Cambridge University Press.

Nair, C. Gopalan. 1923. *The Moplah Rebellion, 1921*. Calicut, India: Norman Printing.

National Sample Survey Office. 1996. "Land Holding Survey: Some Aspects of Household Ownership Holdings," 48th Round, January–December 1992, report no. 399. Department of Statistics, Ministry of Statistics, New Delhi.

Navarro, Moisés G. 1957. "La huelga de Río Blanco." *Historia Mexicana* 6.4:510–533.

——. 1985. *La Confederación Nacional Campesina en la reforma agraria mexicana.* Mexico City: Día en Libros.

——. 2000–2001. *Cristeros y agraristas en Jalisco,* 2 vols. Mexico City: Colegio de México.

Ndlovu, Saul Gwakuba. 2003. "ZAPU and the Liberation Struggle in Zimbabwe." Master's thesis, University of Cape Town.

Neale, Walter C. 1962. *Economic Change in Rural India: Land Tenure and Reform in Uttar Pradesh, 1800–1955.* New Haven, CT: Yale University Press.

Nehru, Jawaharlal. 1921. "Notes on Repression in the United Provinces. *Young India* 18 Aug." In *Collected Works of Mahatma Gandhi,* vol. 24, 469–471. New Delhi: Publications Division, Government of India.

——. 1936. *An Autobiography.* London: Unwin.

——. 1980. "To Rear-Admiral Viscount Mountbatten of Burma," April 17, 1947. In *The Transfer of Power: 1942–47,* vol. 9, ed. Nicholas Mansergh, 304–307. London: His Majesty's Stationery Office.

Nehwati, Francis. 1970. "The Social and Communal Background to 'Zhii': The African Riots in Bulawayo, Southern Rhodesia in 1960." *African Affairs* 69.276:250–266.

Newell, Richard S. 1972. "Ideology and Realities: Land Redistribution in Uttar Pradesh." *Pacific Affairs* 45.2:220–239.

New York Times. 1977. "Guerrilla Camps at Chimoio and Tembue Were Hit by Rhodesians," November 29. http://www.nytimes.com/1977/11/29/archives/rhodesia-reports-killing-1200-in-raids-military-command-says-two.html.

——. 1979a. "Rhodesia Bombs Crowded Camp in Zambia," February 24.

——. 1979b. "Zambia Puts Army on Full Alert after Rhodesia Raids." Nov. 21. https://www.nytimes.com/1979/11/21/archives/zambia-puts-army-on-full-alert-after-rhodesia-raids-muzorewa-gives.html.

Nhamo, Samasuwo. 2002. "An Assessment of the Impact of Economic Sanctions on Rhodesia's Cattle Industry, 1965–1972." *Historia* 47.2:655–678.

Nicholls, Walter. 2009. "Place, Networks, Space: Theorising the Geographies of Social Movements." *Transactions of the Institute of British Geographers* 34.1:78–93.

Njekete, Taurai. 2014. "Understanding ZAPU—the Early Days—Part 2." *Bulawayo 24 News,* December 23. https://bulawayo24.com/index-id-opinion-sc-columnist-byo-59835.html.

Nkomo, Joshua. 1984. *Nkomo: The Story of My Life.* London: Methuen.

Norberto, Valdez. 1998. *Ethnicity, Class, and the Indigenous Struggle for Land in Guerrero, México.* New York: Garland.

North, Douglass C. 1991. "Institutions." *Journal of Economic Perspectives* 5.1:97–112.

North, Douglass, John J. Wallis, and Barry R. Weingast. 2009. *Violence and Social Orders: A Conceptual Framework for Interpreting Recorded Human History.* New York: Cambridge University Press.

Nossiter, Bernard D. 1978. "A Shabby Story." *Washington Post,* September 8.

Núñez Rodríguez, Violeta R. 2004. *Por la tierra en Chiapas . . . El corazón no se vence.* Mexico City: Plaza y Valdez.

Nyerere, Julius K. 1972. *After the Pearce Commission Report.* Dar es Salaam: Printpak Tanzania.

Oberschall, Anthony. 1973. *Social Conflicts and Social Movements.* Englewood Cliffs, NJ: Prentice-Hall.

"Oficina Secreta de Información de la Ciudad de Queretaro." n.d. (circa 1916). Letter 148/16979. Manuscritos de Venustiano Carranza, Centro de Estudios de Historia de México, Mexico City.

Olague, Jesús F., Mercedes de Vega, Sandra K. Ficker, and Laura del Alizal. 1996. *Breve historia de Zacatecas*. Mexico City: Colegio de México, Fondo de Cultura Económica.

Olson, Mancur. (1965) 1971. *The Logic of Collective Action: Public Goods and the Theory of Groups*, rev. ed. Cambridge, MA: Harvard University Press.

Omvedt, Gail. 1976. *Cultural Revolt in a Colonial Society: The Non-Brahman Movement in Western India, 1873 to 1930*. Bombay: Scientific Socialist Education Trust.

Onslow, Sue. 2009. "The South African Factor in Zimbabwe's Transition to Independence." In *Cold War in Southern Africa: White Power, Black Liberation*, ed. Sue Onslow, 110–129. Abingdon, UK: Routledge.

———. 2012. "Robert Mugabe and Todor Zhikov," May 29. Cold War International History Project, Wilson Center, Washington, DC. https://www.wilsoncenter.org/publication/robert-mugabe-and-todor-zhivkov#intro.

Oren, Stephen. 1974. "The Sikhs, Congress, and the Unionists in British Punjab, 1937–1945." *Modern Asian Studies* 8.3:397–418.

Ottaway, David B. 1978. "Rhodesia Bids for Black Support by Opening 'Protected Villages.'" *Washington Post*, September 9. https://www.washingtonpost.com/archive/politics/1978/09/09/rhodesia-bids-for-black-support-by-opening-protected-villages/323fc9af-a3ce-4f2e-ac80-7f9183b14310/?utm_term=.822f667b22da.

———. 1979. "Rhodesians Hit Capital of Zambia." *Washington Post*, April 14. http://www.washingtonpost.com/wp-dyn/content/article/2006/08/10/AR2006081000754.html.

Pacheco, Pedro, Juan Batista, and Teodoro Martinez. 1916. "To Venustiano Carranza." Letter 65/7210, January 12. Manuscritos de Venustiano Carranza, Centro de Estudios de Historia de México, Mexico City.

Paige, Jeffery. 1975. *Agrarian Revolution*. New York: Free Press.

Palley, Claire. 1970. "Law and the Unequal Society: Discriminatory Legislation under the Rhodesian Front from 1963 to 1969, Part 1." *Race and Class* 12.1:15–47.

Palmer, Robin. 1977. *Land and Racial Domination in Rhodesia*. London: Heinemann Educational.

———. 1990. "Land Reform in Zimbabwe, 1980–1990." *African Affairs* 89.355:163–181.

Palmer, Steven. 1988. "Carlos Fonseca and the Construction of Sandinismo in Nicaragua." *Latin American Research Review* 23.1:91–109.

Pandey, Gyanendra. 1978. *The Ascendancy of the Congress in Uttar Pradesh, 1926–34: A Study in Imperfect Mobilization*. Delhi: Oxford University Press.

———. 1979. "Review of *Agrarian Unrest in North India: The United Provinces 1918–1922*, by M. H. Siddiqi." *Indian Economic and Social History Review* 16.3:373–374.

Pandey, Vikash N. 1992. "Dynamics of Property Relations in Colonial Awadh: Towards Peasant Rebellion of 1920s." *Social Scientist* 20.7:29–49.

Panikkar, Kavalam M. 1920. *Indian Nationalism: Its Origins, History and Ideals*. Charing Cross, UK: Faith.

Panikkar, K. N. 1978. "Agrarian Legislation and Social Classes: A Case Study of Malabar." *Economic and Political Weekly* 13.21:880–888.

———. 1989. *Against Lord and State: Religion and Peasant Uprisings in Malabar*. New Delhi: Oxford University Press.

Papp, Daniel S. 1980. *The Soviet Union and Southern Africa*. Strategic Issues Research Memorandum. Carlisle, PA: Strategic Studies Institute, U.S. Army War College. https://apps.dtic.mil/dtic/tr/fulltext/u2/a089399.pdf.

Parikh, A. 1972. "Market Responsiveness of Peasant Cultivators: Some Evidence from Pre-war India." *Journal of Development Studies* 8.2:291–306.

Pastrana, Prudencio Moscoso. 1972. *Jacinto Pérez "Pajarito," el ultimo líder chamula.* Mexico City: Gobierno de Chiapas.

Piramal, Gita. 1998. *Business Legends: G. D. Birla, J. R. D. Tata, Walchand Hirachand, Kasturbhai Lalbhai.* Delhi: Penguin.

Pitchford, Mark. 2011. *The Conservative Party and the Extreme Right, 1945–1975.* Manchester, UK: Manchester University Press.

Plana, Manuel. 2000. "La cuestión agraria en La Laguna durante la revolución." *Historia Mexicana* 50.1:57–90.

Polletta, Francesca, and James M. Jasper. 2001. "Collective Identity and Social Movements." *Annual Review of Sociology* 27:283–305.

Popkin, Samuel. 1979. *The Rational Peasant.* Berkeley: University of California Press.

———. 1988. "Political Entrepreneurs and Peasant Movements in Vietnam." In *Rationality and Revolution*, ed. Michael Taylor, 9–61. Cambridge: Cambridge University Press.

Potter, David C. 1973. "Manpower Shortage and the End of Colonialism: The Case of the Indian Civil Service." *Modern Asian Studies* 7.1:47–73.

Pouchepadass, Jacques. 1974. "Local Leaders and the Intelligentsia in the Champaran Satyagraha (1917): A Study in Peasant Mobilization." *Contributions to Indian Sociology* 8:67–87.

Powell, Robert. 2004. "Bargaining and Learning while Fighting." *American Journal of Political Science* 48.2:344–361.

Prasad, Nandan. 1956. *Expansion of the Armed Forces and Defence Organization, 1939–1945.* Calcutta: Orient Longmans.

"Press Office: Bulletin (Muzorewa Call on Margaret Thatcher)" [Muzorewa asked for meeting]. 1979. INGH 2/21, June 27. Churchill Archive Center, Churchill College, Cambridge, UK.

Preston, Matthew. 2004. "Stalemate and the Termination of Civil War: Rhodesia Reassessed." *Journal of Peace Research* 41.1:65–83.

PricewaterhouseCoopers. 2008. *Healthcare in India: Emerging Market Report, 2007.* https://www.slideshare.net/david_singer/healthcare-in-india-pwc-report.

Pryor, Frederic L. 1992. *The Red and the Green: The Rise and Fall of Collectivized Agriculture in Marxist Regimes.* Princeton, NJ: Princeton University Press.

Puri, Harish K. 1983. "The Akali Agitation: An Analysis of Socio-economic Bases of Protest." *Economic and Political Weekly* 18.4:113–118.

Purnell, Jennie. 1999. *Popular Movements and State Formation in Revolutionary Mexico: The "Agraristas" and "Cristeros" of Michoacán.* Durham, NC: Duke University Press.

Quintana, Alejandro. 2007. "The President That Never Was: Maximino Avilo Camacho and the Taming of Caudillismo in Early Post-Revolutionary Mexico." PhD diss., City University of New York.

———. 2010. *Maximino Avila Camacho and the One Party State: The Taming of Caudillismo and Caciquismo in Post-revolutionary Mexico.* Lanham, MD: Lexington Books.

Radhakrishnan, P. 1989. *Peasant Struggles, Land Reforms and Social Change: Malabar, 1836–1982.* Delhi: Sage.

Raghavaiyangar, Seshayangar S. 1893. *Memorandum on the Progress of the Madras Presidency during the Last Forty Years of British Administration.* Madras: Superintendent of Government Printing.

Rai, Lajpat. 1908. *The Story of My Deportation.* Lahore: Panjabee.

———. 1915. *The Arya Samaj: An Account of Its Origins, Doctrines, and Activities with a Biographical Sketch of the Founder.* London: Longmans, Green.

———. 1916. *Young India: An Interpretation and a History of the Nationalist Movement from Within*. New York: B. W. Huebsch.

Rajendran, Narayana P. 1994. *The National Movement in Tamil Nadu, 1905–1914*. Madras, India: Oxford University Press.

Ramos, María E. R. 1992. *El reparto de tierras y la política agraria en Chiapas, 1914–1988*. Mexico City: Universidad Nacional Autónoma de México.

Randathani, Husain. 2007. *Mappila Muslims: A Study on Society and Anticolonial Struggles*. Calicut, India: Other Books.

Ranger, Terence, 1985. *Peasant Consciousness and Guerrilla War in Zimbabwe: A Comparative Study*. Berkeley: University of California Press.

———. 1997. "Violence Variously Remembered: The Killing of Pieter Oberholzer in July 1964." *History of Africa* 24:273–286.

Ratzinger, Joseph, and Jürgen Habermas. 2007. *The Dialectics of Secularization: On Reason and Religion*. San Francisco: Ignatius.

Ray, Rajat, and Ratna Ray. 1975. "Zamindars and Jotedars: A Study of Rural Politics in Bengal." *Modern Asian Studies* 9.1:81–102.

Raychaudhuri, Tapan. (1983) 2005. "The Mid-Eighteenth-Century Background." In *The Cambridge Economic History of India*, vol. 2, ed. Dharma Kumar and Meghnad Desai, 3–35. Cambridge: Cambridge University Press.

Rebolledo, Miguel. 1915. "To Venustiano Carranza." Letter 46/5062, July 26. Manuscritos de Venustiano Carranza, Centro de Estudios de Historia de México, Mexico City.

Reed, William C. 1993. "International Politics and National Liberation: ZANU and the Politics of Contested Sovereignty in Zimbabwe." *African Studies Review* 36.2:31–59.

Reeves, Peter D. 1964. "The Landlords' Response to Political Change in the United Provinces of Agra and Oudh, 1921–1937." PhD diss., Australian National University, Canberra.

———. 1966. "The Politics of Order: 'Anti-Non-Cooperation' in the United Provinces, 1921." *Journal of Asian Studies* 25.2:261–274.

———. 1991. *Landlords and Government in Uttar Pradesh*. Bombay: Oxford University Press.

Reich, Peter L. 1997. "The Mexican Catholic Church and Constitutional Change since 1929." *Historian* 60.1:77–86.

Reid-Daly, Ronald, and Peter Stiff. 1982. *Selous Scouts: Top Secret War*. Alberton, South Africa: Galago.

Reinhardt, William W. 1972. *The Legislative Council of the Punjab*. Durham, NC: Duke University Program in Comparative Studies on Southern Asia.

Reno, William. 1998. *Warlord Politics and African States*. Boulder, CO: Lynne Rienner.

———. 2001. "How Sovereignty Matters: International Markets and the Political Economy of Local Politics in Weak States." In *Intervention and Transnationalism in Africa: Global-Local Networks of Power*, ed. Thomas Callagh, Ronald Kassimir, and Robert Latham, 197–216. New York: Cambridge University Press.

Renwick, Robin. 2013. *A Journey with Margaret Thatcher: Foreign Policy under the Iron Lady*. London: Biteback.

Report. n.d. Anonymous to anonymous, doc. 85/9547, 6 of 6. Manuscritos de Venustiano Carranza, Centro de Estudios de Historia de México, Mexico City.

Report of the Advisory Commission on the Review of the Constitution of the Federation (Command 1148). 1960. London: Her Majesty's Stationery Office.

Reuter, Ora John, and Thomas F. Remington. 2009. "Dominant Party Regimes and the

Commitment Problem: The Case of United Russia." *Comparative Political Studies* 42.2:501–526.

Reyes, Jesús M. 2006. "Un debate sobre la regulación de cambios y moneda antecedente de un banco central." In *Temas a debate: Moneda y banca en México, 1884–1954*, ed. María E. R. Sotelo and Leonor Ludlow, 113–148. Mexico City: Universidad Nacional Autónoma de México.

Richmond, Douglas W. 1980. "Factional Political Strife in Coahuila, 1910–1920." *Hispanic American Historical Review* 60.1:49–68.

Riddell, Roger. (1980) 2013. "Zimbabwe's Land Problem: The Central Issue." In *From Rhodesia to Zimbabwe: Behind and Beyond Lancaster House (Studies in Commonwealth Politics and History)*, ed. W. H. Morris-Jones and Dennis Austin, 1–13. Oxford: Routledge.

Ridgeway, Stan. 2001. "Monoculture, Monopoly, and the Mexican Revolution: Tomás Garrido Canabal and the Standard Fruit Company in Tabasco (1920–1935)." *Mexican Studies* 17:143–169.

Rifkind, Malcom L. 1968. "The Politics of Land in Rhodesia: A Study of Land and Politics in Southern Rhodesia with Special Reference to the Period 1930–1968." Master's thesis, University of Edinburgh.

Riguzzi, Paolo. 1999. "Mercado, regiones y capitales en los ferrocarriles de propiedad mexicana, 1870–1907." In *Ferrocarriles y obras* públicas, ed. Sandra Kuntz Ficker and Priscilla Connolly, 39–70. Mexico City: Instituto de Investigaciones Históricas, Universidad Nacional Autónoma de México.

Riley, M. F. 1982. "Zimbabwean Nationalism and the Rise of Robert Mugabe." Master's thesis, Naval Postgraduate School, Monterey, CA.

Risely, H. H., and E. A. Gait. 1903. *Report on the Census of India, 1901*. Calcutta: Superintendent of Government Printing.

Ristow, Colby N. 2008. "From Repression to Incorporation in Revolutionary Mexico: Identity Politics, Cultural Mediation, and Popular Revolution in Juchitán Oaxaca, 1910–1920," vol. 1. PhD diss., University of Chicago, 2008.

Robinson, Francis, 1974. *Separatism among Indian Muslims: The Politics of the United Provinces' Muslims*. Cambridge: Cambridge University Press.

Roggero, Franco S. 1997. *Pueblos y nacionalismo: Del* régimen *oligárquico a la sociedad de masas en Yucatán, 1894–1925*. Mexico City: Instituto Nacional de Estudios Históricos de la Revolución Mexicana.

Rose, Arthur H., and J. P. Thompson. 1908. *Imperial Gazetteer of India, Provincial Series: Punjab*, vol. 1. Calcutta: Superintendent of Government Printing.

Rothchild, Donald. 2002. "Settlement Terms and Postagreement Stability." In *Ending Civil Wars: The Implementation of Peace Agreements*, ed. Stephen J. Stedman, Donald Rothchild, and Elizabeth M. Cousens, 117–140. Boulder, CO: Lynne Rienner.

Rothermund, Dietmar. 1967. *The Bengal Tenancy Act of 1885 and Its Influence on Legislation in Other Provinces*. Heidelberg: Südasien-Institut der Universität Heidelberg.

———. 1993. *An Economic History of India: From Pre-colonial Times to 1991*, 2d ed. New York: Taylor and Francis.

Rothermund, Indira. 1999. "Maharashtra's Response to Gandhian Nationalism." In *Region, Nationality and Religion*, ed. A. R. Kulkarni and N. K. Wagle, 69–93. Bombay: Popular Prakashan.

Rouaix, Pastor. 1946. *Genesis de los Articulos 27 y 123 de la Constitución Política de 1917*. Mexico City: Instituto Nacional de Estudios Históricos de la Revolución Mexicana.

Rouquie, Alain. 1987. *The Military and the State in Latin America*. Berkeley: University of California Press.

Rowe, David M. 2001. *Manipulating the Market: Understanding Economic Sanctions, Institutional Changes, and the Political Unity of White Rhodesia*. Ann Arbor: University of Michigan Press.

Roy, Ramashray. 1968. "Dynamics of One-Party Dominance in an Indian State." *Asian Survey* 8.7:553–575.

Rudra, Asok. 1981. "One Step Forward, Two Steps Backwards." *Economic Weekly* 16.25/26:A61–A68.

Rueschemeyer, Dietrich, Evelyn H. Stephens, and John D. Stephens. 1992. *Capitalist Development and Democracy*. Chicago: University of Chicago Press.

Ruiz, Priscilliano. 1915. "To Mariano de Urdaniva." Letter 38/4126, May 3. Doc. 1 of 2, Manuscritos de Venustiano Carranza, Centro de Estudios de Historia de México, Mexico City.

Sachse, F. A. 1917. *Bengal District Gazetteers: Mymensingh*. Calcutta: Bengal Secretariat Book Depot.

Sadomba, Zvakanyorwa W. 2013. Interview by the author. May 3. Harare, Zimbabwe.

Salamini, Heather F. 1978. *Agrarian Radicalism in Veracruz, 1920–1938*. Lincoln: University of Nebraska Press.

Salazar Adame, Jaime. 2011. "La revolución en Guerrero." In *La revolución en los estados de República Mexicana*, ed. Patricia Galeana, 213–232. Mexico City: Siglo Veintiuno.

San Andrés de los Gama, Municipio Temascaltepec. n.d. 276.1/1769. Archivo General Agrario, Mexico City.

Sanchez, Fernando P. 2006. *La política económica de la revolución mexicana, 1911–1924*. Mexico City: Universidad Nacional Autónoma de México.

Sanderson, Steven E. 1981. *Agrarian Populism and the Mexican State: The Struggle for Land in Sonora*. Berkeley: University of California Press.

Sanderson, Susan W. 1984. *Land Reform in Mexico: 1910–1980*. Orlando, FL: Academic.

Sandoval, Javier R. 2009. "Conflictos laborales en el despegue industrial de Nuevo León, México: Ferrocarriles y vidrieros." *Ingenierías* 12.44:42–50.

Sanginés, Pedro S. 2006. "Lucha agraria y revolución en el oriente de Durango: 1900–1929." *Historia Mexicana* 56.1:117–173.

San Juan Lalana, Jurisdicción Villa Alta de San Ildefonso. n.d. 276.1/2309. Archivo General Agrario, Mexico City.

San Juan Nochistlán, Municipio Tequixtepec n.d. 276.1/2089. Archivo General Agrario, Mexico City, box 19, folder 2.

Sanoo, M. K. 1978. *Narayana Guru: A Biography*. Bombay: Bharatiya Vidya Bhavan.

Sanyal, Amal. 2010. "The Curious Case of the Bombay Plan." *Contemporary Issues and Ideas in Social Sciences* 6.1:1–31.

Sareen, Sushant. 2010. "Socio-economic Underpinning of Jihadism in Pakistan." *Strategic Analysis* 35.1:6–11.

Sarkar, Chandiprasad. 1991. *The Bengali Muslims: A Study in Politicization, 1912–1929*. Calcutta: K. P. Bagchi.

Sarkar, Sumit. 1973. *The Swadeshi Movement in Bengal, 1903–1908*. New Delhi: People's.

Sartori, Andrew. 2014. *Liberalism in Empire: An Alternative History*. Berkeley: University of California Press.

Saxena, Mohanlal P. 1935. *Rent Law of Oudh: Being a Commentary on the Oudh Rent Act (Imperial Act, XXII of 1886)*. Hardoi, United Provinces: n.p.

Sayeed, Khalid Bin. 1959. "Collapse of Parliamentary Democracy in Pakistan." *Middle East Journal* 13.4:389–406.

Scarnecchia, Timothy. 2008. *The Urban Roots of Democracy and Political Violence in*

Zimbabwe: Harare and Highfield, 1940–1964. Rochester, NY: University of Rochester Press.

Schoffeleers, J. M. 1978. "Introduction." In *Guardians of the Land: Essays on Central African Territorial Cults*, ed. J. M. Schoffeleers, i–xii. Gwelo, Zimbabwe: Mambo Press.

Schryer, Frans J. 1986. *Una burguesía campesina en la revolución mexicana: Los rancheros de Pisaflores*. Mexico City: Era.

Scott, James C. 1977. *The Moral Economy of the Peasant*. New Haven, CT: Yale University Press.

———. 1987. *Weapons of the Weak*. New Haven, CT: Yale University Press.

———. 2009. *The Art of Not Being Governed*. New Haven, CT: Yale University Press.

Sección de Estadística de la Secretaría de Gobierno. 1910. *Anuario Estadístico del Estado de Chihuahua*. Chihuahua, Mexico.

Secret Agent. n.d. "To Venustiano Carranza [officially, anonymous to anonymous]." Letter 150/17111. Manuscritos de Venustiano Carranza, Centro de Estudios Historia de México, Mexico City.

Secretaría de Educación Pública, Secretaría de la Defensa Nacional, and Instituto Nacional de Estudios Históricos de las Revoluciones de México. 2014. *Diccionario de generales de la revolución*, vol. 2. Mexico City: Instituto Nacional de Estudios Históricos de las Revoluciones de México.

Secretaria de la Camara de Senadores del Congreso de la Union, 32d Legislatura. 1925. "Hoja de servicios del C. Gral. De División Gildardo Magaña, enviada por la secretaría de gobernación, para la ratificación de los grados militares del expresado ciudadano," October 25. Archivo Histórico y Memoria Legislative del Senado de la Republica (México), Mexico City, sec. 2, no. 13.

Secretario de Hacienda. 1916a. "To Venustiano Carranza." Letter 89/10064, July 29, 1 of 5. Manuscritos de Venustiano Carranza, Centro de Estudios de Historia de México, Mexico City.

———. 1916b. "To Venustiano Carranza." Letter 89/10064, July 29, 2 of 5. Manuscritos de Venustiano Carranza, Centro de Estudios de Historia de México, Mexico City.

Secretary of State for India. 1943a. "To War Cabinet." Memorandum CAB/66/41/11, September 22, pp. 43–44. National Archives of the United Kingdom, Richmond, UK.

———. 1943b. "To War Cabinet." Report for the Month of November 1943 for the Dominions, India, Burma, and the Colonies and Mandated Territories, CAB/66/44/34 26, December 26. National Archives of the United Kingdom, Richmond, UK.

———. 1945. "To Cabinet." Memorandum: The Indian Constitutional Question, CAB/129/1, August 18. National Archives of the United Kingdom, Richmond, UK.

Semo, Enrique, Sergio Peña, and Teresa Aguirre. 2006. *Historia económica de México: De la revolución a la industrialización*. Mexico City: Universidad Nacional Autónoma de México, Editorial Océano de México.

Sen, Amartya. 1981. *Poverty and Famines: An Essay on Entitlement and Deprivation*. Oxford: Oxford University Press.

Sen, Shila. 1976. *Muslim Politics in Bengal, 1937–1947*. New Delhi: Impex India.

Sen, S. N. 2006. *History of Modern India*. Delhi: New Age International.

Sengupta, Kalyan K. 1972. "Agrarian Disturbances in 19th Century Bengal." *Indian Economic and Social History Review* 8:192–212.

Seyd, Patrick. 1972. "Factionalism within the Conservative Party: The Monday Club." *Government and Opposition* 7.4:464–487.

Seylon, Raman N. 2004. "Study of Poligar Violence in Late 18th Century Tamil Country in South India." *African and Asian Studies* 3.3:245–272.

Shadow Cabinet: Circulated Paper. 1978. *Conservative Research Document on Bingham Report* [Rhodesia]. Thatcher mss., 2/6/163, September 28. Margaret Thatcher Foundation, Large Scale Document Archive, 1975–1979: Leader of the Opposition Archive. https://c59574e9047e61130f13-3f71d0fe2b653c4f00f32175760e96e7.ssl.cf1.rackcdn.com/BEC0CEBFD4CD4B05B7B0FD23AE742CF4.pdf.

Shafer, Robert J. 1973. *Mexican Business Organizations*. Syracuse, NY: Syracuse University Press.

Sharma, H. R. 1994. "Distribution of Landholdings in Rural India, 1953–1954 to 1981–1982." *Economic and Political Weekly* 29.13:A12–A25.

Shepsle, Kenneth E., and Barry R. Weingast. 1981. "Structure Induced Equilibrium and Legislative Choice." *Public Choice* 37.3:503–519.

Sholk, Richard. 1984. "The National Bourgeoisie in Post-Revolutionary Nicaragua." *Comparative Politics* 16.3:253–276.

Sibanda, Eliakim. 2005. *The Zimbabwe African People's Union, 1961–1987: A Political History of Insurgency in Southern Rhodesia*. Trenton, NJ: Africa World Press.

Siddiqi, Majid H. 1978. *Agrarian Unrest in North India: The United Provinces (1919–22)*. Delhi: Vikas.

Simmons, Colin. 1976. "Indigenous Enterprise in the Indian Coal Mining Industry, 1835–1939." *Indian Economic and Social History Review* 13.2:189–218.

———. 1981. "Imperial Dictate: The Effect of the Two World Wars on the Indian Coal Industry." *World Development* 9.8:749–771.

Simon, John. 1930. *Report of the Indian Statutory Commission*, 2 vols. London: His Majesty's Stationery Office.

———. 1932. *Indian Statutory Commission Report*. Calcutta: Government of India Central Publication Branch.

Simone, Abdou M. 2004. *For the City Yet to Come: Changing African Life in Four Cities*. Durham, NC: Duke University Press.

Singh, Anita I. 1987. *The Origins of the Partition of India, 1936–1947.* Delhi: Oxford University Press.

Singh, Brij Pal. 2005. "Punjab." In *Socio-economic Profile of Rural India*, ed. V. K. Agnihotri, 148–229. Delhi: Lal Bahadur Shastri National Academy of Administration, Mussoorie and Concept.

Singh, Khushwant. 2004. *History of the Sikhs, 1939–2004*. Delhi: Oxford University Press.

Singh, Manmohan. 2004. "Associated Chambers of Commerce and Industry of India, JRD Tata Birth Centenary Celebration." Prime Minister's Address. New Delhi, August 4.

Singh, Nikki-Guninder Kaur. 2003. "The Mahatma and the Sikhs." In *Indian Critiques of Gandhi*, ed. Harold Coward, 171–192. Albany: State University of New York Press.

Sinha-Kerkhoff, Kathika, 2014. *Colonising Plants in Bihar, 1760–1950*. Gurugram, India: Partridge.

Sirsikar, V. M. 1964. "Leadership Patterns in Rural Maharashtra." *Asian Survey* 4.7:929–939.

Sitarammya, Pattabhi, 1969. *A History of the Indian National Congress, Volume 1: 1885–1935*. Delhi: S. Chand.

Sithole, Ndabaningi. 1969. *African Nationalism*, 2nd ed. London: Oxford University Press.

Skocpol, Theda. 1979. *States and Social Revolutions: A Comparative Analysis of France, Russia, and China*. New York: Cambridge University Pres.

Smith, Anthony D. 2003. *Chosen Peoples: Sacred Sources of National Identity*. Oxford: Oxford University Press.

Smith, Donald L. 1974. "Pre-PRI: The Mexican Government Party, 1929–1946." PhD diss., Texas Christian University, Fort Worth.

Smith, Ian. 1997. *The Great Betrayal: The Memoirs of Ian Douglas Smith*. London: John Blake.

Smock, David R. 1969. "The Forgotten Rhodesians." *Foreign Affairs* 47.3:532–544.

Smyth, Regina, Ann Lowry, and Brandon Wilkening. 2007. "Engineering Victory: Institutional Reform, Informal Institutions, and the Formation of a Hegemonic Party Regime in the Russian Federation." *Post Soviet Affairs* 23.2:118–137.

Snow, Peter. 1976. "Switzerland and Robert Mugabe: SYND 26 1976 Interview with ZANU leader Robert Mugabe." *AP Television*, October 26, 1976. http://www.aparchive.com/metadata/youtube/df6ed9d6bcd4295035d71be215a09d16.

Snyder, Richard. 2001. "Scaling Down: The Subnational Comparative Method." *Studies in Comparative International Development* 36.1:93–110.

Soames, Lord. 1980. "From Rhodesia to Zimbabwe." *International Affairs* 56.3:405–419.

Solodnikov, Vassily. (1998) 2013. "The Cold War in Southern Africa." In *Southern Africa in the Cold War, Post-1974*, ed. Sue Onslow and Anna-Mart van Wyk, 165. Washington, DC: Woodrow Wilson International Center for Scholars. https://www.wilsoncenter.org/sites/default/files/CWIHP_SouthAfrica_Final_Web.pdf.

Solomon, Rakesh H. 1994. "Culture, Imperialism, and Nationalist Resistance: Performance in Colonial India." *Theatre Journal* 46.3:323–347.

Sonnichsen, Charles L. 1971. "Colonel William C. Greene and the Strike at Cananea, Sonora, 1906." *Arizona and the West* 13.4:343–368.

"South African Government Cabinet Minutes on Rhodesia, 3 March 1976 to 1 September 1976, South African National Archives, CAB 1/1/6." (1976) 2013. In *Southern Africa in the Cold War, Post-1974*, ed. Sue Onslow and Anna-Mart Van Wyk, 238–240. Washington, DC: Woodrow Wilson International Center for scholars. http://digitalarchive.wilsoncenter.org/document/118528.

Southard, Barbara. 1980. "The Political Strategy of Aurobindo Ghosh: The Utilization of Hindu Religious Symbolism and the Problem of Political Mobilization in Bengal." *Modern Asian Studies* 14.3:353–376.

Spate, O. H. K., and Enayat Ahmad. 1950. "Five Cities of the Gangetic Plain: A Cross Section of Indian Cultural History." *Geographical Review* 40.2:260–278.

Spector, Ronald.1981. "The Royal Indian Navy Strike of 1946: A Study of Cohesion and Disintegration in Colonial Armed Forces." *Armed Forces and Society* 7.2:271–284.

Spence, Daniel O. 2015. "Beyond *Talwar:* A Cultural Reappraisal of the 1946 Royal Indian Navy Mutiny." *Journal of Imperial and Commonwealth History* 43.3:489–508.

Spierenburg, Marja. 1995. "The Role of the Mhondoro Cult in the Struggle for Control over Land in Dande (Northern Zimbabwe): Social Commentaries and the Influence of Adherents. Center for Applied Social Sciences Occasional Paper. University of Zimbabwe, Harare.

Srivastava, Saraswati. 1976. "Uttar Pradesh: Politics of Neglected Development." In *State Politics in India*, ed. Iqbal Narain, 323–369. New Delhi: Meenakshi Prakashan.

Srivastava, Sushil. 1995. *Conflicts in Agrarian Society: Avadh, 1920–1939.* Delhi: Renaissance.

Stauffer, Carl S. 2009. "Acting out the Myths: The Power of Narrative Discourse in Shaping the Zimbabwe Conflict of Matabeleland, 1980–1987." PhD diss., University of KwaZulu-Natal.

Stedman, Stephen J., Donald Rothchild, and Elizabeth M. Cousens, eds. 2002. *Ending Civil Wars: The Implementation of Peace Agreements*. Boulder, CO: Lynne Rienner.

Stern, Jessica. 2000. "Pakistan's *Jihad* Culture." *Foreign Affairs* 79.6 (November–December): 115–126.

Stern, Robert W. 2001. *Democracy and Dictatorship in South Asia: Dominant Classes and Political Outcomes in India, Pakistan, and Bangladesh*. Westport, CT: Praeger.

Stokes, Edward T. 1959. *The English Utilitarians and India*. Oxford: Clarendon.

Stokes, Eric. (1983) 2005. "Agrarian Relations: Northern and Central India." In *The Cambridge Economic History of India*, vol. 2, ed. Dharma Kumar and Meghnad Desai, 36–85. Cambridge: Cambridge University Press.

Stoneman, Colin. 1980. "Zimbabwe's Prospects as an Industrial Power." *Journal of Commonwealth and Comparative Politics* 18.1:14–27.

Suhrawardy, Huseyn S. 1980. "To Sir Eric C. Melville," May 15, 1947. In *The Transfer of Power: 1942–47*, vol. 9, ed. Nicholas Mansergh, 829–831. London: His Majesty's Stationery Office.

Svensson, Isak. 2007. "Fighting with Faith: Religion and Conflict Resolution in Civil Wars." *Journal of Conflict Resolution* 51.6:930–949.

———. 2009. "Who Brings Which Peace? Neutral versus Biased Mediation and Institutional Peace Arrangements in Civil Wars." *Journal of Conflict Resolution* 52.3:446–469.

Talbot, Ian. 1980. "The 1946 Punjab Elections." *Modern Asian Studies* 14.1:65–91.

———. 1988. *Punjab and the Raj, 1849–1947*. Riverdale, MD: Riverdale.

———. 1996. *Khizr Tiwana: The Punjab Unionist Party and the Partition of India*. Richmond, UK: Curzon.

———. 2007. "The Punjab under Colonialism: Order and Transformation in British India." *Journal of Punjab Studies* 14.1:3–10.

Talbot, Walter S. 1901. *Final Report of the Revision of the Settlement of the Jhelum District in the Punjab: 1895–1901*. Lahore: Civil and Military Gazette Press.

Tamarkin, M. 1990. *The Making of Zimbabwe: Decolonization in Regional and International Politics*. London: Frank Cass.

Tamayo, Jaime. 2008. *El obregonismo y los movimientos sociales: La conformación del estado moderno en México (1920–1924)*. Guadalajara, Mexico: Universidad de Guadalajara.

Tannenbaum, Frank. 1929. *The Mexican Agrarian Reform*. New York: Macmillan.

Tarrow, Sidney. 1998. *Power in Movement: Social Movements and Contentious Politics*. New York: Cambridge University Press.

Tauger, Mark B. 2009. "The Indian Famine Crisis of World War II." *British Scholar* 1.2:166–196.

Taylor, William B. 1972. *Landlord and Peasant in Colonial Oaxaca*. Stanford, CA: Stanford University Press.

Tejeda, Carlos. 1915. "To Unknown." Letter 33/3352, March 18. Manuscritos de Venustiano Carranza, Centro de Estudios de Historia de Mexico, Mexico City.

Thakurdas, Purushottamdas, ed. 1945. *A Brief Memorandum Outlining a Plan of Economic Development of India*, 2 vols. Harmondsworth, UK: Penguin.

Thomas, E. F. (1921) 1923. "Order under Section 144 C.P.C.," February 5. In *The Moplah Rebellion, 1921*, by C. Gopalan Nair, app. 3. Calicut, India: Norman.

Tilly, Charles. 1978. *From Mobilization to Revolution*. Reading, MA: Addison-Wesley.

———. 1985. "War Making and State Making as Organized Crime." In *Bringing the State Back In*, ed. Peter Evans, Dietrich Rueschemeyer, and Theda Skocpol, 170–187. Cambridge: Cambridge University Press.

———. 1995. "To Explain Political Processes." *American Sociological Review* 100.6:1594–1610.

Tilly, Charles, and Sidney Tarrow. 2006. *Contentious Politics*. Boulder, CO: Paradigm.
Timberg, Thomas. 1977. *The Marwaris: From Traders to Industrialists*. Delhi: Vikas.
Tobler, Hans W. 1988. "Peasants and the Shaping of the Revolutionary State, 1910–1940." In *Riot, Rebellion and Revolution: Rural Social Conflict in Mexico*, 2d ed., ed. Friedrich Katz, 487–518. Princeton, NJ: Princeton University Press.
Toft, Monica D. 2007. "Getting Religion? The Puzzling Case of Islam and Civil War." *International Security* 31.4:97–131.
"To Unknown." n.d. (circa 1916). Letter 149/17008. Manuscritos de Venustiano Carranza, Centro de Estudios de Historia de México, Mexico City.
"To Venustiano Carranza." 1914. Letter 11/1170, July 31. Manuscritos de Venustiano Carranza, Centro de Estudios de Historia de Mexico, Mexico City.
Tsebelis, George. 1991. *Nested Games: Rational Choice in Comparative Politics*. Berkeley: University of California Press.
———. 2002. *Veto Players: How Political Institutions Work*. Princeton, NJ: Princeton University Press.
Tudor, Maya. 2013. *The Promise of Power: The Origins of Democracy in India and Autocracy in Pakistan*. New York: Cambridge University Press.
Tutino, John. 1990. "Revolutionary Confrontation, 1913–1917: Regions, Classes, and the New National State." In *Provinces of the Revolution: Essays on Regional Mexican History, 1910–1929*, ed. Thomas Benjamin and Mark Wasserman, 41–70. Albuquerque: University of New Mexico Press.
Uadiale, Martin. 2012. "Implication of the Political and Economic Factors in the Rise of 'Boko Haram' Insurgencies in Nigeria." *International Journal of Advanced Legal Studies and Governance* 3.3:81–100.
United Kingdom. 1972. *Rhodesia: Report of the Commission on Rhodesian Opinion under the Chairmanship of the Right Honorable the Lord Pearce (Command, 4964)*, by Lord Pearce. London: Her Majesty's Stationery Office.
———. 1979a. "Cabinet: Carrington Memo Circulated to OD Committee—OD (79) 19 (Rhodesia—Possible Repercussions on British Political and Commercial Interests)," July 19. CAB 148/183. National Archives of the United Kingdom, Richmond, UK.
———. 1979b. "Cabinet: Carrington Memorandum Circulated to Overseas and Defence Policy—OD (79) 19 (Rhodesia)," May 11. Secretary of State for Foreign and Commonwealth Affairs, CAB 148/183. National Archives of the United Kingdom, Richmond, UK.
———. 1979c. "Cabinet: Minutes of Full Cabinet—CC (79) 13th (Rhodesia, Economic Situation, Magistrates' Courts)," August 10. National Archives of the United Kingdom, Richmond, UK.
———. 1979d. "France: No. 10 Record of Conversation (Margaret Thatcher-Valéry Giscard d'Estaing in Paris) [EC (CAP, budget, EMS); energy, G7; Africa; defence, China, refugees]," June 5. PREM 19/41 f77. National Archives of the United Kingdom, Richmond, UK.
———. 1979e. "Incoming Brief: Cabinet Secretary Incoming Brief for Margaret Thatcher ('Rhodesia')" [Margaret Thatcher: "I agree we need care but a little courage is necessary too"], May 4. PREM 19/106 f313. National Archives of the United Kingdom, Richmond, UK.
———. 1979f. "U.S.: Margaret Thatcher Letter to President Carter (Rhodesia)" [Muzorewa visit to Washington, DC], July 7. Thatcher mss., THCR 3/1/1, personal message T40/79T. Churchill Archive Center, Churchill College, Cambridge, MA.
———. 1979g. "U.S.: No. 10 Record of Conversation (Margaret Thatcher-U.S. Secretary

of State Cyrus Vance)" [Rhodesia, the Middle East, Iran, Turkey], May 23. PREM 19/383 f86. National Archives of the United Kingdom, Richmond, UK.

———. 1979h. "Zimbabwe: Margaret Thatcher Letter to Australian Prime Minister Malcolm Fraser," June 5. PREM 19/107 f371 (T20/79T). National Archives of the United Kingdom, Richmond, UK.

———. 1979i. "Zimbabwe: Margaret Thatcher Letter to Lord Soames (Responsibilities as Governor)" [confirms Walls to have direct access to him], December 11. PREM19/116 pt. 2 f71, National Archives of the United Kingdom, Richmond, UK.

———. 1979j. "Zimbabwe: Margaret Thatcher Letter to President Machel of Mozambique (Rhodesia Constitutional Conference)," October 13. Thatcher mss., THCR 3/1/3 (T117E/79T). Churchill Archive Center, Churchill College, Cambridge, UK.

———. 1979k. "Zimbabwe: No. 10 Record of Conversation (MT-Carrington-Australian PM Malcolm Fraser) [CHGM discussions]." National Archives of the United Kingdom, Richmond, UK, PREM19/109 f.202. July 31.

———. 1979l. "Zimbabwe: No. 10 Record of Conversation (MT-Carrington-Tanzanian President Nyerere). [CHGM discussions]." National Archives of the United Kingdom, Richmond, UK, PREM 19/109 f.207. July 31.

———. 1979m. "Zimbabwe: No. 10 Record of Conversation (MT-General Walls) [Walls seeks assurances]." National Archives of the United Kingdom, Richmond, UK, PREM19/116 pt.2 f.162. December 6.

———. 1979n. "Zimbabwe: No. 10 Record of Conversation (MT-Julian Amery): ["Great blunder" not to recognize Muzorewa regime as soon as it was established], July 26. PREM19/108 f71. National Archives of the United Kingdom, Richmond, UK.

———. 1979o. "Zimbabwe: No. 10 Record of Conversation (MT-Kenyan President Daniel Arap-Moi) (plenary) [extract from Rhodesia]." National Archives of the United Kingdom, Richmond, UK, PREM 19/107 f 239. June 13.

———. 1980a. "Namibia: Gilmour minute to Nott ("South Africa") [Namibia and sanctions against South Africa]." National Archives of the United Kingdom, Richmond, UK. PREM19/597 f297. September 10.

———. 1980b. "South Africa: British Consulate-General Cape Town to FCO (Hunt's further talks to PW Botha, Pik Botha, Fourie, De Villiers and General Malan) [Soviet Threat, Rhodesia/Zimbabwe, Namibia]." National Archives of the United Kingdom, Richmond, UK, PREM19.371 f67. April 11.

———. 1980c. "South Africa: British Consulate-General in Cape Town to FCP ("Rhodesia: Political Situation") [UK Ambassador's talks with Pik Botha]." National Archives of the United Kingdom, Richmond, UK, PREM 19/371 f160. February 15.

———. 1980d. "Zimbabwe: Consulate-General Cape Town to UKE Rome ('Rhodesia: Political Situation') [UK Ambassador's meeting with Pik Botha]." National Archives of the United Kingdom, Richmond, UK, PREM 19/345 f179. February 19.

———. 1980e. "Zimbabwe: Consulate-General Johannesburg to FCO ("Rhodesia/South Africa") [South African concerns about voter intimidation and possibility that Mugabe is planning USSR-supported post-election coup]." National Archives of the United Kingdom, Richmond, UK, PREM 19/345 f18. February 28.

———. 1980f. "Zimbabwe: FCO letter to No. 10 (Rhodesia: Message from General Walls") [Carrington and MT how to respond to Wall's message to MT]." National Archives of the United Kingdom, Richmond, UK, PREM 19/346 f204. March 3.

———. 1980g. "Zimbabwe: FCO to UKE Canberra ('Rhodesia') [Carrington's Response to Fraser's letter regarding Rhodesia and Nyerere]." National Archives of the United Kingdom, Richmond, UK, PREM 19/345 f160. February 20.

———. 1980h. "Zimbabwe: MT letter to President Shegari of Nigeria (Situation in Rhodesia)." Thatcher mss., Churchill Archive Center, Churchill College, Cambridge, UK, THCR 3/1/6 (67) (T35A/80). February 21.

———. 1980i. "Zimbabwe: President Machel of Mozambique Letter to Margaret Thatcher (Situation in Rhodesia)." THCR 3/1/6 (78) (T36B/80). Thatcher mss., Churchill Archive Center, Churchill College, Cambridge, UK.

———. 1980j. "Zimbabwe: UKE Salisbury to FCO ('Rhodesia: Formation of the Government')" [Renwick's talk with General Walls], March 4. PREM 19/346 f184, National Archives of the United Kingdom, Richmond, UK.

———. 1980k. "Zimbabwe: UKE Salisbury to FCO ('Rhodesia: Formation of the Government') [Report that Nkomo's party leadership will refuse to participate in a coalition with Mugabe], March 2. PREM19/346 f210, National Archives of the United Kingdom, Richmond, UK.

———. 1980l. "Zimbabwe: UKE Salisbury to FCO ('Rhodesia: Future Policy')" [Assistance and aid to Rhodesia], March 14. PREM19/346 f49. National Archives of the United Kingdom, Richmond, UK.

———. 1980m. "Zimbabwe: UKE Salisbury to FCO ('Rhodesia: Nkomo's Views')" [Soames's meeting with Nkomo], February 19. PREM 19/345 f173, National Archives of the United Kingdom, Richmond, UK.

———. 1981. "Zimbabwe: Julian Amery MP Letter to Margaret Thatcher (Report on Visit to Africa)," November 12. PREM 19/946 f213, National Archives of the United Kingdom, Richmond, UK.

———. 1983a. "Cabinet: Minutes of Full Cabinet, CC (83) 8th (Parliamentary Affairs, Foreign Affairs, EC Affairs, Industrial Affairs," March 10. CAB 128/76 f92. National Archives of the United Kingdom, Richmond, UK.

———. 1983b. "Cabinet: Minutes of Full Cabinet—CC (83) 10th (Parliamentary Affairs, Foreign Affairs, EC Affairs)." CAB 128/76 f105. National Archives of the United Kingdom, Richmond, UK.

———. 1983c. "Commonwealth: No. 10 Record of Conversation (Margaret Thatcher, Howe, Mugabe)" [Heads of government meeting], November 24. PREM19/970 f55. National Archives of the United Kingdom, Richmond, UK.

———. 1985. "South Africa: Charles Powell Record of Conversation ('CHOGM: Heads of Government Retreat at Lyford Cay") [Margaret Thatcher "considerably disillusioned by the double standards applied by a number of the Commonwealth countries], October 21. PREM19/1688 f154. National Archives of the United Kingdom, Richmond, UK.

United Kingdom, Government of India. 1892. "The North Western Provinces Land-Revenue Act, 1873." In *The North-Western Provinces and Oudh Code*, 3rd ed. Calcutta: Superintendent of Government Printing, India.

———. 1893. *Manual of Standing Information for the Madras Presidency*. Madras, India: Superintendent of Government Printing.

———. 1903. *Census of India, 1901*, vol. 15-A. Calcutta: Superintendent of Government Printing.

———. 1908. *Imperial Gazetteer of India, Provincial Series: United Provinces of Agra and Oudh*, vol. 1. Calcutta: Superintendent of Government Printing.

———. 1909. *Imperial Gazetteer of India*, vol. 1. Oxford: Clarendon.

———. 1913. *Census of India, 1910*, vol. 12, pt. 2. Calcutta: Superintendent of Government Printing.

———. 1916. *Report of the Royal Commission on the Public Services in India, 1912*, vol. 1. Calcutta: Superintendent of Government Printing.

——. 1917. *Report on the Production and Consumption of Coal in India*. Calcutta: Superintendent of Government Printing.

——. 1923. *Census of India, 1921*, vol. 1. Calcutta: Superintendent of Government Printing.

——. 1924. *Report of the Indian Tariff Board Regarding the Grant of Protection to the Steel Industry*. Calcutta: Superintendent of Government Printing.

——. 1933. *Census of India, 1931, Volume 9: The Cities of the Bombay Presidency*. Bombay: Government Central Press.

——. 1934. "Franchise for the Provincial Legislative Assemblies." In *Indian Constitutional Reform*, vol. 1, pt. 1, by Joint Committee on Indian Constitutional Reform, 1933–1934, 358–366. London: His Majesty's Stationery Office.

——. 1936. *Government of India Act, 1935*. London: His Majesty's Stationery Office.

——. 1937a. *Agricultural Statistics of the Punjab, 1901–02 to 1935–36*. Lahore: Civil and Military Gazette Press.

——. 1937b. *Returns Showing the Results of Elections in India*. London: His Majesty's Stationery Office.

——. 1963. "Note by the First Secretary of State Attaching Memorandum Prepared by the Central African Office," Southern Rhodesia, April 3. National Archives of the United Kingdom, Richmond, UK.

——. 1966. "Note by the Secretary of State for Commonwealth Affairs." Draft White Paper on Rhodesia, November 23. National Archives of the United Kingdom, Richmond, UK.

——. 1980a. "Record of Interview between Rear-Admiral Viscount Mountbatten of Burma and Pandit Nehru," April 1, 1947. In *The Transfer of Power: 1942–47*, vol. 10, ed. Nicholas Mansergh, 70. London: His Majesty's Stationery Office.

——. 1980b. "Record of Mr. Henderson's Conversation with Master Tara Singh," January 19, 1947. In *The Transfer of Power: 1942–47*, vol. 9, ed. Nicholas Mansergh, 513. London: His Majesty's Stationery Office.

"United Kingdom, Government of India, 1886. Oudh Rent Act." 1900. In *A Reprint of the Rent Rulings of the Judicial Commissioner of Oudh from 1871 to 1895 (Complete Series) with an Index*, comp. R. G. F. Jacob. Lucknow: Murray.

United Kingdom, Government of India, E. H. H. Edye, and W. R. Tennant. 1923. *Census of India, 1921: United Provinces of Agra and Oudh*, vol. 16, pt. 2. Allahabad: Superintendent of Government Printing, United Provinces.

United Kingdom, Government of India, and John C. Faunthorpe. 1922. "Report on Eka Movement," May 13. *United Provinces Gazette*, pt. 8. 271–287.

United Kingdom, Government of India, Government of Bengal. 1940. *Report of the Land Revenue Commission Bengal*. Calcutta: Superintendent of Government Printing, Bengal Government Press.

——. 1946. "Minutes: Cabinet Meeting." CAB/128/8, December 10. National Archives of the United Kingdom, Richmond, UK.

United Kingdom, Government of India, and V. N. Mehta, Deputy Commissioner, Pratapgarh. 1920. "To the Commissioner, Fyzabad Division," November 11. File 753 of 1920, Revenue Department. Uttar Pradesh State Archives, Allahabad.

United Kingdom, Government of India, and A. C. Turner, Superintendent, Census Operations. 1933. *Census of India, 1931: United Provinces of Agra and Oudh*, vol. 18, pt. 2. Allahabad: Superintendent of Printing and Stationery, United Provinces.

United Kingdom, House of Commons. 1903. *Statement Exhibiting the Moral and Material Progress and Condition of India: During the Year 1901–02 and the Nine Preceding Years*. London: His Majesty's Stationery Office.

———. 1918. "Explanatory Memorandum: East India Accounts and Estimates: 1917–1918." London: His Majesty's Stationery Office.

United Press International. 1976. "Rhodesia Bows to Kissinger's Plan," September 25.

United States. 1977a. "Rhodesia: Proposals for a Settlement," Secretary of State Cyrus Vance to U.S. Embassies, Lagos, Pretoria, Lusaka, Dar es Salaam, Maputo, Gaborone, London, Paris, Ottawa, Bonn, Tehran, and the Hague, August 20. 1977STATE1999049_c . https://aad.archives.gov/aad/createpdf?rid=197810&dt=2532&dl=1629.

———. 1977b. "Secretary of State, [Cyrus] Vance Minute to [Jimmy] Carter (Briefing Notes for Carter's Meeting with Margaret Thatcher)," September 12. NLC-128-12-12-7-6. Jimmy Carter Presidential Library and Museum, Atlanta.

Un Observador. 1929. *La rebelión militar contra el gobierno legítimo.* San Antonio, TX: Self-Published.

Upadhya, Carol. 1997. "Social and Cultural Strategies of Class Formation in Coastal Andhra Pradesh." *Contributions to Indian Sociology* 31.2:169–193.

Uppal, J. S. 1969. "Attitudes of Farm Families toward Land Reforms in Some Punjab Villages." *Journal of Developing Areas* 4.1:59–68.

U.S. Central Intelligence Agency. 1976. "Rhodesian Nationalist Factions and Leaders." Report, January 1. General CIA Records, doc. no. CIA-RD85T00353R000100270012–4. https://www.cia.gov/library/readingroom/docs/CIA-RDP85T00353R000100270012-4.pdf.

U.S. Department of State. (1974) 2013. "Rhodesia: A Breakthrough toward Settlement?" In *Southern Africa in the Cold War, Post-1974*, ed. Sue Onslow and Anna-Mart van Wyk. Washington, DC: Woodrow Wilson International Center for Scholars. http://digitalarchive.wilsoncenter.org/document/118526.

———. 1976a. "Prospects for Change in South Africa," William G. Bowdler, U.S. Embassy, Pretoria, to Secretary of State, Washington, DC, November 19. U.S. Department of State, 1976PRETOR05292_b.

———. 1976b. "Rhodesia Conference: Closing Statement by the Patriotic Front." U.S. Mission, Geneva, to Secretary of State Henry Kissinger, Washington, DC, December 15 1976GENEVA09959_b.

———. 1976c. "Rhodesia Conference: Deadlock Worsens," Reinhardt from U.S. Mission, Geneva, to Secretary of State Henry Kissinger, Washington, DC, November 18. U.S. Department of State, 1976GENEVA09959_b.

———. 1976d. "Rhodesia Conference: November 11 Meeting with Ivor Richard," U.S. Embassy, London, to U.S. Mission, New York, November 12. U.S. Department of State, 1976STATE278398_b.

———. 1976e. "Rhodesia: Ivor Richard Negotiations," U.S. Embassy, Pretoria, to Secretary of State Henry Kissinger, Washington, DC, December 24. U.S. Department of State, Document No. 1976PRETOR05873, File No. P840098-2157. https://aad.archives.gov/aad/createpdf?rid=69217&dt=2082&dl=1345.

———. 1977a. "Rhodesia: Owen's Mood," U.S. Embassy, London, to Secretary of State, Washington, DC, July 14. U.S. Department of State, 1977LONDON11569_c. https://aad.archives.gov/aad/createpdf?rid=161110&dt=2532&dl=1629.

———. 1977b. "South Africa: Article by David Martin," U.S. Embassy, London, to Secretary of State, Washington, DC, September 12. U.S. Department of State, 1977LONDON15175_c, NARA.

———. 1977c. "ZANU Representatives Comment on UK-US Proposals," U.S. Embassy, Dar es Salaam, to U.S. Embassy, Gaborone, December 8. U.S. Department of State, 1977DARES04885_c, NARA. https://aad.archives.gov/aad/createpdf?rid=286248&dt=2532&dl=1629.

——. 1979. "Meeting with Prime Minister Abel Tendekai Muzorewa of Rhodesia." White House Statement, July 11.U.S. National Security Adviser. 1976. "Memorandum of Conversation between Balthazar Vorster, prime minister of South Africa, and U.S. Secretary of State Henry Kissinger," June 24. In *Foreign Relations of the United States, 1969–1976, Volume 28, Southern Africa*. https://www.fordlibrarymuseum.gov/library/document/0314/1553485.pdf.

U.S. Senate. 1919. *Importation of Sisal and Hemp*. Report by the Subcommittee of the Committee on Agriculture and Forestry, 64th Congress, vol. 2. Washington, DC: U.S. Government Printing Office.

Utas, Mats. 2012. "Introduction: Bigmanity and Network Governance in African Conflicts." In *African Conflicts and Informal Power*, ed. Mats Utas, 1–34. London: Zed Books.

Vanderwood, Paul. 1981. *Disorder and Progress: Bandits, Police, and Mexican Development*. Lincoln: University of Nebraska Press.

Vas, J. A. 1911. *Eastern Bengal and Assam District Gazetteers: Rangpur*. Allahabad, India: Pioneer.

Vásquez, Victor R. M. 1985. "El regimen de García Vigil." In *La revolución en Oaxaca, 1900–1930*, ed. Victor R. M. Vásquez, 184–238. Oaxaca, Mexico: Instituto Estatal de Educación Pública de Oaxaca.

Vázquez, Germán, Tuxtla Gutiérrez, Chiapas. 1912. Letter to Juan Sánchez and Francisco I. Madero, Mexico City. Francisco Madero Collection, Archivo General de la Nación, Mexico City, box 2, folder 23–2, pp. 000815–000823.

Velez, Ildefondso V. 1970. *Historia de la Revolución Mexicana en Coahuila*. Mexico City: Biblioteca del Instituto Nacional de Estudios Históricos de la Revolución Mexicana.

Venugopal, Rajesh. 2010. "Sectarian Socialism: The Politics of Sri Lanka's Janatha Vimukhti Peramuna (JVP)." *Journal of Modern Asian Studies* 44.3:567–602.

Vera, María T. T. 2005. "Las ligas de resistencia, emancipación o corporativismo (análisis del discurso)." In *Anuario de historia de la Universidad Juárez Autónoma de Tabasco*, vol. 1, 179–198. Villahermosa, Mexico: División Académica de Ciencias Sociales y Humanidades, Programa Integral de Fortalecimiento Institucional, Cuerpo Académico de Historia, Cultura y Vida Cotidiana, Secretaria de Educación Pública.

Viceroy of India. 1942. "To Secretary of State for India." Letter, CAB/65/25/30, March 6. National Archives for the United Kingdom, Richmond, UK.

Vida Nueva: Órgano de la sociedad recreativa "Balún-Canán." 1914. Comitán, Chiapas, October 1.

Vinci, Anthony. 2006. "Greed-Grievance Reconsidered: The Role of Power and Survival in the Motivation of Armed Groups." *Civil Wars* 8.1:25–45.

Viqueira, Juan Pedro, and Mario Humberto Ruz, eds. 1995. *Los rumbos de otra historia*. Mexico City: Universidad Nacional Autónoma de México and Centro de Investigaciones y Estudios Superiores en Antropología Social.

Vora, Rajendra. 2009. *World's First Anti-Dam Movement: Mulshi Satyagraha, 1920–1924*. Ranikhet, India: Permanent Black.

Voss, Stuart F. 1990. "Nationalizing the Revolution: Culmination and Circumstance." In *Provinces of the Revolution: Essays on Regional Mexican History, 1910–1929*, ed. Thomas Benjamin and Mark Wasserman, 273–317. Albuquerque: University of New Mexico Press.

Wadhwa, D. C. 1981. "Transferability of Raiyati Holdings in Bihar: A Long Journey, 1793–1950." *Economic and Political Weekly* 16.38:1532–1544.

Wagle, Dileep M. 1981. "Imperial Preference and the Indian Steel Industry, 1924–1939." *Economic History Review* 34.1:120–131.

Waldman, Selma. 1975. "Armed Struggle in Zimbabwe: A Brief Chronology of Guerrilla Warfare 1966–1974." *Ufahamu* 5.3:4–10.

Walker, Andrew. 2012. "What Is Boko Haram?" *United States Institute for Peace Special Report* 308:1–16.

Walter, Barbara F. 2002. *Committing to Peace: The Successful Settlement of Civil Wars*. Princeton, NJ: Princeton University Press.

Warman, Arturo. 2004. "La plataforma política del Zapatismo." In *Revuelta, rebelión y revolución: La lucha rural en México del siglo XVI al siglo XX*, 2d ed., ed. Friederich Katz. Mexico City: Era.

Warner, Nick. 1981. "Times of Darkness: Ethnicity and the Causes of Division within the Rhodesian Guerrilla Groups." Master's thesis, Australian National University, Canberra.

Washbrook, David. 1973. "Country Politics: Madras 1880 to 1930." *Modern Asian Studies* 7.3:475–531.

———. 1977. *The Emergence of Provincial Politics: The Madras Presidency 1870-1920*. Cambridge: Cambridge University Press.

Wasserman, Mark, 1973. "Oligarquía y intereses extranjeros en Chihuahua durante el porfiriato." *Historia Mexicana* 22.3:279–319.

———. 1993. *Persistent Oligarchs: Elites and Politics in Chihuahua, Mexico, 1910–1940*. Durham, NC: Duke University Press.

Waterbury, John. 1993. *Exposed to Innumerable Delusions: Public Enterprise and State Power in Egypt, India, Mexico, and Turkey*. New York: Cambridge University Press.

Waterbury, Ronald. 1975. "Non-revolutionary Peasants: Oaxaca Compared to Morelos in the Mexican Revolution." *Comparative Studies in Society and History* 17.4:410–442.

Watts, Carl P. 2002. "Killing Kith and Kin: The Viability of British Military Intervention in Rhodesia," *Twentieth Century British History* 16.4:382–415.

———. 2006. "The Rhodesian Crisis in British and International Politics, 1964–1965." PhD diss., University of Birmingham, Birmingham, UK.

———. 2012. *Rhodesia's Unilateral Declaration of Independence: An International History*. New York: Palgrave Macmillan.

Weber, Max. (1922) 1978. *Economy and Society: An Outline of Interpretive Sociology*. Berkeley: University of California Press.

Weiner, Myron. 1959. "Changing Patterns of Political Leadership in West Bengal." *Pacific Affairs* 32.3:277–287.

Weinstein, Jeremy M. 2006. *Inside Rebellion: The Politics of Insurgent Violence*. New York: Cambridge University Press.

Weitzer, Ronald. 1990. *Transforming Settler States: Communal Conflict and Internal Security in Northern Ireland and Zimbabwe*. Berkeley: University of California Press.

Weldon, Jeffrey A. 2003. "El congreso, la maquinaras políticas locales y el 'maximato': La reformas no reeleccionistas de 1933." In *El legislador a examen: El debate sobre la reelección legislativa en México*, ed. Fernando F. Dowrak, 33–53. Mexico City: Cámara de Diputados Fondo de Cultura Económica.

Wells, Allen. 1992. "All in the Family: Railroads and Henequen Monoculture in Porfirian Yucatán." *Hispanic American Historical Review* 72.2:159–209.

West, Michael O. 2002. *The Rise of an African Middle Class: Colonial Zimbabwe*. Bloomington: Indiana University Press.

Weyl, Nathaniel, and Sylvia Weyl. 1955. "La reconquista de México: Los días de Lázaro Cárdenas." *Problemas Agrícolas e Industriales de México* 7.4:119–334.

White, Luise. 2003. *The Assassination of Herbert Chitepo: Texts and Politics in Zimbabwe*. Bloomington: Indiana University Press.

———. 2011. "Normal Political Activities: Rhodesia, the Pearce Commission, and the African National Council," *Journal of African History* 52.3:321–340.

———. 2015. *Unpopular Sovereignty: Rhodesian Independence and African Decolonization*. Chicago: University of Chicago Press.

White, Nicholas J. 2014. *Decolonisation: The British Experience since 1945*. 2nd ed. London: Routledge.

Wickham-Crowley, Timothy P. 1992. *Guerrillas and Revolution in Latin America: A Comparative Study of Insurgents and Regimes since 1956*. Princeton, NJ: Princeton University Press.

Wilkie, James W. 1966. "The Meaning of the Cristero Religious War against the Mexican Revolution." *Journal of Church and State* 8.2:214–233.

———. 1967. *The Mexican Revolution: Federal Expenditure and Social Change since 1910*. Berkeley: University of California Press.

Wilkinson, Anthony R. 1973. "Insurgency in Rhodesia, 1957–1973: An Account and Assessment." *International Institute for Strategic Studies, Adelphi Paper* 13.100:23–29.

———. (1980) 2013. "The Impact of the War." In *From Rhodesia to Zimbabwe: Behind and Beyond Lancaster House (Studies in Commonwealth Politics and History)*, ed. W. H. Morris-Jones and Dennis Austin, 110–123. Oxford: Routledge.

Wilkinson, Steven I. 2006. *Votes and Violence: Electoral Competition and Ethnic Riots in India*. New York: Cambridge University Press.

Williams, L. F. Rushbrook, Director of Public Information, Government of India. 1924. *India in 1923–24: A Statement Prepared for Presentation to Parliament in Accordance with the Requirements of the 26th Section of the Government of India Act (5 and 6 Geo. V, Chap. 61)*. Calcutta: Government of India Central Publication Branch.

Wolf, Eric R. 1969. *Peasant Wars of the Twentieth Century*. New York: Harper and Row.

Womack, John. 1969. *Zapata and the Mexican Revolution*. New York: Vintage.

Wood, Conrad. 1987. *Moplah Rebellion and Its Genesis*. New Delhi: People's.

Wood, Elisabeth. 2003. *Insurgent Collective Action and Civil War in El Salvador*. New York: Cambridge University Press.

Wood, J. R. T. 2012. *A Matter of Weeks Rather than Months: The Impasse between Harold Wilson and Ian Smith: Sanctions, Aborted Settlements and War 1965–1969*. Bloomington, IN: Trafford.

Woodhead, John. 1945. *Famine Inquiry Commission: Report on Bengal*. Delhi: Government of India Press.

Woodward, Susan L. 1995. *Balkan Tragedy: Chaos and Dissolution after the Cold War*. Washington, DC: Brookings Institution.

Wright, H. R. C. 1954. "Some Aspects of the Permanent Settlement in Bengal." *Economic History Review* 2:204–215.

Yates, George T., III. 1972. "The Rhodesian Chrome Statute: The Congressional Response to United Nations Economic Sanctions against Southern Rhodesia." *Virginia Law Review* 58.3:511–551.

Yong, Tan Tai. 1994. "Maintaining the Military Districts: Civil-Military Integration and District Soldiers' Boards in the Punjab, 1919–1939." *Modern Asian Studies* 28.4:833–874.

———. 1995. "Assuaging the Sikhs: Government Responses to the Akali Movement, 1920–1925." *Modern Asian Studies* 29.3:655–673.

———. 2005. *The Garrison State: The Military, Government and Society in Colonial Punjab, 1849–1947.* New Delhi: Sage.

Young, John. 1997. *Peasant Revolution in Ethiopia: The Tigray People's Liberation Front, 1975–1991.* New York: Cambridge University Press.

Younkin, Helen B. 1916. Doc. 93/10474, September 1. Manuscritos de Venustiano Carranza, Centro de Estudios de Historia de Mexico, Mexico City.

Zamosc, Leon, 1986. *The Agrarian Question and the Peasant Movement in Colombia: Struggles of the National Peasant Association*, 1967–1981. Cambridge: Cambridge University Press.

Zebadúa, Emilio. 1995. "Los bancos de la revolución." *Historia Mexicana* 45.1:67–98.

Zimmerman, Matilde. 2000. *Sandinista: Carlos Fonseca and the Nicaraguan Revolution.* Durham, NC: Duke University Press.

Index

Page numbers followed by the letter *f* refer to figures. Page numbers followed by the letter *t* refer to tables.

Vasabjit Banerjee is an Assistant Professor in the Department of Political Science and Public Administration at Mississippi State University. He is also a Research Associate in the Department of Sociology at the University of Pretoria. Visit him online at https://vasabjitbanerjee.com/.